Electroencephalography

IN CLINICAL PRACTICE

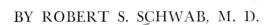

BY ROBERT S. SCHWAB, M. D.

Director of the Brain Wave Laboratory,
Massachusetts General Hospital,
and Associate in Neurology,
Harvard Medical School

ILLUSTRATED

W. B. SAUNDERS COMPANY

PHILADELPHIA · LONDON · 1951

TO

D. M. S.

who gently stimulated, inhibited and polarized this effort

Preface

THE PURPOSE of this book is to discuss the uses and limitations of electroencephalography in the diagnosis and study of diseases of the nervous system. The book is, therefore, primarily intended for neurologists, internists, psychiatrists and neurosurgeons. It is not a manual for the electroencephalographer, nor in any sense a textbook in this field.

It represents essentially the personal experiences and viewpoint of a neurologist who has been active in clinical electroencephalography for twelve years. Electroencephalography achieves its best results when it is thoroughly combined and correlated with the usual diagnostic procedures of the neurologist, psychiatrist and neurosurgeon.

For the neurologist this procedure should stimulate curiosity about the relationship of known areas of pathology to the function of the brain itself. The psychiatrist will find the test most useful in eliminating from psychotherapy those patients in need of surgery or specific medical treatment. The examination should be of value to the neurosurgeon in encouraging operative intervention in some patients or withholding it from others.

Since electroencephalography is essentially the tool of these specialists, they should know something about its history and principles so that they themselves can understand it as well as direct its application efficiently. They should not be forced to depend on a host of non-medical experts. Therefore the first two chapters of this book will cover the history and the relation of electrophysiology and anatomy of the brain to electroencephalography.

Boston, Massachusetts   ROBERT S. SCHWAB

    April, 1951

Acknowledgments

SINCE THIS BOOK is neither a reference book nor a manual, the reader is referred to Gibbs' Atlas,[3] Cohn's Electroencephalography,[2] and the standard volume by Walter, Hill[4] et al. for further details. The complete bibliography by Brazier[1] covers the large number of references not included here. In fact, the short bibliographies at the end of each chapter are more for historical interest, to encourage further reading of original work and to supplement the author's material.

The author is grateful to his colleagues, John A. Abbott, Mary A. B. Brazier and John S. Prichard, for their helpful criticism, to Mrs. Prichard for editorial assistance, and to Dr. Stanley Cobb for advice. Proofreading by Michelle B. Dell of Paris and Mrs. Harriet Cabot, and secretarial assistance of Mrs. Mary Conley and Miss Theresa Delaney are most appreciated. The valuable aid of Mr. M. J. McCann, Jr., of the Massachusetts General Hospital Photographic Department and Mrs. Edith Tagrin of the Medical Art Department is gratefully acknowledged.

THE AUTHOR

[1] Brazier, M. A. B.: Bibliography of Electroencephalography, 1875–1948. Electro-Encephalography and Clinical Neurophysiology, Montreal, 1950.

[2] Cohn, R.: Clinical Electroencephalography. New York, McGraw-Hill Book Co., 1949.

[3] Gibbs, F. A., and Gibbs, E. L.: Atlas of Electroencephalography, 2nd ed. Cambridge, Mass., Addison-Wesley Press Inc., 1950.

[4] Hill, D., and Parr, G. (Editors): Electroencephalography: A Symposium on its Various Aspects. London, Macdonald & Co., Ltd., 1950.

Contents

CHAPTER I

Historical Summary

THE BRAIN is the most delicate, the least understood and the most important of the organs in any living creature. Since it is isolated in a protecting bony shell and is supersensitive to drying, trauma or manipulation, the brain is far more difficult to study directly than organs in the abdominal and pleural cavities. It is only in the last fifty years that we have learned much about its pathology, growth and function, and something of its physiological and electrical properties.

In 1790 Galvani[6] demonstrated two fundamental electrical properties of muscles: first, that contraction would occur on *electrical* stimulation; second, that during a contraction (induced by pinching) an electric current was produced. From this observation it was logical to assume that the nerve leading to the muscle and the brain controlling the nerve would have similar electrical properties.

Indeed, in 1875 Caton[5] in England showed that the exposed brain of a rabbit produced electrical disturbances which he recorded. This work was more or less forgotten and remained buried as a brief note of a meeting.* In 1899, with the invention and development of the sensitive string galvanometer by Einthoven, physiologists and clinicians were able to study electrical phenomena produced by contraction of muscle in the limbs or the heart. By 1910 the electrocardiogram and its relationship to disease of the heart were known to most well-informed physicians. These electrical discharges were strong enough (1 millivolt) to move directly, without *amplification,* the sensitive quartz thread of the string galvanometer. Even though the movement as such was small, it could be *enlarged* optically with light and mirror so that an adequate-sized tracing could be seen on a strip of moving film. The brain, sur-

---

* In 1950 H. R. Viets uncovered a four page report by Caton[5a] suggesting that he was probably recording direct current potentials.

1

rounded by its membranes, spinal fluid, bony envelope and scalp, produced currents too feeble to activate such direct-recording equipment. Not until the discovery and development of the vacuum tube amplifier by DeForest and Fleming were tools available to investigate the electrical properties of the central nervous system.

In 1918 a young medical student, Donald McPherson, working at the physiological laboratories at the Harvard Medical School under Alexander Forbes, was curious enough, in the course of some experiments, to put two electrodes on the exposed brain of a cat. He led these to the input of an amplifier and ran the output into a string galvanometer. Much to his surprise, when the film was developed, he noted regular 10-per-second waves that were unlike the spikes and paroxysmal bursts that he had picked up from muscles. He showed this tracing to his Chief, who felt that, even if it were unusual, it was possibly an artifact and was out of line with the investigation assigned to his young assistant. The record was, therefore, put away in a desk and the matter forgotten. It was not until 1944, in clearing out some material of one of the laboratories at Harvard, that this early tracing of electroencephalographic waves from an animal's brain was uncovered. Dr. McPherson had long abandoned experimental physiology and had gone into the practice of psychiatry in Boston.

Progress in the experimental and clinical investigation of biological problems does not advance unless leads are followed up. So it was not until 1924, in Germany, that a psychiatrist, Hans Berger, saw the possibility of measuring electrical currents produced by the living brain and using these recordings as a diagnostic approach to some of the puzzles and problems connected with psychiatry. There was available at this time a reasonably satisfactory vacuum tube amplifier which would increase 100 times the voltage that was fed into its input. Berger, therefore, thought that, if he could record from electrodes inserted into the scalp of a living human being and amplify this current by means of his vacuum tube amplifier, he would then have potentials sufficiently strong to be registered on the ordinary electrocardiographic string galvanometer. He used two platinum needles, which were inserted into the scalp against the cranium of a patient in his clinic. Berger was gratified to see that by this method he was able to record regular and clearly defined electrical waves coming from the human brain. He found in his early experimental work, which was published for the first time in 1929[4] that the normal human being at rest with eyes closed produced from the occipital and parietal regions a rhythmical wave occurring ten times per second of a voltage of about 50 microvolts, which is about one-twentieth of that from the heart. These were the first waves he encountered, and he called them "alpha waves." He also found that, when his subject opened his eyes and looked at objects, these waves disappeared and were replaced by a faster rhythm which occurred about eighteen to twenty times per second and had an amplitude of some 20 or 30 microvolts. This faster rhythm, which was the second type he encountered, he called "beta waves." He found that these faster, low-voltage waves also occurred over the motor region. These two patterns, which he felt were normal discharges from the brain, he called the "electroencephalogram."

Berger continued his work, vigorously publishing a total of eleven papers, from 1929 to the beginning of the war in 1939. His first publications were received by physiologists and neurologists with a tremendous amount of skepticism. It has been known that living tissue produces electricity and that this activity is in direct proportion to the amount of movement or energy produced. The muscle of the heart or a limb is a good example of this concept. When the muscle is at rest, no electrical discharge is produced. When the muscle contracts, it produces work and electrical current. Berger's report that the brain was producing runs of 10-per-second waves when the eyes were closed and their part of the brain at rest, which disappeared when the subject opened his eyes and saw, was in direct contrast to this notion of the direct relationship of electrical energy to function. Because of this, much skepticism was focused on his work. From 1929, when his work first appeared, until 1933 the general attitude toward electroencephalography was one of belief or disbelief. One could hear among young workers in the field of neurology and physiology such questions as, "Do you believe in the Berger rhythm?"

One of the best-known neurophysiologists in England and a winner of the Nobel Prize was E. D. Adrian of the University of Cambridge, who had done pioneer work on recording the electrical activity of nerves, sense organs and muscles. He was very much interested in this work of Berger's, but also skeptical. Some of the skepticism directed against Berger's work was along technical lines: that he was picking up artifacts from air-borne sources or due to noise in his amplifiers, and that the matter was simply one of misidentification of phenomena. Adrian felt that this could be settled clearly. He had at his disposal a well-protected laboratory (from the standpoint of exclusion of aerial electrical waves), and he had some of the best-made oscillographs and amplifiers at that time. He carefully set up the experimental conditions devised by Berger, using electrodes embedded in the scalp and excluding completely the possibility of air-borne or other artifacts. He found that Berger was correct about the 10-per-second and the faster 18-per-second waves, and confirmed fully his observations. In 1934 Adrian[1] called this activity "the Berger rhythm," which established Berger's observations and brought his work, which was all in German, to the workers in the English-speaking world.

In 1934, in the United States, Hallowell Davis, working at Harvard, and Herbert Jasper, working in Providence, Rhode Island, began to experiment with the recording of electrical activity from the brain. Which of these workers obtained the first electrical tracing from the human brain in America is not clear, since the two almost coincided in the timing of their first recording. It was late in 1934, and neither of the investigators is particularly concerned with the priority of their work, since Berger was the pioneer and regional confirmations of this sort are not important.

Davis' work at the Harvard Medical School soon involved Frederic Gibbs,[7] who was working at the Neurological Unit at the Boston City Hospital. Gibbs suggested the possibility that patients during minor seizures might have unusual discharges from the brain. He found that during a petit mal seizure the normal rhythm was replaced by prominent 3-per-second wave and spike. This component of the electroencephalogram, which is typical of this particular clinical condition, began the important correlation of epilepsy and electroencephalography. From then on, various workers throughout the world began to take up the electroencephalographic recording from the intact skull of the human being, both in normal states and in neurological and psychiatric disorders. It was soon found that it was not necessary to puncture the scalp with a needle, but that, by applying a conducting paste to the scalp and attaching a metal electrode, such as a solder disk, to this area, the waves could be recorded with the same ease as when the needle was introduced into the skin.

From 1936 on, laboratories all over the world began to build electroencephalographic amplifiers and recording equipment. There was no standardization. Some laboratories, like that of Grey Walter, who was then at a neuropsychiatric hospital in London, recorded their tracings on a smoke drum or viewed the actual details of the discharge through a cathode ray oscilloscope. The workers at Harvard used a Western Union Telegraph recording instrument which produced the tracings on a half-inch paper tape. From 1936 to 1940 all kinds of recorders and amplifiers were used, and much of the material, both published and available in records, is difficult to correlate. During this time those going into this field had not the benefit of literature or textbooks. It was very much like the early days of roentgenography or electrocardiography. In order to join the field, one contacted one of the workers to get some rough ideas and technique, and then started off, without experience or knowledge, and learned the techniques through error, trial and tribulation, harnessing the problems of artifacts, lineborne interference, faulty instruments and inadequate recorders. In spite of these handicaps, fundamental work was accomplished during this period.

In England, in 1936, Grey Walter[10] applied the technique for the localization of the slow wave found in tumors so that they could be located on the surface of the scalp with a reasonable amount of accuracy. Travis,[9] working in Iowa, showed that the electroencephalographic pattern of a subject remained constant from day to day and week after week. He felt that every subject's tracing was part of his identification, like the finger print, or the retinal pattern in the eye.

In 1937, at the Massachusetts General Hospital, a two-channel machine was introduced. Since the operation and maintenance of this apparatus required funds not then available, an effort was made to use this technique in the same way as x-ray or other laboratory tests by charging the patient for the examination. Thus the first clinical electroencephalographic laboratory in a hospital was established. From that time on the number of electroencephalographic laboratories throughout the world increased rapidly. Workers in the field agreed that every large neuropsychiatric unit should have one available for clinical investigation, diagnosis or neurophysiological studies. At first they were mostly located on the eastern seaboard, but they soon spread to the West Coast of the United States, to the South, to Canada, down to South America and throughout Europe. By the beginning of the second World War, electroencephalographic laboratories were found in all the large neuropsychiatric centers throughout the world.

When the war began in Europe, this technique was picked up by the medical divisions of both warring powers, and efforts were made to utilize it in the selection of aviators, in the localization of intracranial lesions and for a host of neurophysiological experiments. Denis Williams[11, 12] had a set of apparatus at his disposal at Oxford, England, during the early part of the war to study intracranial injuries and published much important work on this subject. The school founded by Berger* in 1929 is still in existence, and records available at the conclusion of the war[2] showed that Tönnies, Kornmüller and others in Germany were trying to utilize this technique in various efforts related to their armed services.

In America the Armed Forces were at first a little reluctant to accept this technique and its claims, but after military officers had visited a laboratory, they recognized the application of this technique to their problems. By the time the United States entered the war in 1941, the Navy was utilizing the facilities of the Massachusetts General Hospital in Boston and had made arrangements to set up a laboratory of their own in the training station in Newport, Rhode Island. The Canadian Air Force was busily engaged in electroencephalographic investigation of aviators to see if the technique in some way could select the successful from the unsuccessful pilot. The United States Army was setting up laboratories in some of their large Air Centers. The procedure was being accepted then by the Armed Services as well as by institutions and important centers throughout the world.

During the war, progress was made in both instrumentation and in the collection of electroencephalographic tracings. Numerous papers appeared in the war publications, during the time of combat and afterwards, showing the value of the test both in the localization of intracranial lesions and in the identification of some cases of epilepsy.

---

* Berger retired from active laboratory work in 1935 and died in 1941. A personal account of his laboratory by a junior associate appeared in 1949[8] and a *Festschrift* volume in 1949.

After the war there was a rather large increase in the amount of apparatus available. The war years, with the intense demand for radio, radar and other technical equipment, curtailed the development of electroencephalographic apparatus. When hostilities ceased, the manufacturing concerns making amplifiers, recorders and other equipment associated with this apparatus could produce more and more. By 1947 there were in America five or six manufacturers of apparatus, some of high standards and others of doubtful standards. The equipment, which during the early development of the apparatus was cumbersome and heavy, now became consolidated, streamlined, and more practical and reliable. As an example, in 1938 a six-channel electroencephalographic machine consisted of twelve separate amplifiers, a switch box unit, and a recording set, all of which weighed somewhere around 1000 pounds and took from two to eight hours to set up. Unless it was mounted on a large wheel base, it was not portable. Since 1948 the six- and even eight-channel machines produced by a number of different manufacturers have been incorporated on a console wheel base with all the units built into it, the total weight of which is under 350 pounds, so that it can be wheeled about a hospital by a technician.

From the days of 1934 and 1935, when the question under discussion was whether or not one believed in the existence of the Berger rhythm, until the present time in 1950, when the procedure is a routine part of the usual neuropsychiatric hospital record, is a story of rapid growth.

Since the war a number of societies devoted to the work of electroencephalography have been formed. The first, "The E.E.G. Society" in England, was established to standardize, supervise and raise the quality of work throughout the British Isles.

The American Society was started in 1946, and there are in addition in the United States four regional electroencephalographic societies, all very active. There are also French, Swiss, Danish and Italian societies in this field. These workers are doing their utmost to raise the standards and quality of the work and to coordinate the investigation in different parts of the world so that some sort of uniform recording will be possible. They hope to keep out of the field unscrupulous exploiters of new techniques who might mislead and bilk the public because of its complexity and novelty.

The journal of "Electroencephalography and Clinical Neurophysiology," an international quarterly, was founded at the first International E.E.G. Congress in London in 1947, and has successfully completed its first year of publication. In 1949 a second International E.E.G. Congress was held in Paris. At this meeting an *International Federation of Electroencephalographic Societies* was formed.

In 1950 the various organizations in electroencephalography throughout the world are busy developing means for examination and certification of commercial apparatus, training and qualification of both technicians and physicians in the laboratories, and screening and supervision of published material.

This new specialty is not only acquiring the maturity and dignity of other special branches of medical diagnosis. It is doing more than that by keeping a place in its ranks for the basic scientists—physicists, physiologists, engineers and psychologists—who contributed so much to its early dynamic growth and who will surely play vital roles in broadening its scope and future development.

REFERENCES

1. Adrian, E. D., and Matthews, B. H. C.: The Berger Rhythm; Potential Changes from the Occipital Lobes in Man. Brain, *57:*355–385, 1934.
2. Alexander, L.: Neuropathology and Neurophysiology, Including Electroencephalography, in Wartime Germany. Combined Intelligence Objectives Subcommittee, Item No. 24, File No. XXVII–1, 23–36.
3. Archives für Psychiatrie und Nervenkrankheiten und Zeitschrift für die Gesamte Neurologie und Psychiatrie. Berger Memorial Issue, *183:* 1949, Springer-Verlag, Berlin-Charlottenburg 2.
4. Berger, H.: Über das Elektrenkephalogramm des Menschen. Arch. f. Psychiat., *87:*527–570, 1929.
5. Caton, R.: The Electric Currents of the Brain. Brit. Med. J., 2:278, 1875.
5a. Caton, R.: Researches on Electrical Phenomena of Cerebral Gray Matter. Tr. Internat. Med. Congress, 9th Session, Section VIII (Physiology), Washington, D. C., 1887, Vol. III, pp. 246–249.
6. Galvani, L.: De Viribus Electricitatis in Motu Musculari Commentarius. Memoirs of the Institute of Sciences. 7: 1791, Bologna, Italy.
7. Gibbs, F. A., Davis, H., and Lennox, W. G.: The Electro-encephalogram in Epilepsy and in Conditions of Impaired Consciousness. Arch. Neurol. & Psychiat., *34:*1133–1148, 1935.
8. Ginsberg, R.: Three Years with Hans Berger—A Contribution to his Bibliography. J. Hist. Med. & Allied Sc., *4:*361–371, 1949.
9. Travis, L. E., and Gottlober, A.: How Consistent Are an Individual's Brain Potentials from Day to Day? Science, *85:*223–234, 1937.
10. Walter, W. G.: The Location of Cerebral Tumours by Electroencephalography. Lancet, 2:305–308, 1936.
11. Williams, D.: The EEG in Acute Head Injuries. J. Neurol. & Psychiat., *4:*107–130, 1941.
12. Williams, D.:: The EEG in Chronic Post-traumatic States. J. Neurol. & Psychiat., *4:*131–148, 1941.

The Relation of Neurophysiology to Electroencephalography

THE RECORDING of the potential changes between two points on the scalp produced by the electrical activity in the brain is called *electroencephalography*. Like electrocardiography and electromyography, it depends on the fundamental property of the living nerve cell to produce electrical potentials during any change in its physical or chemical state. This correlation of electrical with chemical activity is a common occurrence in inorganic chemical reactions also and therefore cannot be identified with "life" of the biological cell.*

THE NERVE CELL

The nerve cell (human) is a concave rectilinear structure averaging 0.02 mm. in diameter (Figs. 1, 2) and containing a nucleus and nu-

---

* The usual analogies have been purposely omitted from this book, since they complicate and confuse conception rather than clarify. An example of this comes up at once when a nerve is compared to a telegraph wire. The wire conducts impulses as does a nerve; it is usually insulated by a non-conductor comparable to the myelin sheath of the nerve. It is long compared to its diameter, as is a nerve fiber. Often many wires lie in a cable, as does a nerve fiber in a trunk. Cutting both the wire and nerve severs continuity, and no impulses pass. So far so good. But the wire—all wires, big, small, copper, lead, silver, hot, cold—conducts at nearly the same rate, 186,000 miles a second. A nerve fiber of large diameter conducts its spike impulses at 100 meters a second ($\frac{1}{16}$ mile per second), which, when contrasted to the speed of an electric impulse along a wire, has a ratio of 1 to 2,976,000. (The rate of a tortoise versus a jet propelled plane has a ratio of 1 to 5648). A telegraph wire requires a return wire to complete the circuit. A nerve impulse needs only *one* fiber. A nerve uses oxygen, sugar and enzymes in its conduction—a wire has no chemical reactions. More is lost by the exceptions and differences than is gained by the similarities.

8

cleolus as in other living cells. At one end are a number of short, wavy-shaped fine filaments called dendrites, which, in general, are for the purpose of reception of stimuli from the cellular environment. At the other end of the cell (diagonally across) emerges a vastly longer, single, larger filament called the axone. It is the effector organ by which the individual cell influences other structures or other cells. The far end of the axone, which may be several feet long, branches into finer filaments which are in contact with another nerve cell, a gland or muscle cell. The entire central nervous system is composed of billions of these cells, called neurones, as well as supporting structure (glia) and nutritive elements (vessels and spaces filled with spinal fluid).

The cellular part of these neurones requires more nutrition and oxygen for survival than do the long, tenuous axones. In the central nervous system where the cells predominate, such as in the cerebral cortex, the basal ganglia or in the anterior horns of the spinal cord, the appearance is gray with a rich blood supply. Where there are chiefly axones or conducting parts of the neurone, the color is white and the blood supply comparatively meager (one fiftieth to one hundredth of that in the gray matter). In general the dendrites are short, 1 to 2 mm., and the axones 20 mm. to nearly a meter. There are, however, millions of short connecting cells (Golgi type) whose dendrites are about as long as the axones, and these are called internuncial nerve cells. The whole network is far more complicated than any diagram can illustrate, and the number of possible alternate pathways is astronomical.

We shall return to these networks later in this chapter. Let us consider the simple, isolated nerve cell. The nucleus and surrounding cytoplasm, where higher metabolic activity ensues as compared to the cell membranes, have a negative charge which results in a potential difference of as much as several millivolts between the interior of the cell and the outside surface. At this point it is well to emphasize an important point in electrical phenomena in general. Electric charges or potential differences can be produced in three ways: (1) by movement of a conducting loop of metal in an electro-magnetic field as in a magneto or dynamo; (2) by friction of a rough surface against an insulated surface as in an electrostatic machine (rubbing a piece of glass with a chamois cloth); (3) by chemical reactions of many sorts in which no mechanical motion is involved (dry battery).

In the nervous system there is, of course, *no* motion or friction, so that the electrical properties are *always* due to chemical reactions. Thus it is ridiculous to argue whether life in the central nervous system is electrical or chemical. They are both so intimately correlated with each other that separation is impossible.

The negative charge or potential difference of the nerve cell nucleus and the cell membrane is related to the concentration of potassium (K) ions in the cytoplasm of the nerve cell. As the charge is reduced, potassium ions leave through the cell membrane. Indeed, it is possible to reverse this potential difference by concentrating potassium ions outside. Sodium ions play an opposite role.

In the nervous system there are four different types of communication from one nerve cell to another:

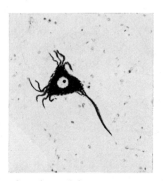

Fig. 1. Microphotograph of a normal human nerve cell in the lumbar anterior horn showing nucleus, dendrites, and axone (Nissl stain) X 1000. The latter have been slightly touched with a pencil since the cresyl violet does not stain them. (From Dr. C. Kubik.)

1. Direct electrical spread, through tissue, of the change in the potential differences due to alterations in the electrical field about a nerve cell. This occurs in the body or brain at a rate of many miles per second.
2. Conduction of an impulse along an axone (nerve spike) at rates of *3 mm. per second* to *125 meters per second,* according to the

Fig. 2. Diagram of nerve cell and axone to illustrate relation of cell body size to actual length of axone in a motor fiber from the anterior horn to muscle in foot. Cell is 2 cm. in diameter in drawing which is 1000 times actual size. With this scale the broken line represents one kilometer (3000 feet) of axone.

diameter of the fiber. This is one of the most important properties of all nervous tissue.
3. Direct spread of the chemical products of nerve cell metabolism by diffusion through tissue in which they are soluble. This varies from 1 to 10 cm. per second, according to the size of the molecule and other chemicals in the area.

4. Indirect spread, by means of the circulation of the blood through the nervous systems, of distant metabolic or glandular products produced by the nerve impulse. This takes twenty to thirty seconds to cause an effect. For example: an impulse from a nerve cell contracts a muscle fiber which produces lactic acid. This chemical affects other nerve cells when it reaches them via the blood stream.

In a living person all four forms of communication are in use and deliver their message after four different periods of time have elapsed: namely, instantly for (*1*); five to ten milliseconds for (*2*); one to two seconds for (*3*); and twenty to thirty seconds for (*4*).

ABBREVIATIONS USED IN FIGURES		
Anal.	=	Analyzer, Analysis
Ant.	=	Anterior
Chan.	=	Channel
E. Cort. G.	=	Electro-corticogram
E. E. G.	=	Electroencephalogram
E. K. G. E. C. G.	=	Electrocardiogram
E. M. G.	=	Electromyogram
F.	=	Frontal
L.	=	Left
Mic. V., M. V.	=	Microvolt
Mot.	=	Motor
Occ. Occip.	=	Occipital
Par.	=	Parietal
Phar., Pharyn.	=	Pharyngeal
Post.	=	Posterior
R., Rt.	=	Right
Sec.	=	Second
Temp.	=	Temporal
Tymp.	=	Tympanic
Vert.	=	Vertex

Only the first and second of these systems are concerned directly with the origin of the brain waves. The other two are important in modifying these electrical rhythms by chemical means and must always be considered.

THE NERVE IMPULSE

The propagation of an impulse down the axone is associated with a negative potential spike (Fig. 3) and the shift of potassium ions to the exterior of the fiber. This produces a potential difference between a more proximal point *A* (Fig. 4) outside the fiber and a more distal point *B*. This potential is accompanied by further migration of potassium ions to the outside and new electrical discharges which are the moving action spike of the nerve impulse. The propagation spike is possibly followed by a small production of heat, utilization of glucose and oxygen, and formation of carbon dioxide. After the action *Wave* has passed, the process reverses, more slowly, to reestablish the potential difference which allows the fiber to conduct again. Oxygen and glucose are consumed in this catabolism. The changes in the cell wall or axone wall which are associated with this potassium ion shift are believed to be tied up with a complicated enzyme system possibly based on acetylcholine and esterase equilibrium.*

When the electrical spike with its concomitant potassium ion changes reaches the end of the axone which branches into several small filaments, it produces an electrical change in these terminals which affects either dendrites of other cells or the end plates in muscles or glands.

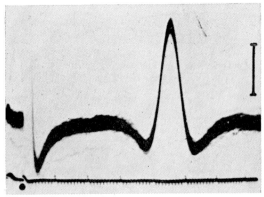

Fig. 3. Human nerve action spike obtained from surface electrodes over median nerve above elbow by technique of superimposing 50 separate traces on the cathode ray oscilloscope. Black dot shows time of stimulus at wrist about 30 cm. away. Time scale in 0.1 and 1 milliseconds. Calibration 30 microvolts. (From Dr. George Dawson: J. Neurol., Neurosurg. & Psychiat. Volume 12, 1949.)

The axone spike moves in large diameter fibers 125 meters per second and in small C fibers as slow as 3 to 4 mm. per second. Internuncial fibers have intermediate rates of conduction. In other words, the rate of conduction increases with fiber diameter. Since no nerve fiber has the same diameter throughout its length and no two fibers are of exactly the same diameter, the conduction rate in the nervous system is a most complicated variable at all times.

Such a spike recorded through suitable amplifiers and an oscillograph on a two-dimensional paper or film gives a false idea of its characteristics. It is really a two-dimensional plane moving at right angles to the long axis of the fiber. This movement sets up complicated patterns of electrical fields that are three-dimensional as the impulse goes down the nerve. Such fields diminish in intensity as the square of the distance

* For further details of the complicated electrical and chemical phenomena associated with the nerve impulse the reader is referred to the textbooks by Fulton,[3] Brazier,[1] and Lorente de Nó[5]—the order here indicating the degree of detail and specialization in the texts.

and are present in the surrounding tissue even though the myelin sheath is a fair insulator.

In the myriads of circuits in the central nervous system, millions of rising and collapsing three-dimensional electrical fields are always in

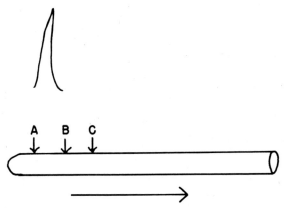

Fig. 4. Diagrammatic picture showing propagation of the nerve impulse along the axone. The negative spike is over points A and B. Between B and C negativity increases as ions go from B to A, making C positive to B which "fires" the portion between B and C.

evidence, interfering with each other—cancelling, adding, in such a complicated way that mathematics of the most elaborate sort fail to devise expressions to handle them. These fields make up the first form of communication mentioned previously. The most reasonable explana-

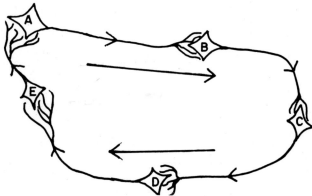

Fig. 5. Diagram of a simple loop containing five neurones. → shows impulse direction.

tion of the rhythmic spontaneous activity found in the brain is a combination of the effects of the first two forms of cell-to-cell communication. We know that the neurones are interconnected by being arranged in trains of closed circuits or loops. In such a chain (Figs. 5, 6 and 7) cell *A* can affect *B* and so on until there is a continuous circuit of activity. As loops I, II, III, and so forth may be in the same area, interplay of loop I on loop II, and so on, may alter the characteristics of each other in such a way that they run in synchrony.

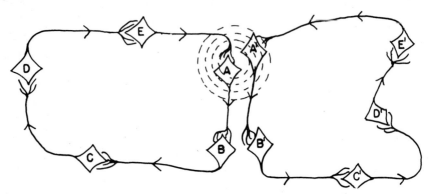

Fig. 6. Diagram of two adjacent five-neurone-loops indicating influence of the electrical field produced by activity of cell A on cell A′ in the second loop.

Eccles[2] feels that the field effect of short axons on the dendrites may alter the sensitivity by polarization or neutralization on a partial scale of the positive surface charge, so that for a brief period these dendrites are refractory (inhibition). This will set up pulsations in cell sensitivity, and, with enough neurones in an area all interlocked in a network,

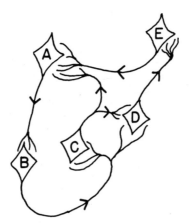

Fig. 7. Diagram of a more complicated five-neurone-loop. → shows impulse direction. Note there are three different pathways from cell B to cell A.

rhythmic undulations in the electric activity will result. At 100 meters per second as a conducting rate for large fiber, a 10-cm. loop with five synapses, each with a delay of one millisecond, would circulate 140 times per second. At small fiber speed of 2.5 meters per second, a 5-cm. diameter loop with ten synapses would take 140 milliseconds, or seven per second. So in the central nervous system we have an opportunity of various loop rates from 140 per second to six per second. The few mathematical calculations of loop rates that have been made lead to a loop rate of ten per second.

It is necessary to note the difference between an impulse that may occur a number of times a second and a continuous wave like a sine wave with the same number of beats per second.

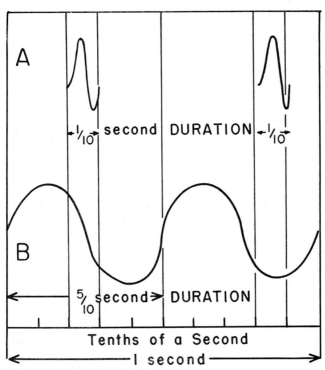

Fig. 8. Diagram showing the difference in duration of two types of waves with the same frequency (two per second).
A shows a wave of duration $\frac{1}{10}$ sec. with no activity for $\frac{5}{10}$ sec. between each wave.
B shows a continuous sine wave of $\frac{5}{10}$ sec. duration where the frequency, 2, is the reciprocal of the duration $(2 = \frac{1}{0.5})$

An impulse has a certain *duration,* which is usually expressed in milliseconds instead of fractions. It may be followed by a period of no activity before the next impulse begins. A sine wave, on the other hand, is a continuous function without such interruptions in activity between each wave. The number of impulses or waves per second is the *frequency*. The reciprocal of the frequency is equal to the duration in a continuous function only when there are no periods of inactivity. (See Fig. 8.)

For example: The electrical impulse caused by the contraction of a muscle fiber lasts 10 milliseconds. In a normal voluntary muscular contraction forty impulses per second occur. The period of no activity between impulses is about fifteen milliseconds. A sine wave of the same frequency, namely, forty per second, has a duration for each wave of twenty-five milliseconds.

Brain waves as recorded from the scalp from electrodes several centimeters apart and as far from the underlying cortex closely resemble sine waves. Electrical activity from needle electrodes 1 mm. apart deep within the brain resembles repetitive impulses of extremely short duration with periods of no activity between them.

Physicists[7] have shown that multiple sources of repetitive impulses that are only partially synchronous can give at distant and widely separated electrodes (because of alteration of form by intervening tissue) a composite picture that looks like the pattern of a waxing and waning sine wave.

Therefore brain waves as we usually see them probably are smoothed out and composite patterns of repetitive impulse activity of the nerve cell and its fiber.

The first theoretical explanations of rhythmic electrical waves in the brain assumed a large number of closely interconnected cells such as we see in a silver preparation of Cajal in the occipital calcarine cortex (area 17). With various loops synchronized, they beat at 10 cycles per second. Then physiologists began to interfere surgically with the projecting pathways from the thalamus to these regions. They noted disappearance of the cortical rhythms and so postulated the need of two separate nerve cell stations connected together by relatively long loops of axones (corticothalamic networks). Terms such as "scanning" or "sweep circuits" crept into the physiological language from television engineers. Recently, Kristiansen[4] has confirmed the earlier work of Spiegel[10] that with more careful surgical isolation of a piece of cortex there remains a clear 10-per-second rhythm *not* dependent on connections to any structures deep or superficial. Shinners[9] also reported that a child with no cerebral cortex had 10-per-second waves in the thalamus. We are thus back to where we began to speculate—namely, that if there are enough healthy nerve cells interconnected in any one place in the nervous system, spinal cord, thalamus or cortex, we can find these 10-per-second rhythms.

These concepts can therefore be stated concerning the origin of the electroencephalogram:

In local regions of the nervous system where cell populations are high there will be enough "loops" interconnected and interaffected by action spikes and field effects to produce an independent synchrony of electrical waves at ten per second. When two or more such cell stations are closely tied together by afferent loops (corticothalamic networks), more synchrony and higher voltage waves at ten per second appear.

The arrival in the brain of sensory stimuli affect these spontaneous electrical rhythms in a number of ways. The earlier physiologists conceived the central nervous system as a rising and falling of axone spikes directly proportioned to central activity, but electroencephalography rather seriously altered this simple concept. In brief, the number of electrical spikes moving along various axone paths was supposed to be highest during intense mental effort and nearly absent during sleep (poetically described in Sherrington's[8] monograph). In sleep, actually, activity of a "spontaneous" sort is maximal and during active mental work minimal. Possibly the total number of spikes moving along in sleep and the alert states is not very different, but variation in arrangement is the important point.

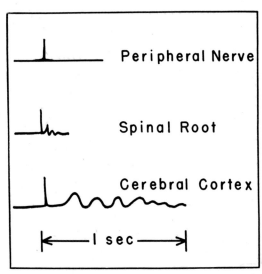

Fig. 9. Diagrammatic representation showing the increasing complexity of the pattern associated with the nerve impulse the higher it goes in the nervous system.

In the peripheral nerve the spike discharge is relatively simple (Fig. 9). After it enters the cord at the posterior root it becomes more complicated, and still more so when it reaches the cortex. In addition, throughout the central nervous system there are spare circuits going all the time which may be altered as the impulse goes by or through them.

This, of course, is oversimplified, but may be summarized as follows:

The waxing and waning of localized spontaneous activity is modified (modulated is another favorite word, borrowed from communication engineers) by impulses from a distant receptor. It is further altered by the local effects of the short loops in its vicinity which were also affected in their properties by the same impulses.

The best-known example of such an effect is that of a visual stimulus on the occipital alpha rhythm. This 10-per-second regular sine wave discharge is "blocked" when the visual stimulus reaches the calcarine cortex from the retina (Fig. 10). The number and variety of such direct and indirect effects on the total electrical pattern of a human brain directing its owner through city traffic, for example, are matters of sufficient complexity and mystery to interest mathematicians.*

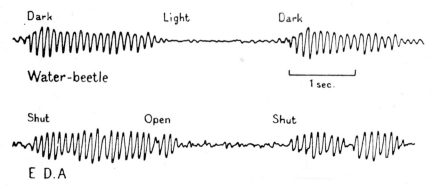

Fig. 10. The effect of light and dark on the alpha rhythm of man and insect. (From Adrian.)

In conclusion, it may be of interest to note that in a motor response to a light in the eye, the time taken (reaction time) is about 150 to 170 milliseconds, or 1/6 second. This is composed of the following parts:[6]

Light to retina, no delay.................... 0
Retinal response..........................20 milliseconds
Retina to calcarine occipital cortex via lateral geniculate ....20 milliseconds
Calcarine cortex via occipital associative areas (18 and 19) to frontal motor and temporal associative areas and thence to the motor Betz cells in area IV..........................95 milliseconds
Motor area IV down pyramidal tract to anterior horn cell and then out motor nerve to muscle and plate and muscle contraction.....17 milliseconds

Note the short motor or effector time, *17 milliseconds,* 40 milliseconds for sensory time and 95 milliseconds for associative time within the brain.

The *95 to 110 milliseconds* associative time suggests that 1/10 second (10 per second) may be a necessary period to traverse, modify and utilize the loop networks in the brain that constitute voluntary activity and that the 10-per-second alpha is a fundamental property of such a system.

REFERENCES

1. Brazier, M. A. B.: The Electrical Activity of the Nervous System. London, Sir Isaac Pitman & Sons Ltd. In press.
2. Brooks, C. McC. V., and Eccles, J. C.: An Electrical Hypothesis of Central Inhibition. Nature, *159:760–764,* 1947.

* Professor Wiener's fascinating book on "Cybernetics" gives a readable and not too technical approach to this problem.[11]

3. Fulton, J. F.: Physiology of the Nervous System. 3rd ed. New York, Oxford University Press, 1949.

4. Kristiansen, K., and Courtois, G.: Rhythmic Electrical Activity from Isolated Cortex. EEG Clin. Neurophysiol., *1*:265–272, 1949.

5. Lorente de Nó, R.: A Study of Nerve Physiology. Rockefeller Institute Med. Res., 1947, Vol. 131 and 132.

6. Monnier, M.: L'Electro-Rétinogramme de L'Homme. EEG Clin. Neurophysiol., *1*:87–108, 1949.

7. Prast, J. W.: An Interpretation of Certain EEG Patterns as Transient Responses of a Transmission System. EEG Clin. Neurophysiol., *1*:370, 1949.

8. Sherrington, C.: Quoted by Adrian, E. D.: The Physical Background of Perception. New York, Oxford University Press, 1947, 16–17.

9. Shinners, B. M., Hamby, W. B., and Krauss, R.: The Electrical Activity of the Thalamus and Cortical Remnants in a Case of Schizencephaly. EEG Clin. Neurophysiol., *1*:522, 1949.

10. Spiegel, E. A.: Comparative Study of the Thalamic, Cerebral and Cerebellar Potentials. Am. J. Physiol., *118*:569–579, 1937.

11. Wiener, N.: Cybernetics, or Control and Communication in the Animal and the Machine. New York, John Wiley & Sons, Inc., 1948.

The Normal and Abnormal Electroencephalogram

GENERAL CONSIDERATIONS

THE MOST important features of the electroencephalogram are the frequency and amplitude of the discharges. In order to understand the tracings and their clinical interpretations, it is essential to have some clear descriptions of these features and to group them according to their normal and abnormal characteristics.

Frequency

Historically, the first recordings studied in man by Berger consisted of the 10-per-second waves from the occipital area of the scalp. These he called "alpha waves" (Fig. 11). Their disappearance when the eyes were opened, so carefully investigated by Adrian,[1] led the latter to include this feature in their definition. Therefore, if we follow this trend, we must assign another letter to this same frequency wave if it is encountered other than in the occipital area or if repression by light on opening the eyes is absent. Since many parts of the human brain are accessible to electroencephalography and there is a variety of physiological responses similar to this visual phenomenon, we would exhaust the alphabet and have the most cumbersome and complicated classification imaginable. In spite of the charm of retaining historical descriptions, throughout this book the identification by the few letters in common use will be restricted to frequency bands. The specific area of the brain from which any particular activity is obtained will precede the letter used. Any relevant or important physiological alteration of the activity will follow the letter.

Some may prefer to retain the more classical conception of the word "alpha" and use the number of the frequency for activity in the same band when encountered in other areas or situations. Any system of classification that embraces clarity and simplicity can be followed until the international committees have resolved these problems into universally acceptable forms.

It is conventional to arrange any frequency spectrum so that the slow components are on the left and the fast on the right. The spectrum of the frequency of the electroencephalogram as followed in this book consists of six different bands:

1. The slowest on the left consists of waves from ½ per second through 3 per second and is called the *delta band*.

2. The intermediate slow from 4 through 7 per second is called the *theta band*. (Walter, in the course of his investigations, assigned these letters, and they are generally accepted.)

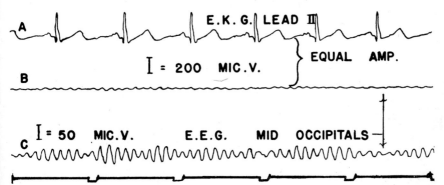

Fig. 11. Comparison of voltage and frequency of the electrocardiogram and occipital alpha rhythm in man. The top line shows lead II of the electrocardiogram with the usual amplitude of such recording. The second line shows the almost imperceptible alpha rhythm at this degree of amplification. The third line shows the prominent alpha when the gain is increased four times over the usual value needed for electrocardiography. The bottom line shows the time in seconds. Calibration signals as indicated.

3. The waves from 8 through 13 per second compose the *alpha band*.

4. The intermediate fast 14 through 17 per second is as yet unnamed.

5. The fast waves consist of frequencies of 18 through 30 per second and are called the *beta band*.

6. Any frequencies above 30 (which are unusual) are included in the *very fast band*, also as yet not associated with any specific letter. We must have such a band on the right of the spectrum which includes recurring short duration spikes, the frequencies produced by some drugs, and those rhythms believed by some to be obscured by the slower frequencies (Fig. 12).

Amplitude

The problem of amplitude of the waves of these six frequency bands should be simple. No letters or names are involved, and the amplitude is usually expressed as the number of microvolts from the top to the bottom of a wave.

It is simple enough to measure amplitude by ruler or caliper *from peak to opposite peak* and compare this to the upward or downward deflection of the calibration signal. This gives the voltage in microvolts and agrees with modern electronic practice. The voltage from an electrical source in a fluid-like medium (brain-skull-scalp) decreases with the square of the distance from that source. Voltage increases as interelectrode distances become larger, with lowered interelectrode resistance, and with increase in electrode size. Furthermore, the particular

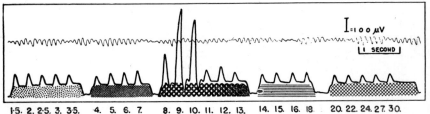

Fig. 12. A normal electroencephalogram from the left occipital region, alpha type, showing frequency analysis with Walter automatic analyzer. The analysis is shown by continuous heavy line under the electroencephalogram. The amount of activity in any one 10-second-period (epoch) of any frequency present is shown by the vertical height of this line above *baseline* values. (This is approximately the height of identifying band markings.) The slow (delta) band is shown by large dots on left with five frequency bands 1.5 through 3.5 below. There is no activity here as the heavy analyzer pen line is at baseline or zero setting.

The intermediate slow band (theta) is shown by small dots 4 through 7, and shows a trace of activity at 7.

There is a good deal of activity in the alpha band. The highest peak is 9 per second with nearly as much in the 10, and half as much in the 8, a trace at 12. There is none in intermediate, fast or beta groups in this case.

position of the two electrodes in respect to the lines of force of the electric field bears a direct relationship to the amplitude. See *Field* in Glossary.)

Therefore the voltage measurements of the electroencephalogram depend on *all* these variables. The distance from the source and the exact position of the electrodes on the electric field are rarely known. Interelectrode distances, resistance and size vary considerably. Finally, the cut-off characteristics of the apparatus, which include recording pen frequency response curves, filters in the circuit, and to some extent the amplifier characteristics themselves, reduce or increase the amplitude registered on the paper by significant amounts. The latter depend on the wave form as well as the duration of the impulse being studied.

Therefore any absolute measurements of voltage of the electroencephalogram are nearly impossible. It is possible, by keeping some of these variables in mind, to determine whether voltages are low, normal or high in respect to calibration signals, normal controls, previous examinations of the same person or from one part of the head to another. The accuracy of voltage in microvolts of an electroencephalogram when compared to the calibration signal depends largely, then, on the recordist's skill, care and knowledge of many of the variables just mentioned.

With the preceding paragraph in mind, the voltages encountered in the electroencephalogram vary from 5 to 1000 microvolts (or 1 millivolt).

THE NORMAL ELECTROENCEPHALOGRAM

The characteristics of the normal electroencephalogram have been determined from the study of the tracings of many thousands of persons in good physical health and free of neurological abnormalities. Various series of normals in different parts of the world show almost complete agreement in these features.

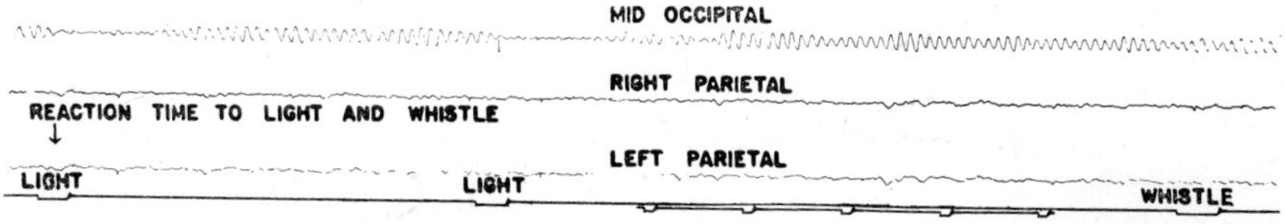

Fig. 13. Normal electroencephalogram showing normal alpha response to light as well as the motor reaction time. Both are compared to the effect of a whistle. The light flashed on at beginning of signal showing on fourth line and motor response (closing a key) is shown at end of signal. When compared to the time signal (between light and whistle) the reaction time is 0.3 second, alpha disappearance time 0.2 second, and recovery of alpha 1 second.

In any classification or description of this type it is essential that the records be taken under certain standard conditions. Any deviations from these must be accurately described and the interpretation altered accordingly. These are:

1. The gain setting on each amplifier should be arranged so that 1 cm. of deflection of the pens above or below the base line is equivalent to 100 microvolts of the calibration signal.
2. The conventional paper speed of 3 cm. (or 2.5cm.) per second should be used.
3. Standard electrodes and placements should be used (see Chap. IV).
4. (a) The subject must be awake.
   (b) His blood sugar should be normal (above 90 mg. per 100 cc.).
   (c) He should not be taking sedatives, alcohol or other drugs likely to affect the record.
   (d) He should be in a comfortable chair or bed, relaxed and quiet, in a semi-dark room, which is cool and free of distracting sights and sounds.

For the sake of convenience the normals will be divided into three groups: adults, 20 to 70 years; adolescents, 14 to 20 years; and children, 0 to 14 years.

Normal Adults

The frequencies are almost all in the alpha and beta bands. The alpha is found mostly in the occipital and parietal regions. Its voltage is 25 to 100 microvolts, averaging about 50. The waves usually appear in spindles of rising and falling amplitude which last one to two seconds. Such occipital alpha is promptly reduced or disappears on opening the eyes (Fig. 13). It may be present as much as 90 per cent of the time or as little as 1 per cent. The two sides of the head are usually symmetrical in voltage, duration and shape of the spindles, and in the percentage time of the rhythm and its frequency. The frequency remains constant and, on an analyzed record, shows a dominant peak with some activity below and above this (one cycle different).[2] See Figure 12.

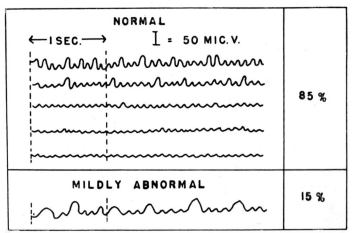

Fig. 14. Diagrammatic distribution of the electroencephalogram in 100 normal controls.

Minor differences in symmetry of the two sides of 10 to 20 per cent in any of these elements are normal, but not usual.

The beta band, more irregular than the alpha, is found over the frontal and temporal areas and has an amplitude of 5 to 30 microvolts. In many normals with little alpha, the beta is found in all areas. Its frequency averages 18 to 30 per second without the sharp dominant frequencies of the alpha. In some normals its amplitude is so low that the tracings look flat and the rhythm is difficult to identify.

The majority of normals have records of various distributions of alpha and beta frequencies. The actual patterns, in any given subject, are remarkably constant from minute to minute as well as from examination to examination.

Approximately 85 per cent of normals have records which agree with these descriptions. In the remaining 15 per cent, other rhythms are encountered[3] (Fig. 14).

In some normals theta activity is found in the temporal regions. It is usually of low amplitude (20 to 40 microvolts), only present about 25 per cent of the time and does not occur in runs or spindles.

In other normals some low-voltage (10 to 20 microvolts) delta activity is found in the frontal regions, usually less than 10 per cent of the time and, like the theta, not in runs or spindles.

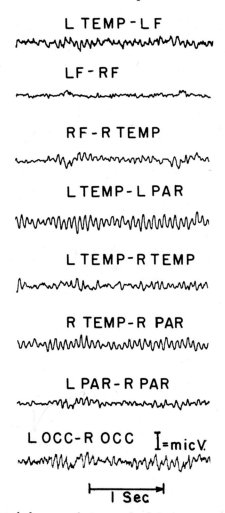

Fig. 15. Electroencephalogram of a normal adult (23 years, male) with a strong 14-per-second intermediate fast dominant rhythm. Subject was fully awake at the time.

A few normals show a rhythm in the intermediate fast band (14 to 18 per second) of 20 to 50 microvolts. Its significance is far from clear, and a few believe that it is an abnormal finding (Fig. 15).

Therefore, in a normal record a small amount of delta, theta or intermediate fast may be seen.

This constancy of pattern is a fundamental property of normal records. This means that the usual variations of blood sugar, blood pressure and fluid balance do not affect these stable patterns.

Another important feature of the normal adult electroencephalogram is its stability under mild induced changes in physiological environment. These are used, under the term "activation," to bring out latent or hidden electroencephalographic abnormalities in certain patients (Figs. 16 and 17). (See Chapter IV, page 66, for details of this technique.)

For example, three minutes of moderate overbreathing (at 20 liters per minute) does not usually change records. Nor does 500 mg. of metrazol at 100 mg. per minute intravenously. On the other hand, slight

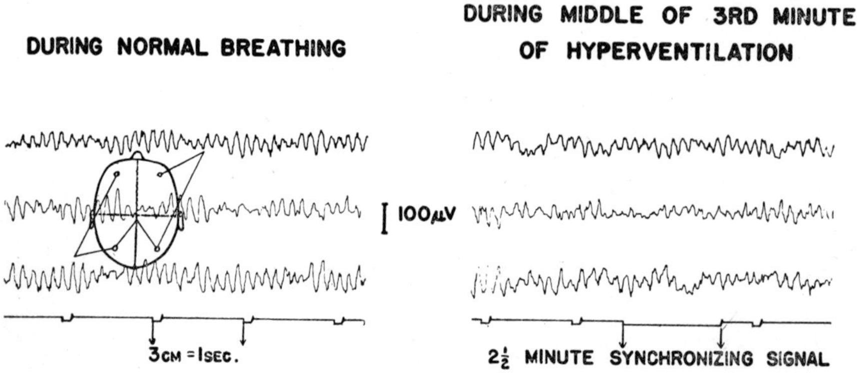

Fig. 16. Electroencephalogram of a 23-year-old, normal female, during normal breathing and during third minute of voluntary hyperventilation at a rate of 25 liters per minute. Except for slight slowing of the alpha there is no change in the record. Subject had eaten two hours before the test.

changes from such forms of activation are found in some normal persons, and even the most carefully selected normals will show definite and severe abnormalities if the activation is carried too far. Thus criteria of normality are relative matters and must be regarded only in such terms.

The Normal Adolescent

The frequency bands found in normal young people are essentially the same as in adults. A little more temporal theta, less constancy in patterns, and a far greater vulnerability to activation, especially by hyperventilation, are allowed. This is only partly due to the natural tendency of youth to do things more vigorously, which may result in overbreathing at rates of 30 to 35 liters per minute. It may also be caused by various minor delays in full maturation of the nervous system, not in themselves pathological, but common enough in adolescents. Some young men do not reach full maturity in this respect until twenty-five years of age, but they are normal physically and intellectually.

In working with any group of normals these findings must be kept in mind.

The Normal Child

At birth the electroencephalogram is irregular, asymmetrical and rather formless, and what rhythm is seen is in the slow delta band. No responses similar to the occipital alpha disappearance with light can be seen.

During the first year the delta activity becomes more regular, and

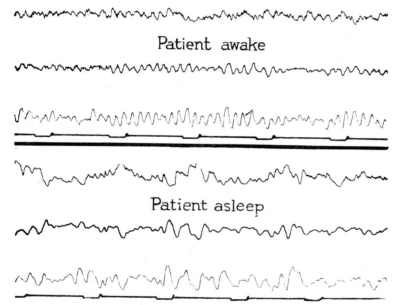

Fig. 17. The effect of sleep on the electroencephalogram of a normal subject. Symmetry is preserved and there are no seizure patterns.

symmetry is found in the two sides. Opening the eyes represses the occipital rhythm (Fig. 18).

From then on there is a gradual increase in the frequency of the dominant rhythm from 3 per second until the alpha band is reached at the age of ten; but the voltage may be 150 microvolts. By fourteen years of age this occipital frequency is nine to ten waves per second, and normal levels of voltage are found. Slow waves over the frontal and temporal regions are gradually replaced by the normal beta band by the age of sixteen. See Henry's Monograph on this subject.[4]

The age frequency charts of Lindsley[6] and Smith[7] are essential to differentiate the normal records of children from the abnormal (Fig. 19).

Far greater latitude in allowing for slower temporal lobe frequencies must be accepted in children than in adults in the normal records.[5]

There is little constancy in pattern or resistance to activation in the young child. Overbreathing of an involuntary sort due to anxiety may produce 3-per-second delta waves during one examination and be ab-

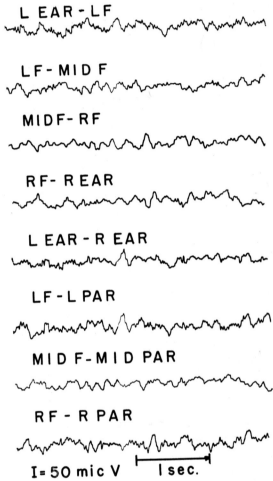

L EAR - L F

L F - MI D F

MIDF - RF

RF - R EAR

L EAR - R EAR

LF - L PAR

MID F - MID PAR

RF - R PAR

I = 50 mic V   I sec.

Fig. 18. Electroencephalogram of a normal 13-month-old infant. Note symmetry, normal slow waves for age and absence of paroxysmal activity.

sent in another. Voluntary overbreathing nearly always produces delta waves in the normal child.

Symmetry of the child's electroencephalogram is one of the best indications of a normal record. The appearance of paroxysms of high-voltage slow waves and spikes, or other high-voltage fast waves, is usually an indication of abnormality. The same standard conditions described before are important with children. It is, of course, far more difficult to secure a relaxed state with quiet in a child than in an adult. The technician who deals with children must possess a number of traits that will reassure the apprehensive child and bring out cooperation and confi-

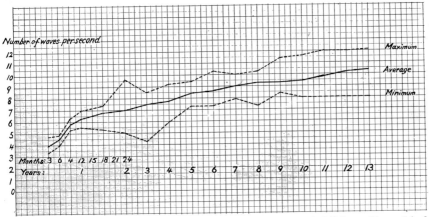

Fig. 19. Table of alpha rates versus age in normal infants and children. (From Lindsley, D. B.: J. Genet. Psychol., 55:197–213, 1939.)

BRAIN WAVE PATTERNS

Normal

Slow 9-11 per sec.	Fast 18-24 per sec.	Mixed Type

Abnormal

Slow 3-6 per sec.	Fast 16-22 per sec.	Mixed (Wave Spike)
Found In	**Found In**	**Found In**
Epilepsy - { Fugue States, Behavior Types, Convulsions } Deep Sleep Low Blood Sugar or Oxygen Deep Anaesthesia Severe Alkalosis Brain Tumor, Abscess, Hematoma Encephalitis or Head Injury Some Psychoses Some Behavior Disorders Infancy	Epilepsy - { Convulsions (Grand Mal), Focal Seizures } Infiltrating Tumors Light Anaesthesia Some Psychoses	Epilepsy { Lapses - (Petit Mal), Convulsions } Rare Tumors

Fig. 20. Summary table of the most frequent normal (alpha, beta and mixed) and abnormal (slow, fast and mixed) frequencies in the electroencephalogram.

dence. In some instances in which asymmetrical or focal activity is to be found, natural sleep or that induced by drugs will bring this out. The normal sleep record is, of course, bilaterally symmetrical.

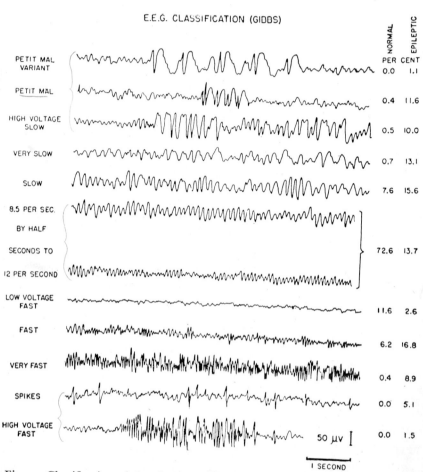

Fig. 21. Classification of the electroencephalogram used by the Gibbs. The upper three and the bottom two tracings illustrate seizure discharges. The tracings central to these illustrate dominant frequencies which are either slow or fast. Frequencies from 8½ to 12 per second, and those marked low voltage fast, are considered normal. The signal at the bottom line marks a deflection caused by 50 microvolts, and the horizontal line, one second of time. At the right is the distribution of each type of record found in 1000 control adults and in 730 adult epileptics. (From Lennox, W. G.: The Practitioner, *164*:432, 1950.)

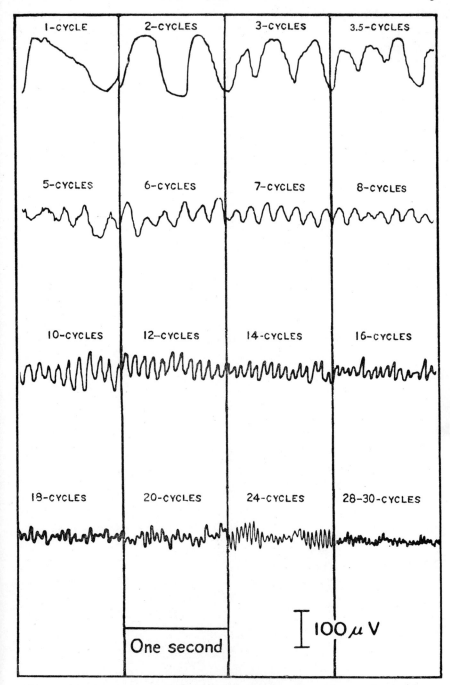

Fig. 22. Actual samples of 16 different frequencies commonly seen in the electro-encephalogram. (Taken from unpublished summary chart of Dr. A. J. Derbyshire and Dr. L. J. Ravitz, Harper Hospital, Detroit, Michigan.)

When overbreathing is done, a far greater amount of induced delta activity is normal in children than in young adults. It is usual to disregard it unless it is extreme, asymmetrical or associated with paroxysms of slow and fast waves in components suggestive of seizure patterns.

In no group of normals is it more difficult to be dogmatic than in that of young children. Extreme caution is essential in calling records abnormal. Repeat examinations are an excellent way to arrive at cor-

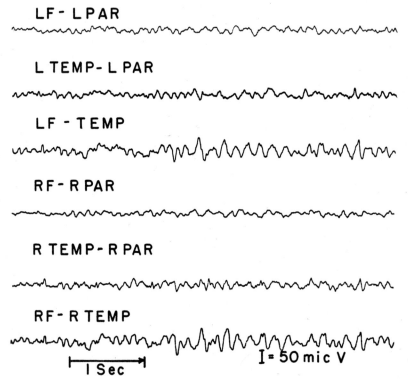

Fig. 23. Electroencephalogram showing a mild bilateral degree of abnormality consisting of runs of 6 per second (theta) in both temporal-frontal areas. This is an early case of multiple sclerosis in a male, 24 years old.

rect interpretation. A trend toward better stabilization and reduction in slow waves over a year or so in a particular child is of considerable aid in assessing the electroencephalogram as normal. On the other hand, a trend in the opposite direction is strongly suggestive of an abnormality in the brain.

THE ABNORMAL ELECTROENCEPHALOGRAM

The abnormal record is best subclassified into four groups: (1) very abnormal, (2) moderately abnormal, (3) mildly abnormal, and (4) borderline. The significance and clinical correlations with the different types of abnormalities will not be discussed in this chapter, since they are fully covered in Chapters V, VI, VII and IX, but the following sum-

mary tables are worth comparing. Note how they cover the six examples
of abnormal records that follow (Figs. 20, 21 and 22).

Since considerable time has been spent describing the characteristics
of the normal electroencephalogram, effort can be saved by stating that

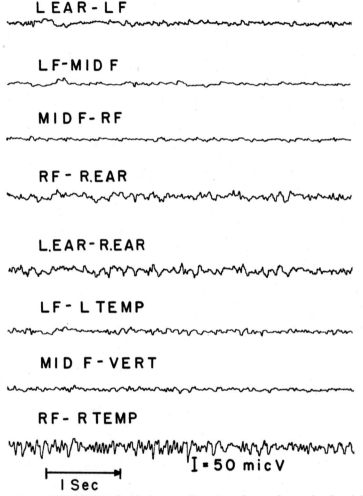

Fig. 24. A record showing a focal abnormality of moderate degree in the right temporal area consisting of high voltage beta (20 per second) as well as some superim-
posed theta. There is also some of this theta at the right ear. A 44-year-old female one
month after removal of a right temporal tumor.

any records not fitting into these groups are, by definition, *abnormal*.
They should fall into one of the four subgroups just mentioned. It
should be recognized that the borderline group might have in it some
normal records with mild or insignificant deviations. If a physiological
phenomenon is outside normal limits, it is, therefore, "abnormal" even
though the deviation is insignificant or inconsistent clinically. It is use-

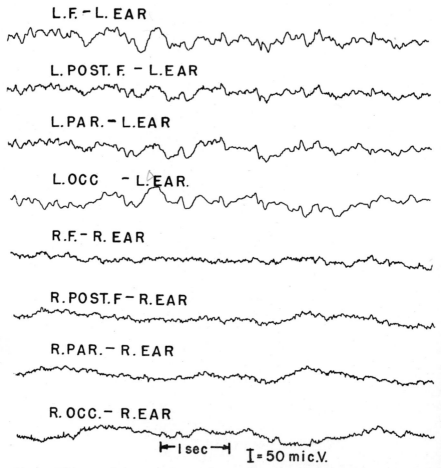

Fig. 25. This record shows moderate abnormality all over the left side of the head. The right side is normal. Left ear to right ear run (not shown) also normal, showing left ear not source of abnormality. Abnormal waves are delta and theta. Deep left side inoperable brain stem tumor with pressure relieved by operation in which a rubber tube runs from lateral ventrical to cisterna magna (Torkildson procedure). Two years postoperative. Male, 33 years old.

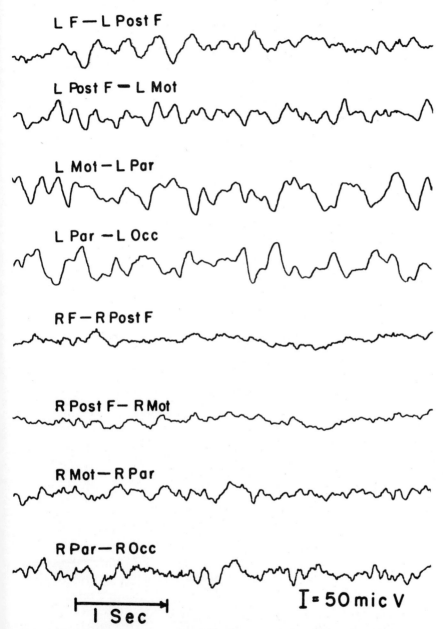

Fig. 26. Severe abnormality on the left side, more marked in the parietal than the frontal region, in a 17-year-old male who was recovering from a traumatic brain laceration with hemiparesis and aphasia ten days after injury. The right side was mildly abnormal especially in occipital region, but the marked asymmetry of the record is important. The abnormality consists of delta with some theta as well. Voltage is greatly increased.

ful to have this group, but it is not logical to include it in the normal divisions.

The various abnormal disturbances cover all the six frequency bands of the spectrum as well as a variety of amplitudes. Their distribution over the scalp, as well as in time, is an important feature of the type of abnormality. This involves the use of terms "diffuse asymmetrical" or "focal" to indicate whether the abnormal activity is seen in all leads or only on one side of the head or in only one area as a focus (Figs. 23, 24 and 25).

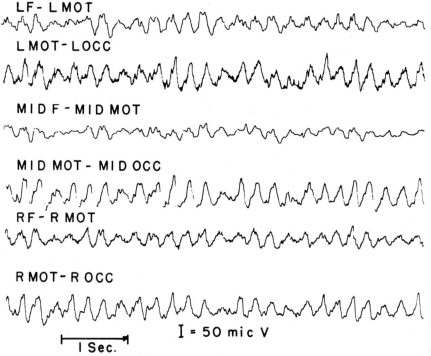

Fig. 27. Severe bilateral diffuse abnormality consisting mainly of 4 to 5 per second theta of greatly increased voltage in all leads. This is a case of a 51-year-old epileptic male with considerable intellectual deterioration.

The distribution in time involves terms such as "rare," "scattered," "paroxysmal" or "continuous," depending on the amount of the activity per minute of record (Figs. 26 and 27). Another relation of abnormality to time is whether a certain pathological electrical activity is bilaterally synchronous or not (Fig. 29). Abnormal sensitivity to mild or moderate activation is another factor of abnormality, the degree of which depends on what activity is uncovered by this means. All these data can best be summarized in a table which also includes the features of the normal electroencephalogram.

This table is for comparison, is essentially diagrammatic, and should not be used for interpreting records. The record must be interpreted as a whole unit (Fig. 28).

	DELTA BAND 1½ thru 3½	THETA BAND 4 thru 7	ALPHA BAND 8 thru 13	INTERMEDIATE FAST 14 thru 17	BETA BAND 18 thru 30	VERY FAST	SPIKES	COMPLEXES WAVE & SPIKE
SEV AB	Very slow or Extreme high volt. or Continuous	High volt Diffuse, parox or focal	Extremely high volt Cont in Front or Temp	Very high volt Continuous	Volt very high Focal or parox	If present high volt as well	Many or Focal of High volt	Nearly Cont or many parox
MOD AB	Diffuse c̄ high volt Focal c̄ high volt Parox c̄ high volt.	Mod. voit Diffuse, parox or focal	Absence of alpha in one occip Parox or focal in Front or Temp with inc volt	Focal or parox High volt	Parox or focal c̄ inc volt over 100 mic V	Occ seen	Mod. no More with activation	In runs & single & parox. more with activation
MILD AB	Diffuse c̄ low volt. Focal c̄ low volt. Parox. c̄ low volt.	Mod. volt and Scat. Temp and Front.	More asymmetry Volt over 150 mic.V Occip alpha fails to respond to light	Diffuse high volt	High volt 50 to 100 mic V Diffuse	Rare	Scat. low volt. except when activated	Scat. except when activated.
BORDERLINE	Scat. low volt. in Frontals	Scat low volt in Temporals Rare to scat in Frontals	Asym or slight inc in volt	Diffuse low volt	Inc volt 30 to 50 Mic.V Prominent in Front	Rare	Rare except when activated	Rare except when activated.
NORMAL	Rare low volt. in Frontals	Rare low volt in Temporals	2 to 90% 20 to 100 mic.V mostly in occip Reduc. on opening the eyes	Rare to scat Low volt	Irreg. and general distribution 5 to 30 mic. V.	Prob absent	None	None

Fig. 28. Summary table of various abnormalities in relation to frequency, voltage, amount and distribution.

The technique of such interpretation and the application of this material for clinical purposes are covered in Chapter IX.

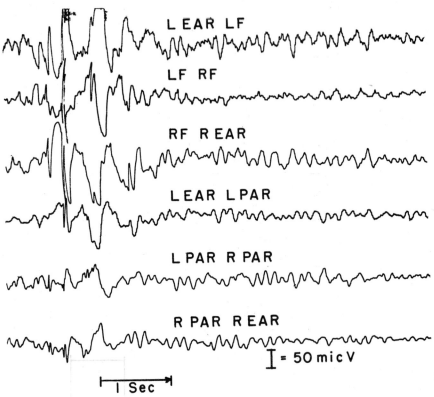

LEAR LF

LF RF

RF R EAR

L EAR L PAR

L PAR R PAR

R PAR R EAR

I = 50 mic V

1 Sec

Fig. 29. A severe paroxysmal type of abnormality consisting of a short run of spike and waves, bilaterally synchronous, more prominent in both frontals, and often called seizure patterns. In this case they occurred frequently without activation in a 16-year-old epileptic who had frequent grand and petit mal type of seizures. In addition there are theta and sharp waves bilaterally.

REFERENCES

1. Adrian, E. D.: Cortical Rhythms. J. Nerv. Ment. Dis., *81*:55–56, 1935.
2. Davis, H., and Davis P. A.: Action Potentials of the Brain in Normal States of Cerebral Activity. Arch. Neurol. & Psychiat., *36*:1214–1224, 1936.
3. Gibbs, F. A.: Cortical Frequency Spectra of Healthy Adults. J. Nerv. Ment. Dis., *95*:417–426, 1942.
4. Henry C. E.: Electroencephalograms of Normal Children. Monograph of the Society for Research in Child Development. Washington, D. C., Nat. Res. Council, 1944, XI, 71 pp.
5. Jasper, H. H.: Electroencephalography in Child Neurology and Psychiatry. Pediatrics, *3*:783–800, 1949.
6. Lindsley, D. B.: A Longitudinal Study of the Occipital Alpha Rhythm in Normal Children; Frequency and Amplitude Standards. J. Genet. Psychol., *55*:197–213, 1939.
7. Smith, J. R.: The Frequency Growth of the Human Alpha Rhythms During Normal Infancy and Childhood. J. Psychol., *11*:177–198, 1941.

CHAPTER IV

Technique

RECORDING APPARATUS

THERE ARE NOW a number of manufacturers of electroencephalo-graphic equipment in the United States and abroad. It would not be proper in this book to recommend those manufacturers who produce the most reliable apparatus. An alphabetical list would be of no value. The reader who is interested is referred to the American Electroencephalographic Society, which has published a pamphlet on the minimum requirements of such apparatus.[2] The present apparatus available commercially is considerably improved in appearance, ruggedness and performance over the equipment available before World War II. Most of the modern equipment is built into one unit and is mounted on wheels. Some of these sets operate entirely on the output from the commercial 110 volt alternating current, requiring no storage batteries or even dry cells. Equally good equipment requires, for its first two stages of amplification, a storage battery to heat the filaments and B batteries for the plates. The use of chargers which are continually in operation while the set is turned on eliminates the need of multiple storage batteries or charging them during the night. B battery power requirements for the plates of the pre-amplifiers is now so improved in efficiency that a good set of B batteries will last four to six months. Partial operation by means of B batteries and storage cells is nearly balanced in weight and space (needed for the voltage regulator). Undoubtedly, as electronics advances and better vacuum tubes and equipment become available, the use of B batteries and storage batteries may be entirely eliminated by means of light weight, satisfactory voltage regulators and power supplies. Such apparatus can then be plugged in in the same way as a heater or an electric toaster and be ready to function. The cost at the present time depends on the number of channels or units that one desires. In earlier days, one was often satisfied with one or two channels, but the modern demands on the apparatus, particularly that involved in the localization of intracranial lesions, makes so few channels highly unsatisfactory. Less than 4 channels is considered inadequate. Six channels is the usual choice of most neuropsychiatric laboratories, but many prefer 8 channels for better localization and accuracy. The cost per channel is around 500 dollars, so a 6-channel machine would cost from 2500 to 3500 dollars with all the parts and maintenance equipment delivered. The period of life, with proper care, should be at least five years and may run as high as eight or nine years. A new principle of recording or radical improvements in efficiency might, of course, render obsolete apparatus that was otherwise working satisfactorily before the elapse of such periods.

The technique of operating, setting up and maintaining any particular instrument is fully covered in the instruction manual that the manufacturer supplies and will be omitted here. The recording equipment now available is strongly built of excellent material, but it is still an instrument of *extreme delicacy* and *precision*. It amplifies exceedingly small electric discharges one to two million times and may do this from eight different sources simultaneously without the slightest interference of one channel with another. Therefore this equipment should be handled with the greatest care and respect. The instructions and advice of each manufacturer should be thoughtfully and diligently followed.

EXAMINATION ROOM

Formerly it was essential to enclose the subject in a grounded, screened room, called a faradic cage, in order to keep out the air-borne 60-cycle current from the wires and power lines that run through hospitals and laboratories. The newer equipment is so well balanced and well shielded in its cabinet that it is not necessary to have any form of shielding in order to obtain satisfactory records. The subject must not be too close to unshielded electric light and power wires, and the laboratory should be 100 feet or so away from diathermy machines or sparking commutators of high-powered motors. In some institutions the wiring is antiquated and unshielded, producing a 60-cycle current air-borne interference intense enough to make shielding necessary. In all modern buildings the lighting circuits are in grounded metal conduits, so that there is usually little need of shielding. If one is building a laboratory in which electroencephalographic apparatus is to be installed, the actual cost of adding the shielding during construction is so small and the trouble so slight that one should do it in order to exclude the possibility of interference from air-borne currents from unknown sources, connected possibly with television or other newer develop-ments. On the other hand, it is expensive and difficult to convert the inside of an ordinary room into a satisfactory shielded cage.

The general advice to the beginner in this field is first of all to try out the apparatus in the situation where he plans to use it, and then assess the air-borne or other interference. If it is zero or minimal, there is no need to worry about shielding. If there is a good deal of 60-cycle artifact on the recording pen, an electronic engineer should be consulted.

Some workers are firm in insisting that the apparatus and patients be in the same room so that the recorder can watch closely what is going on during the actual recording. On the other hand, there are some who feel that the subject should be isolated in a quiet, possibly soundproof, room with the apparatus and technician in another place. In this case conversation and the sound of the machine in operation will not dis-turb or distract the subject. It is highly desirable, however, to have a window of some sort between the observer and the subject. This en-ables the recordist to identify movement producing artifacts and to see whether the patient is comfortable, asleep or having a convulsion. This is the usual set-up in most hospitals and has proved to be the most prac-tical. The apparatus in such an arrangement can be adjusted, moved or taken over for other functions without disturbing the patient.

The examination entails no particular preparation of the subject. The patient should have eaten within an hour or so of the examination to insure a normal blood sugar. If he has not eaten in that time, he may be given a 50-gm. dose of glucose in some water with a little lemon juice in order to bring the blood sugar up to a normal value. As will be shown later, a fasting blood sugar of 60 or 70 mg. per 100 cc. may in-troduce abnormal waves into the electroencephalogram which would give a false reading. The patient can either sit in a comfortable chair or lie on a stretcher or bed, depending upon the facilities in the laboratory. The recumbent position is perhaps easier for the technician and more comfortable for the subject, but in a number of laboratories chairs are preferred. It is essential that the subject be comfortable and relaxed, so that he can be quiet and eliminate voluntarily the tenseness of the neck and head muscles which would interfere with the recording.

ELECTRODES

The electrodes used in the laboratories at the present time are not standardized. The use of needles which Berger used in 1929 has been generally abandoned, but there are a few laboratories that find that a hypodermic needle (No. 26) can be inserted into the scalp as quickly as the application of a surface electrode (Fig. 30, *A*). For the ordinary recording of an electroencephalogram this technique is all right, and most patients do not object to having half a dozen or more needles stuck into the skin, provided the needles are sharp and the introduction

A

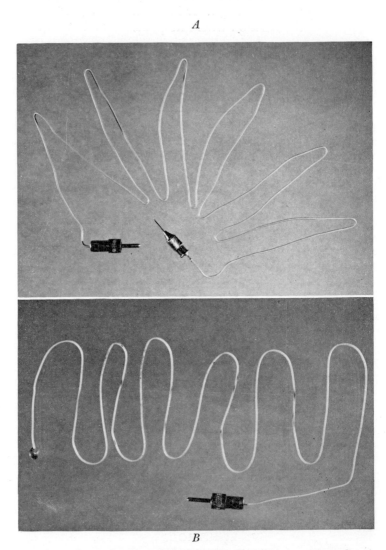

B

Fig. 30 *A*. A needle electrode made from a No. 26 stainless steel hypodermic needle soldered to the electrode wire. This type of electrode can be quickly inserted into the scalp with minimum discomfort.

B. The usual solder disk electrode which can be made in the laboratory by a technician. It is 5 mm. in diameter and is shown on the left side of the picture. It is attached to the electrode wire as shown in the picture. At the bottom is the connecting jack that is plugged into the electrode box.

is done with efficiency.* In most laboratories, however, a surface electrode is applied. There are a number of these. The first one was introduced by Gibbs in 1935 and consists of a simple 1 cm.-solder disk, that can be made by the technicians in the laboratory, in which is embedded a tinned copper wire insulated except at the tip. The other end of this wire is attached to a suitable plug which goes to the switchboard (Fig. 30, B).

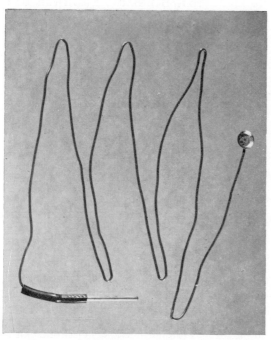

Fig. 30 C. Five millimeter electrode made from pure silver and soldered to the connecting wire. This electrode is just as easy to attach as that shown in Fig. 30 B and eliminates the artifact from bimetallic currents occasionally found with solder. The connection to the electrode box is shown at the bottom.

Since normal resistance of the skin would preclude picking up these currents, it is necessary to lower this by the application of an electrode paste. This paste is often the same as is used in the electrocardiographic laboratory. It is a mixture of soap, pumice, calcium chloride, salt and water, and is rubbed into the skin until a redness occurs. Some laboratories remove, with acetone or ether, the natural oil of the skin before applying the paste. After the electrode paste is rubbed into the skin, the electrode is placed on top of this small amount of paste and is held there

* Grass[11] obtained some laboratory evidence that the stainless steel needle, which is the usual metal of the hypodermic, has a property of distorting and reducing the amplitude of the higher frequency waves. Therefore, the slow-fast components such as are encountered in petit mal may be distorted by such electrodes and identification may be difficult. Platinum-iridium or silver plated steel would not have this objection, but are not readily available.

with a rubber supporting structure, adhesive tape, collodion dressing or, in some places, elastic attachments to fit onto a head gear of one sort or another. The usual method is to drop some collodion on top of the electrode and let this dry from a compressed air jet or from a small rubber bulb held in the hand. Hair dryers can be used for this purpose. If done neatly and carefully, such electrodes remain in place without producing artifacts for one to twelve hours. Recently there has been introduced a paste made from Bentonite, which can be obtained from

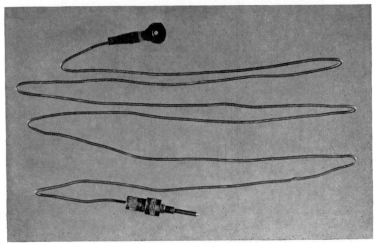

Fig. 30 *D*. This is the type of electrode designed and used by Dr. Jasper. It consists of a silver cup covered by a felt ring. The silver cup is carefully chlorided and the felt pad is kept moist with saline. This electrode eliminates both bimetallic artifacts from solder and due to the chloriding of the silver and the contact with the sodium chloride in the pad is also very free of any polarization currents. Is is not as easy to attach to the scalp as the previous three electrodes but it has given excellent service over the years for the Montreal group.

any pharmacist, which is mixed with calcium chloride, salt and water. This mixture* is placed on the prepared skin in a small lump, and the electrode is embedded in this and no further covering is used.

In some laboratories, because solder consists of two metals and may produce a *bimetallic* voltage artifact an electrode of silver is used. To reduce polarization voltage artifacts the silver electrodes may be carefully chlorided. Jasper[14] in Montreal uses a silver-chlorided cup on

* Bentonite paste usually has the following formula: Bentonite, 75; calcium chloride (saturated solution), 15; sodium chloride (saturated solution), 10; glycerine, 5. The calcium chloride may cause an irritative dermatitis in some sensitive persons, particularly if the paste is applied after too vigorous rubbing with acetone (abraded skin) or if it is left on too long, three to six hours, or if it is not washed off after the test. Usually the incidence of such complication is less than one in 1000 applications and clears up after a few days. Desquamation, erosion and even permanent scarring of the skin can occur if care is not taken in using this paste. It is better to keep the amount of calcium chloride down to the lowest level that prevents drying of the paste.

E

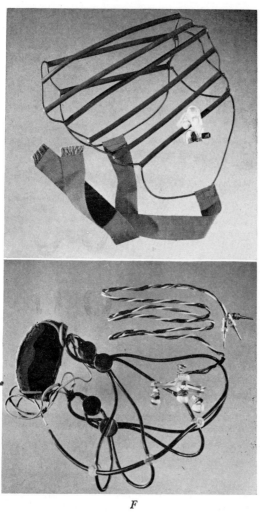

F

Fig. 30 *E*. The "beauty rest" elastic cap and the translucent plastic electrode holder designed and used by Walter. The electrode is made of silver which is carefully chlorided and covered with a cloth pad which is soaked in saline. Artifacts are eliminated in the same way as Fig. 30 *D*. After the "beauty rest" is snapped on to the patient's head the electrode attaches easily by inserting the curved part under the elastic strap. This type of electrode is in general use in Europe and has been quite satisfactory in all of their laboratories.

F. The elastic cap and tripod electrode designed by Rémond in Paris. The head rest is attached to the head in a similar way as the Walter one. Actually 3 electrodes are incorporated into each tripod which appears in the center of the picture slightly to the right. Each tripod consists of a silver chlorided electric element covered with cloth soaked in saline in the same way as the Walter one. The three are placed on the scalp in an appropriate position to be studied and the center hook under the spring is pushed down to engage one of the supporting elastic bands. In this way 15 electrodes can be put on the head in a very short time. Some patients object to the tightness of the elastic cap. In the hands of some workers this electrode arrangement is not as satisfactory as the individual ones. Some of the laboratories in France find it very practical and efficient.

which a felt ring is attached and which has proved very practical for his group (Fig. 30, *D*). He uses a heavy unit, so that, if it remains attached, one can be assured that there is electrical continuity with the scalp. Walter[23] in England, and most of the workers there, use a commercial form of hairdresser beauty-wave cap which goes over the head. Between the rubber strands a plastic electrode holder is inserted which contains a silver element that has been chlorided and is surrounded by a felt pad soaked in saline. The elastic property of the beauty headdress holds the electrodes firmly against the scalp and allows recording to take place. The notable advantages of this technique are that the electrode can be moved from time to time without disturbing the patient, and more accurate localizations are possible than with the fixed placements in use in many laboratories (Figs. 30, *E, F*).

SPECIAL ELECTRODES AND THEIR PLACEMENT

Basal Leads

The usual scalp electrodes record activity mostly from the convex surface of the brain. Disturbances or normal rhythms from the under surface of the frontal and temporal lobes and from midline structures deep within the brain are so attenuated by the actual distance of the scalp electrodes that their presence may be entirely missed because of the activity at the convexity.

Grinker and Serota[12] in 1939 devised a stilette electrode that could be inserted through the nose into the mucous membrane and bone in the posterior nasopharynx. Activity at the base of the brain can be recorded from such an electrode, but the risk and complication of its application have discouraged its use. Jasper[16] recently has used an insulated needle inserted via the mouth and under radiological control in the foramen ovale. It lies 1 cm. from the under part of the tip of the temporal lobe.

The present author[20] devised a nasal electrode, the tip of which was inflatable to insure contact instead of perforating tissue. It often produced artifacts from movement in the pharynx and required cocainization of the patient before insertion.

In 1949 MacLean[18] in our laboratory developed a simple nasal electrode made of heavy insulated silver tubing shaped so that it could easily be inserted without cocainization and would remain in place without discomfort or artifact (Fig. 30, *G*). With one in each nostril a pair of basal leads is obtained. In the same year Arellano[3] working in our laboratory added to this basal coverage by devising an electrode that could be placed against the tympanic membrane in each ear (Fig. 30, *H*).

By means of such basal electrodes the activity of the base of the brain can be recorded, thus greatly enlarging the scope of electroencephalography.

G

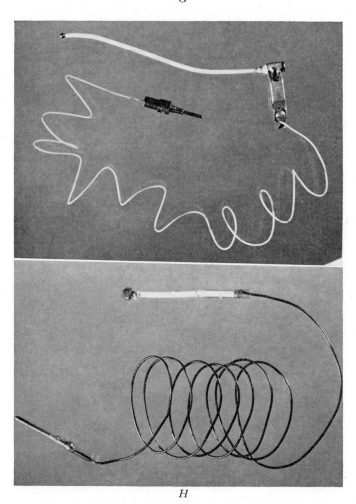

H

Fig. 30 G. The pharyngeal electrode designed by MacLean. This electrode is slipped into the nose and requires only a little lubrication with mineral oil to slide easily into the nasopharynx. The silver tip lies against the posterior pharyngeal wall. The body of the electrode is solid copper which can be adjusted to fit the normal curve of the nasal passage. It is covered with an insulating enamel. The right hand or outer side of this electrode is free of insulation and a clip is attached to this as is shown. This clip carries the wire that runs to the electrode box and serves to orient the electrode in the proper plane in the nasal passage. Usually two such electrodes are inserted to give bipolar pharyngeal recording.

H. The tympanic electrode designed by Arellano. This consists of a rigid copper wire covered with enamel. On the tip at the left is a small felt hemisphere which is attached to the electrode and rests against the tympanic membrane after insertion. When this is inserted the felt hemisphere is soaked in saline to insure good contact. The right side of the electrode is soldered to the lead in wire which goes to the electrode box.

Dural Leads

Jasper introduced the dural lead in 1941.[14] He seized the opportunity afforded by the burr holes made for the purpose of ventriculography to place sterile silver electrodes on the dura mater itself just before the neurosurgeon incises this membrane for the passage of the ventricular needle.

Recording can be done in the operating room, or the patient can be sent to the electroencephalographic laboratory after the scalp and bone have been prepared, a sterile dressing covering and holding the electrode in place. This lead is still 0.5 cm. away from the brain, but is naturally in a better position for the recording of electrical activity in the brain under it. The obvious disadvantage is that complete coverage of both cerebral hemispheres is impossible, since only two burr holes are made for simple air studies. On the other hand, it does furnish an opportunity to record from the brain with the dura intact and the normal spinal fluid covering of the cortex in situ. As will be shown later, the recording from the exposed cortex is complicated by artifacts from drying of the brain surface and the effects of room air on it.

It is, however, a procedure that delays the air studies, introduces some risk of infection, and may not be near the area of pathological electrical activity. It has not met with much enthusiasm in most clinics, but may be of increasing physiological interest as more and more electroencephalographic investigators are associated with prefrontal leucotomy projects.

Cortical Leads

Berger was the first to place electrodes on the exposed human brain in the operating theatre.[5] He noted that the direct electrocorticogram, as such records are called, had higher voltages and a broader band of frequencies than from scalp leads. Jasper[15] and Penfield extensively developed this technique in the search for epileptic foci and scars which could then be excised. Walker[22] and his co-workers in World War II further expanded this technique by better design of the electrode holder. Specially built cortical electrodes and holders that can be autoclaved and clamped onto the opened skull in the operating room are now commercially available (Figs. 30, *I* and *J*). They consist of eight to ten electrodes connected to a suitable length of shielded cable which is also sterile. The end of this can be handed to the electroencephalographic technician and connected to the apparatus, which may be outside the operating theater. Since the modern machines are portable, it is not essential to have a separate set of apparatus for this purpose.

The details of the technique of recording cortical potentials during neurosurgical procedures are sufficiently complicated to be omitted from this book. They are well covered, for those who are interested, in the articles by Jasper and Walker.

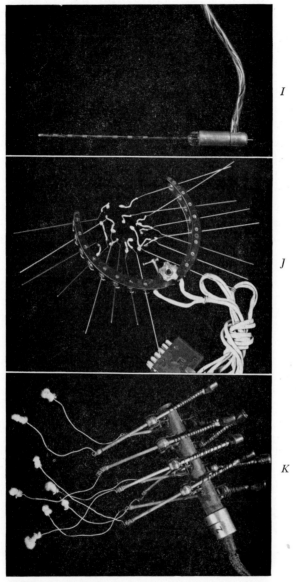

Fig. 30 *I*. The depth electrode showing the concentric silver rings each of which acts as a separate electrode.

J. The cortical electrode holder for recording in the operating room as designed by Grass.

K. The cortical electrode holder designed and used by Jasper and his workers at Montreal.

Subcortical Leads

Walter published a paper in 1946[24] showing that excellent recording from deeper structures of the brain can be obtained from a bipolar electrode made from a silver ventricular needle. The two active elements are carefully chlorided. This needle can be slowly pushed into the brain substance and the electrical record studied until a pathological disturbance is seen. With this needle, deep tumors and abscesses have been localized. It also is an excellent method to explore the electrical activity of the deep structures in the human brain and should furnish valuable knowledge.

Meyers[19] devised a depth electrode consisting of a row of six or seven silver rings 1 cm. apart, insulated from each other, and each running to a lead wire in the center of the electrode, which has a diameter of 2 to 3 mm. (about the same as a ventricular needle). This electrode gives a recording from several different layers below the surface at the same time and has many possibilities of localization of deep lesions as well as the study of normal activity from all the deep and basal structures.

ELECTRODE PLACEMENTS

There has been no real standardization of the electrode placements used in the world at the present time, but no doubt there will be within the next few years. It is generally agreed that, for an ordinary study, a minimum of eleven electrode placements should be used, four on each side of the head, one on the vertex, and two attached to either the ears or the mastoid process, which are close to the temporal lobe.* When exact localization is required, as many as twenty-four to thirty electrodes are used in an examination. The placement of these varies according to the laboratory and the type of clinical localization desired. More are usually concentrated over the area of suspected disease.

Jasper and Kershman[14] in Montreal have worked out a comprehensive method of electrode placement and measurement which they use in all their localizing studies to quote from their monograph on the subject:

A set of forty standard positions, twenty over each hemisphere, are measured from skull landmarks. A complete set of electrodes are never necessary in the examination of any single patient. The fourteen most commonly used positions for an exploratory examination are those marked in Figure 31.

The mid-sagittal line, from nasion to inion, is divided into six equal parts. The five mid-points are called pre-frontal (pf), frontal (F), central (C), parietal (P) and occipital (O). A line is drawn from the prefrontal point to the middle of the zygomatic arch on either side to form the prefrontal line of electrodes. Likewise, lines are drawn from the frontal point to the pre-auricular point, the central to the external auditory meatus, the parietal to the post-auricular point, and the occipital to

* These four on each side are roughly placed as follows: (1) over frontal pole at average hairline, (2) over motor area above and midway from ear to midline, (3) over parietal area, and (4) near occipital pole.

the mastoid crest. Electrodes are placed along these lines at 3 cm. intervals measuring and numbering from the mid-sagittal line in each case (o5 and o6 are measured 4 cm. from o3 and 4 as the only exceptions).

All even numbers appear to the right hemisphere and all odd numbers on the left hemisphere so as to facilitate reference to one hemisphere. For example, position C3 would indicate the mid-central region on the left, while position C4 the homologous region on the right. Likewise, C7 and C8 would indicate the mid-temporal regions of the left and right hemispheres respectively. The occipital line from these measurements falls at the upper border of the occipital lobe so that an additional position 2 cm. above and to one side of the inion is used for the occipital pole leads, Op1 and Op2.

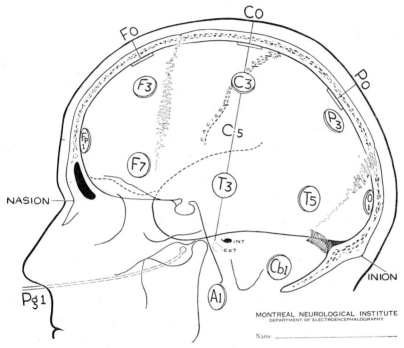

Fig. 31. Diagram of some of the electrodes used in the Montreal placements. Odd numbers are on the left; even numbers are on the right. The dotted line on the left of the picture indicates the relationship of pharyngeal electrodes if used.

They feel strongly that localization without this method is subject to error. Abbott,[1] working in the Massachusetts General Hospital laboratory, has devised a method of using templets from which electrode measurements and placements can be obtained, and this work will soon be published.

Most laboratory workers, however, simply place the electrodes by eye over what they consider to be symmetrical lines on both sides of the head, with two electrodes over the frontal area, two over the motor area, two over the parietal and two over the occipital region on each side. In deference to this placement by eye it is well to remember that the thickness of the skull varies and that the actual convolutions of the brain vary tremendously from person to person, so that even with the most exact measurement of the scalp, one could not state definitely that a particular cerebral area was directly below it. For most cases of cerebral localization by the electroencephalogram careful placement of the electrodes by eye by an experienced technician covers most of the needs. When more time is available and exact correlation with clinical findings is desired, measuring the positions of the electrodes is perhaps worthwhile.

In the school set up by Gibbs[9] (which represents in America a rather large proportion of the workers in electroencephalography) the electrodes on the two ears are hooked together as a common reference electrode and connected with ground, and the eight or more scalp electrodes placed on the surface of the skull are each connected to this "double-ear-ground" electrode and the recording thus obtained. Gibbs calls this "monopolar" recording. In other laboratories the ears are not grounded and are kept separate, since they are regarded as active electrodes, which they undoubtedly are. This school feels that only two electrodes should be observed in each channel, and this is called "bipolar" recording. In some laboratories both methods are used at each examination, which would appear to be the more conservative and practical method of getting the best out of both schools. Furthermore, if an indifferent electrode is desired, a satisfactory place for it is over the seventh cervical vertebra. If one has eight channels, it is possible to include eight scalp electrodes at the same time and obtain a record without adjusting the apparatus. The main point is that all areas of the scalp should be covered for a reasonable amount of time, such as two or three minutes for each area, so that nothing occurs paroxysmally or regionally that will be missed. Most laboratories, after a preliminary run with the patient breathing normally and as relaxed as he can be, then try to activate something by overbreathing. The patient is told to breathe in and out deeply about fifteen or twenty times a minute for a period of three minutes. The record is taken during this time and for one to three minutes of normal breathing in addition before the end of the examination. (See Activation, page 66.)

After the recording is completed the electrodes are removed with a little water and acetone. If the skin is sensitive and reddened by the procedure, a little cold cream may be applied. Complications from allergic skin sensitivity to the ingredients of the usual electrode pastes are exceedingly rare (less than 0.1 per cent). When they are encountered, a dermatologist should be consulted.

TECHNIQUE OF LOCALIZATION

There are essentially three methods of determining which electrodes are nearest a particular source of electrical activity in the electroencephalogram.

Monopolar Localization

The first method is called "monopolar" and requires an indifferent electrode as remote as possible from the activity being studied. Gibbs advocates using as an indifferent electrode the two ears linked together and grounded. A large number of followers of Gibbs use this system. The advantage of having both ears and "mother earth" at the same potential is questionable (Fig. 32).

Since the ear is right over the temporal lobe, it is invariably an active lead. By connecting the opposite ear on the same lead, some of this activity cancels out. A better indifferent lead is one over the seventh

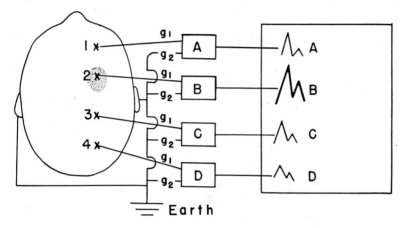

MONOPOLAR TECHNIQUE (GIBBS)

Fig. 32. Diagram of a 4-channel electroencephalograph connected to the right side of a patient's head in the monopolar technique designed and used by Gibbs. Note that both ears are connected together and run to the ground as well as to each of the channels of the electroencephalogram. A disturbance such as that at electrode No. 2 will give increased amplitude in channel B as is shown in the picture. On the other hand, if the brain under the ear on either side is active some confusion may result in the picture.

cervical vertebra but in this case the readily identifiable electrocardiogram appears as an artifact.

The other scalp electrodes are each connected via an amplifier to the indifferent lead, and recording takes place.

If a disturbance or particular activity is close to a certain electrode, this one will show the greatest amplitude (Fig. 33).

Bipolar Localization

The second method is called "bipolar." Two electrodes, 5 or 6 cm. apart, are attached to the scalp in a variety of places, and the records are obtained from pairs of electrodes and compared with other pairs in different areas on the head. No indifferent, or common, electrode is used, and the entire examination depends upon the presence of abnormal activity in a certain pair that distinguishes it from others (Fig. 34). This technique is less likely to pick up abnormal waves from a deep lesion than the so-called monopolar system. This method is not generally used alone, but when combined with the first method of recording has proved very satisfactory. If only a few pairs of closely spaced electrodes are used, the localized abnormality from a small tumor may not be picked up at all. As many as twenty pairs may be

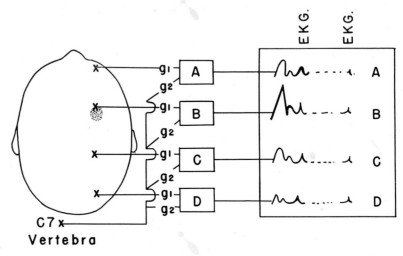

MONOPOLAR TECHNIQUE

Fig. 33. The monopolar technique devised by Brazier and Casby in which the seventh cervical vertebra is used as the indifferent electrode. Many think this method is superior to that of Gibbs. The electrocardiographic artifact which usually is obtained is not troublesome and can readily be identified. It is possible by using a potentiometer connected to another area in the cervical region to eliminate the artifact entirely.

necessary if this method is to be relied on alone. If the distance between the electrodes is large, say 5 to 6 cm., this objection is reduced, but then the sharpness of the localization is less clear.

Phase Reversal

The third method is called "phase reversal" and was first applied to the localization of tumors in the brain by Walter in 1936.[25] The principle of this technique depends on the fact that electrical waves behave like sound waves or waves in water by spreading out in all directions from their point of origin. At any instant of time the picture of this center of origin shows waves pointing in opposite directions and therefore having opposite polarity or sign (Fig. 35).

The amplifiers used in electroencephalography are constructed so that when grid 1 at the input is negative to grid 2, the pen in the writing unit is deflected up. Making grid 2 negative to grid 1 pro-

duces a downward deflection. A number of electrodes in the vicinity of
a particular source of electrical activity are placed equidistant on a
straight line. This line of electrodes must be of sufficient length so that
the electrodes at each end are on opposite sides of the disturbance to

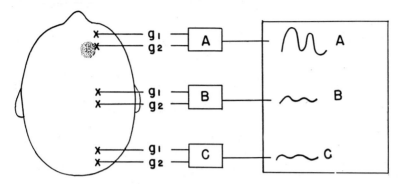

BIPOLAR TECHNIQUE

Fig. 34. Electroencephalographic recording using 3 channels each connected to its
own two electrodes. A disturbance such as is picked up by amplifier A, if small
enough not to spread to the other channels, may be localized as in the diagram.
This technique is useful when combined with other forms of localization. The rhythm
at B and C is not related to that of A.

be localized. This is attained in electroencephalogram localization by
a low prefrontal and postoccipital electrode, in the longitudinal line,
and both ears in the lateral lines.

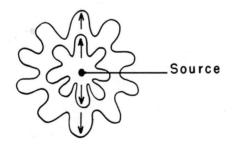
Source

REVERSAL   OF   WAVES
AT SOURCE

Fig. 35. A diagram of a source of a wave activity showing the spread of the wave
front in a circular fashion in all directions. This results in a reverse of phase at opposite points on the circle.

The amplifiers of a multi-channel electroencephalograph are arranged
so that each grid points in the same direction along this line of electrodes. Therefore the place of origin of the electrical activity, or in
other words its localization, will show up as a change in direction of the
waves. This will appear on the record as a reversal of sign of the par-

ticular activity and will show on the paper a 180-degree reversal in phase of the wave form.

The pairs of electrodes showing this change in direction or phase reversal are 1 and 2 and 3 and 4. Numbers 5 and 6 are of the same sign as 3 and 4 and are, therefore, in phase. The location of the activity is between 1 and 4 at either 2 or 3 (Fig. 36).

In order to localize more specifically whether number 2 or number 3 is closest to the focus of activity, another channel, B, is connected to them in the same direction, so that electrode number 2 goes to grid 1 and number 3 to grid 2. In such an arrangement, grid 2 of channel A

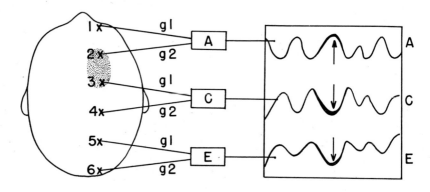

PHASE REVERSAL TECHNIQUE
(SIMPLE)
(BIPOLAR)

Fig. 36. A diagram of the application of the principles shown in Fig. 35 to three amplifiers recording as in the figure. Note that the disturbance between electrodes 2 and 3 shows a phase reversal between amplifiers A and C but does not tell whether the disturbance is at electrode 2 or 3.

and the grid 1 of the new channel B are attached to the same electrode number 2, and also grid 2 of B and grid 1 of C are joined together by means of the common electrode number 3.

A fifth channel, D, is connected in a similar way to number 4 and number 5 electrodes. Such an arrangement now clearly shows that the reversal of phase is centered at electrode number 3. It is here that the particular electrical activity being studied is localized. When amplifiers are interconnected in this way, they are said to be "linked" (Fig. 37).

This method can be used to localize any recurring wave form or impulse, provided the duration of the event is long enough to be identified as occurring at the same time in all channels of the record. There should be exact line-up of all writing pens one above the other on a line perpendicular to the edge of the paper. If this precaution is taken, repetitive activity of frequencies as fast as fifteen per second is not too difficult to identify as occurring simultaneously in a number of channels, especially if the paper speed can be advanced to 6 cm. per second. Very short duration impulses or waves such as a five-milliseconds spike, unless they are isolated from each other by a sufficient period of no activity at least 100-milliseconds long, are difficult to localize by this technique. Slow waves of three to four per second present their focus most clearly by such a method.

If enough channels are available, a second line of electrodes is arranged to cross the presumed focus at a 90 degree angle. This will establish the localization in a second dimension and is routine in such studies.

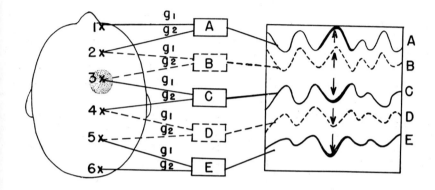

PHASE REVERSAL TECHNIQUE
(LINKED AMPLIFIERS)
BIPOLAR

Fig. 37. By adding two amplifiers to the diagram of Fig. 36 (these are shown in their traces in dotted lines) the phase reversal technique is made more accurate and the disturbance at electrode 3 is clearly localized in the diagram.

VOLTAGE DEPRESSION

In addition to the three methods of localization just described, the appearance of an area of absence of electrical activity can be considered a site of a lesion.

It is important in the recording of these tests to be sure that accurate calibrations are made before and after every examination, that the same setting of the amplifiers is noted and that if any changes are made deliberately they be clearly shown at the appropriate place on the record. The speed of paper generally adopted in this country by the American Electroencephalographic Society and by most of the European societies is 3 cm. per second, although a few laboratories abroad and in this country prefer the electrocardiographic speed of 2.5 cm. per second. In long records, or if there is a paper shortage, it is often economical to record at 1.5 cm. per second, which is half-speed on the usual recorder. It is always best in such cases to have samples here and there of recording at standard speed. In order to see the detail of fast activity or to compare the property of a wave that appears in more than one channel simultaneously, it is convenient from time to time to run the paper at the fast speed of 6 cm. per second. Most modern machines are equipped with three speeds and a convenient gear change, so that this can be done during recording with great ease.

It is important to note the changes in speed on the record every time they occur, and, in presenting records either for publication or for clinical demonstration, it is mandatory to show on the record both the *calibration* and a *time scale* (Fig. 38). The standard amplification settings in general use produce 1 cm. of pen movement for 100 microvolts fed into the amplifier. With abnormal brain waves of higher amplitude, such as are found during seizures, it is necessary to reduce this amplification by factors of 2 or 4 or even 8 as soon as they occur in order to prevent amplifier blocking with resulting distortion of the record. It is desirable to have on the machine a *master gain control* which can do this instantly in all channels. Most manufacturers will supply this on request. When the voltage of some of the components is so low as not to be readily identifiable, increasing the gain is recommended. Whenever departure is made in amplification settings from the standard value, such information must be written on the paper at the time and, of course, kept in mind in examining the record later. A number of the commercial apparatus available have a variable filter circuit to exclude extraneous potentials such as from muscle or from movement. These filters, of course, distort the record, but this is legitimate, provided the operator knows what their characteristics are and indicates what filter setting he is using on the record at the time it is taken. The instruction manual of the manufacturer should fully cover the use of such filters.

The training of technicians and of the interpreter of the record and filing and handling reports are covered in Chapter IX.

ARTIFACTS

An artifact in the electroencephalogram is defined as any disturbance in the record not produced by potentials from the brain. These occur from four sources: (1) air-borne, (2) instrumental, (3) electrode, (4) biological.

1. The first includes air-borne 60-cycle alternating current waves that radiate from unshielded 60-cycle equipment, such as old type diathermy machines, x-ray apparatus or motor commutators. Unshielded light or power wires that carry current will radiate this interference. It is also sometimes picked up from the air by direct current lighting wires, telephone or signal wires, and re-radiated in the laboratory.

The patient acts as an aerial and picks up this 60-cycle air-borne current and transmits it via the electrodes to the electroencephalogram recorded. In unusual situations where the laboratory is close to a radio

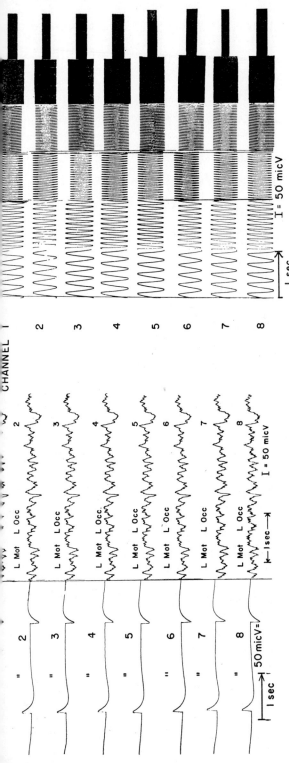

Fig. 38 *A.* A calibration signal of 50 microvolts fed into all of the 8 channels of an electroencephalographic machine showing the similarity of response to this common signal.

B. This shows the same apparatus recording from 2 electrodes between the left motor and the left occipital areas. Each channel is connected to these same two electrodes. This is called a voltage calibration or channel comparison to be sure that each channel is recording the activity in an identical manner.

C. A response of an 8-channel electroencephalograph with no filters in the circuit to a sine wave signal of the same amplitude but of different frequencies. The frequencies are indicated by the numbers above the figure and represent cycles per second. Note that the amplitude is well preserved in this type of machine through a sine wave of 60 per second. At 100 per second the ink-writer is incapable of following the amplitude accurately and there is a loss of approximately 70 per cent in amplitude at this point. Also, note that on channel 3 there is an individual loss of amplitude to the frequency 20 but it recovers its full values above this. This sometimes happens due to the individual pen unit having a specific period at this frequency of its own. It is usually too cumbersome to calibrate in routine procedures with a sine wave calibrator. There is little evidence that the brain wave activity follows the sine wave pattern above 20 cycles per second.

station such as a shortwave police unit, the ink writer may respond as a receiver and in a distorted ghostly way say "Calling all cars—a drunk on 5th and Main."

The 60-cycle frequency is simple to identify, especially if the paper

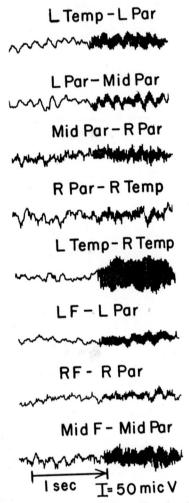

Fig. 39. This shows the 60 cycle artifact in all channels.

speed is increased to 6 cm. per second, when the exact 60-per-second sine waves will appear (see Fig. 39).

An electronic engineer can usually spot the source of this artifact and, by applying condensers or proper shielding, eliminate it. Other forms of air-borne artifacts are annoying. Closing and opening of relays and switches make single or multiple spikes that are picked up in the same way. Telephone dial switches radiate in this way, but are easy to control by condensers. Again the engineer can usually take care of this problem (see Fig. 40).

2. Defects in the apparatus itself may produce a large variety of artifacts, and the reader is referred to the manuals for the technique in

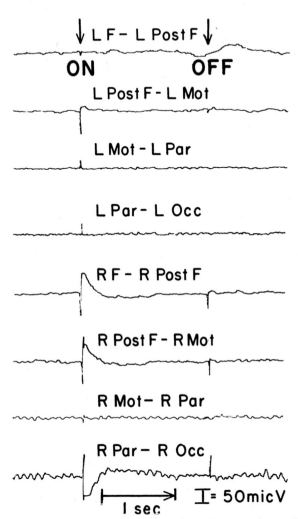

Fig. 40. An artifact from the opening and closing of a large air conditioning switch adjacent to the machine. Note the artifact at the instant of closing the switch and then opening it.

locating and identifying them. Briefly, they are due to noisy batteries, defective vacuum tubes, burned-out condensers, loose connections, short circuits, defective apparatus shielding, inadequate or absent ground connections or broken continuity of any of the wires in the apparatus (see Fig. 41).

Well-trained technicians can usually correct such artifacts. If they are unable to do so, an engineer must be called.

3. The electrode, if it is loose or improperly applied, will produce artifacts from movement on the scalp. If the connecting wire from the electrode to the switch box is defective, conspicuous artifacts will result. Bad polarization of an electrode will cause artifacts (see Fig. 42).

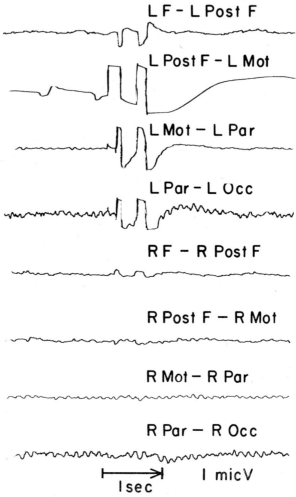

Fig. 41. An artifact due to a defective tube in channel 2. Note that the artifact is picked up in the first four channels.

Reapplying the same electrode or a new one usually takes care of such problems. Further electrode artifacts can result from a person moving around a subject having an electroencephalogram and disturbing the electrodes, or because the patient in moving disturbs the electrodes or shorts their wires. Such artifacts are easy to spot, and direct

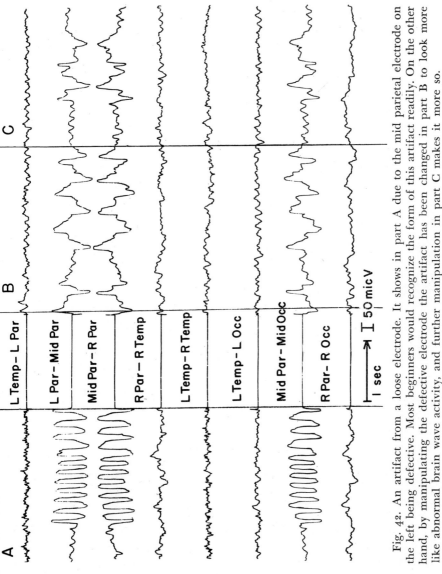

Fig. 42. An artifact from a loose electrode. It shows in part A due to the mid parietal electrode on the left being defective. Most beginners would recognize the form of this artifact readily. On the other hand, by manipulating the defective electrode the artifact has been changed in part B to look more like abnormal brain wave activity, and further manipulation in part C makes it more so.

observation of the subject facilitates this. Sweating, causing short-cir-cuiting of the electrodes, is another source of trouble (see Fig. 43).

4. Biological artifacts are due to (*a*) electrocardiogram transmitted to the scalp electrode and greatly increased in amplitude if an indiffer-ent lead is in use. Identification of this is made absolute if one channel is used to record the electrocardiogram (Fig. 44).

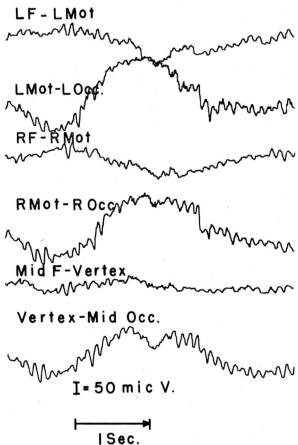

LF-LMot

LMot-LOcc.

RF-RMot

RMot-R Occ

Mid F-Vertex

Vertex-Mid Occ.

I=50 mic V.

I Sec.

Fig. 43. The slow undulation due to movement artifacts which were superim-posed on the electroencephalogram. A similar slow wave undulation is caused by ex-cessive sweating in the scalp.

(*b*) Muscle discharges reaching the scalp electrodes. Neck, face and jaw muscles are close enough to do this; so they must be relaxed. Swal-lowing or coughing introduces a muscle discharge artifact as well as a movement artifact (Fig. 45).

(*c*) The potential difference between the cornea of the eye and the retina is a direct current, and the condenser-coupled electroencephalo-graphic amplifiers would not respond to it, but when a direct current field is moved, as during an eye blink or nystagmus, the fields become

alternating and are picked up by the electroencephalogram recorder.
Eye movements are avoided by fixation or by either a technician or the
patient's gently holding a pad over them. Biological artifacts are recognized by experience and are usually identifiable or can be eliminated
(Fig. 46).

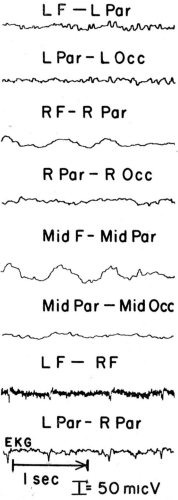

Fig. 44. An artifact produced by the electrocardiogram is shown in channel 8 at the
   bottom of the figure. There is also an artifact from 60-cycle-current in channel 7.

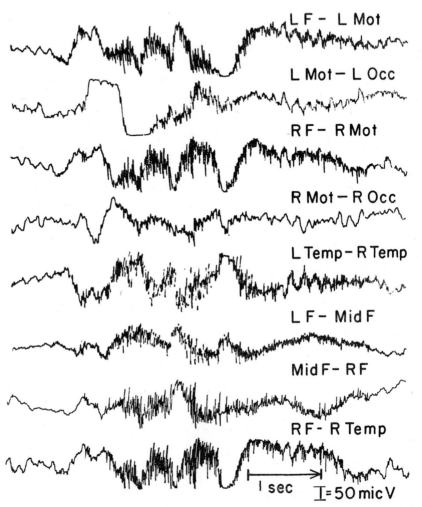

Fig. 45. Muscle artifact appearing in all 8 channels produced by the patient gritting his teeth together. Muscle artifact is one of the easiest to recognize.

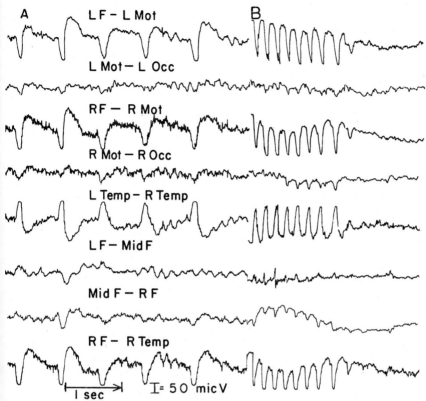

Fig. 46 *A*. An artifact produced by blinking the eyes in a natural way. Note that a component of this is picked up as far back as the occipital-motor lead.

B. The patient is voluntarily blinking his eyes as fast as he can, and the production of the artifact is seen.

SPECIAL TECHNIQUES

Activation of Abnormal Activity

When a normal electroencephalogram of a patient is inconsistent with the clinical state, activation may be undertaken. There are ten different procedures and four or five combinations of two of these, all of which have been used to some extent successfully.

Hyperventilation (Voluntary). This is the simplest and most widely used method, as well as the safest. The patient, while the record is being taken, is told to breathe in and out *deeply* at a rate of 20 to 25 per minute for three minutes. If this is properly done,[7] a moderate alkalosis develops which causes a constriction of the cerebral capillaries. Under such an altered environment abnormal waves may appear and diagnostic patterns be evoked. Normal children and young adults, however, produce some slow waves on overbreathing, so that the time of

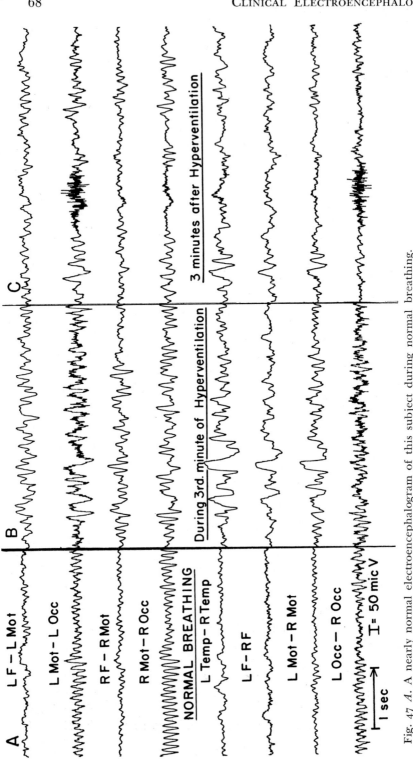

Fig. 47 *A.* A nearly normal electroencephalogram of this subject during normal breathing.
B. The electroencephalogram during the third minute of voluntary overbreathing. This shows high voltage slow delta waves on both sides, slightly more on the left, and indicates a bilateral abnormality at this time.
C. The same record taken three minutes after overbreathing had stopped and when the patient was breathing normally shows the

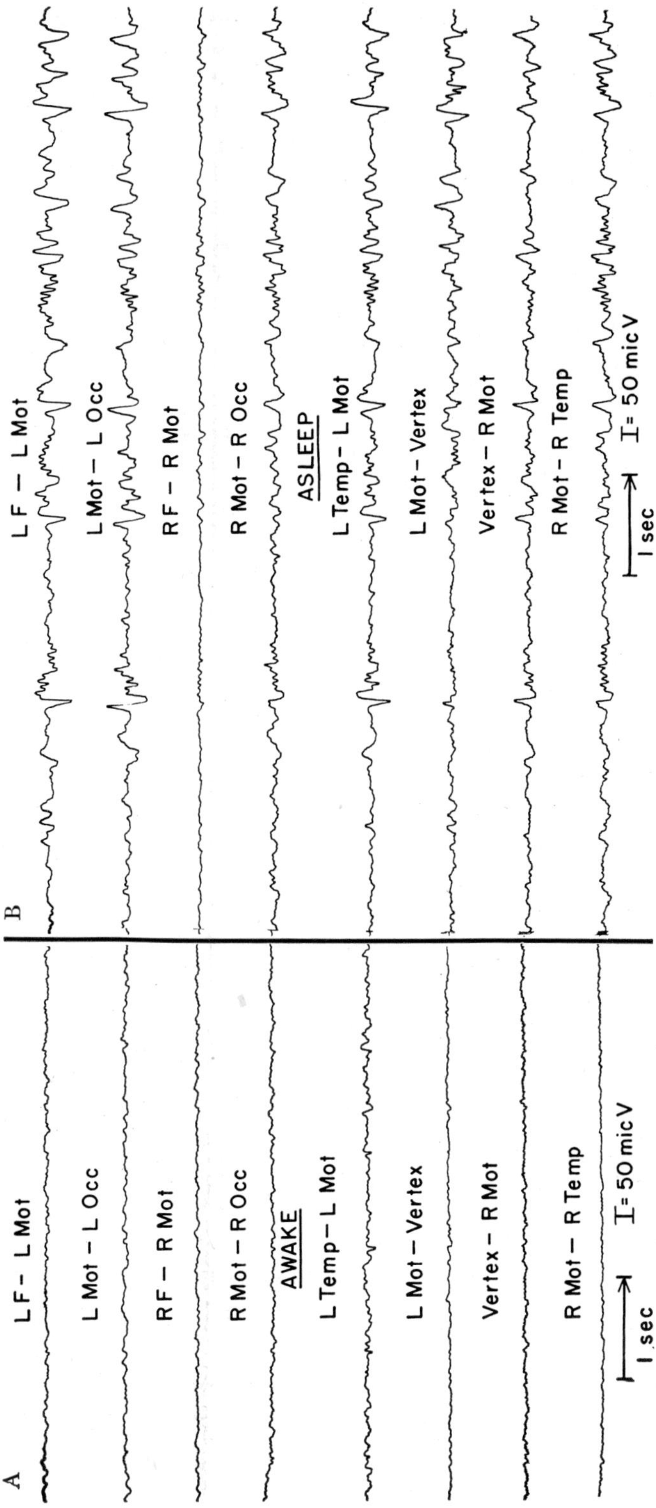

A

LF — L Mot

L Mot — L Occ

RF — R Mot

R Mot — R Occ

AWAKE
L Temp — L Mot

L Mot — Vertex

Vertex — R Mot

R Mot — R Temp

I = 50 mic V   1 sec

B

LF — L Mot

L Mot — L Occ

RF — R Mot

R Mot — R Occ

ASLEEP
L Temp — L Mot

L Mot — Vertex

Vertex — R Mot

R Mot — R Temp

I = 50 mic V   1 sec

Fig. 48 A. The electroencephalogram with no clear-cut abnormality when the patient is awake. B. The patient is asleep from 300 mg. Nembutal taken one-hour previously. The sleep record shows activation of a strong spike focus in the left motor region as shown in the chart. This patient had temporal lobe seizures with increased reflexes on the right side.

appearance as well as the amount and intensity of the "breakdown" to abnormal waves must be carefully considered. The time to return to the previous normal level is important (Fig. 47).

Measuring the minute respiratory volume quantitatively adds greatly to the value of overbreathing. This can be done by means of an ordinary basal metabolism machine,[21] special recording flow meters or other devices. The number of liters breathed per minute should be determined for three minutes prior to hyperventilation, during the overbreathing, and for one minute afterwards. This recording is done at the same time the electroencephalogram record is taken. If the respiratory trace is on another recorder, some crossed signal device is essential. It is possible by electronic means to record the liters breathed per minute directly on the electroencephalographic tracing. Apparatus has been built to record the amount of carbon dioxide in the expired air directly on the electroencephalographic paper and indicate the state of alkalosis this way.

Hyperventilation (Involuntary). An apprehensive or disturbed patient, especially a child having the test for the first time, may overventilate during most of the procedure. Activation of abnormal activity may result from this and mislead the interpreter of the record. A subsequent examination free of anxiety would then be normal and lead to an erroneous therapeutic effect. Experienced technicians are usually able to prevent such situations.

Sleep. During *natural or drug-induced sleep,* abnormalities and specific patterns often appear. This method of activation has been developed by Gibbs, who considers it very useful. It requires a relatively quiet room and specific knowledge of the appearance of the electroencephalogram in the sleep records of normals (Fig. 48).

Low Blood Sugar. The blood sugar may be lowered by fasting or by insulin and the record then taken. Here, too, the abnormalities brought out must be considered in the light of the hypoglycemic tracings of normals. Blood sugar levels of 70 alter the normal only slightly, whereas a severe degree of induced abnormality by this means is significant.

Low Oxygen. The oxygen in the inspired air can be reduced from 20 to 12 or 14 per cent without much visible change in the electroencephalogram of a normal person, whereas the abnormal brain may show a considerable amount of abnormal activity.

Photic (Flickering Light). By using a bright light that illuminates the entire retina on both sides and that can be made to flicker at various rates (a stroboscope is the best one to use), activation can be produced in certain conditions, whereas no abnormal waves are produced in normal subjects. Walter[26] showed that seizure patterns in some children are easily elicited by specific frequency flashes by this means (four to six per second (See Fig. 49).

Sound. Sound, even loud and unexpected, does not usually activate a normal-appearing record. Certain epileptics do have seizures (Arellano[4]) associated with certain specific sound frequencies (musicogenic or audiogenic seizures). Grossman[13] has shown that, during sleep, tones may bring out differences in the evoked cortical electroencephalographic responses that help to localize deep lesions, whereas in a normal the responses are symmetrical (Fig. 50).

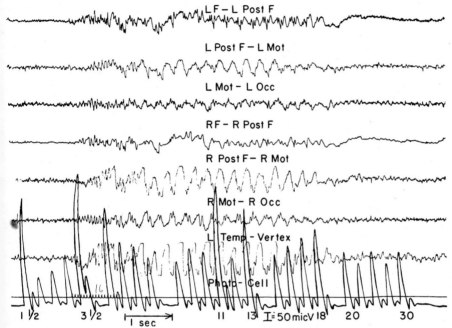

Fig. 49. With an otherwise normal record but subject to occasional seizures usually attributed to rapid changes in illumination in her environment, this person, at the age of 40, in a responsible position, came in for investigation. The record shows the seizure produced by activation from a flashing stroboscopic light at 16 flashes per second. At the bottom of the picture to the left can be seen the photo cell recording from the flashes. After about the 14th flash all of the electroencephalogram is responding at this frequency. The flash was discontinued after running for one second. The wave and spike seizure continued to develop and lasted 4½ seconds and was present on both sides. The analysis of channel 5 is shown by the large spiky lines under the photo cell responses. It is noted that there are frequencies in the slow band at 1½ and 3½ and in the intermediate band at 4 and 5; in the alpha band at 11 and 13; in the intermediate fast at 18; and some at 20 and 30 in the fast band.

Emotional Stresses. In a normal, an artificially produced emotional stress does not alter the electroencephalogram. It may, however, produce some overbreathing, and this effect or the disturbing stress alone can in specific situations activate the record of a few patients.

Hydration. The use of pitressin added to a large intake of fluid produces, in the hands of some workers, a fair degree of activation in epileptics who have normal interseizure records. It is, on the other

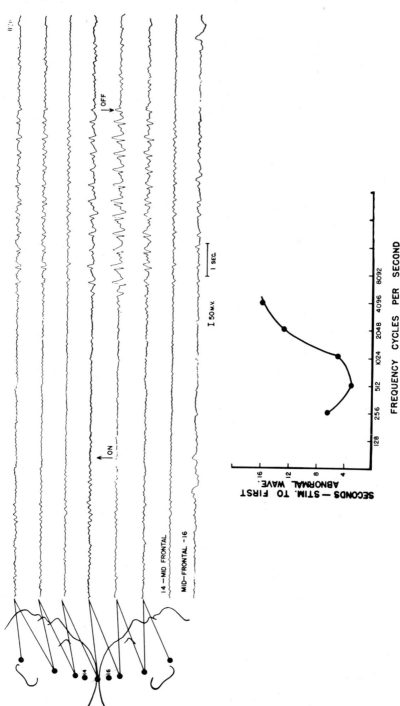

Fig. 50. Activation of a normal electroencephalogram by a pure tone at 512 per second. The tone goes on as marked by the arrow and continues until the reverse arrow opposite the word "off" is encountered. The spell begins approximately four seconds after the onset of the tone and stops immediately that the sound is discontinued. At bottom of picture is graph of tone frequency to latent period. Note 512 per second activates in the shortest time—4 seconds. (From Arellano, Schwab and Casby: EEG

hand, a long, tedious and complicated procedure and therefore not much in favor.

Carotid Sinus Pressure. A few patients have irritable carotid sinuses. They usually have seizures or syncopal spells, and their electroencephalographic records are generally quite normal. With pressure on the carotid sinus (one channel of the electroencephalograph should be used to record lead II of the electrocardiograph), changes appear in the electroencephalogram (associated with the pulse slowing in some cases) which are abnormal. The ordinary person will be unaffected.

Metrazol.* A review of this technique and modifications of it were described by Kaufman in 1949. There are three methods: (1) a slow intravenous injection of metrazol diluted with an equal amount of saline at a rate of 100 mg. of the drug per minute; (2) a rapid intravenous injection of 200 mg. of undiluted metrazol; (3) an intramuscular injection of a fixed amount (500 to 800 mg.) that would be gradually absorbed after a period of time. The three methods have their advantages and disadvantages, and it would not be within the scope of this book to go into them in detail. It would seem, however, that slow intravenous injection of the diluted drug in a subconvulsive amount carries the most promising results. Activation of petit mal usually occurs at 100 to 150 mg. (one to two minutes). Other forms of epilepsy show abnormality at 300 to 500 mg. It is usual to stop at 600 mg. if no activation occurs. (The convulsive dose at this rate is 900 to 1200 mg. in normals.) The normal person, therefore, will show nothing if this procedure is followed. Some patients may report irritability, a sensation of fearfulness, and headache and trembling, but in general side effects are minimal and disappear rapidly. The amount of drug injected is accurately known, the procedure takes little time, and the persistence of the effect is much shorter. As soon as activation is established, the injection is stopped, because in a few patients the presence of the drug in the circulating blood in the brain might produce a seizure. A dose of 60 to 120 mg. of sodium luminal or, better still, 0.5 to 1 gm. of tridione may be injected intravenously, which nearly always quiets the disturbance set up by the metrazol and prevents the occurrence of a generalized seizure. Instead of this, an oral barbiturate may be given. There is no advantage in having the abnormal discharges persist for more than a few minutes, and after they have been identified and perhaps localized it is unnecessary to expose the patient to the hazards and unpleasantness of a generalized seizure (Fig. 51).

Metrazol alone, in the hands of some clinicians, has been quite satisfactory as an activating agent. In some patients, however, the subconvulsive level is so close to the convulsive that either nothing is found

---

* The intravenous use of metrazol requires, of course, that the electroencephalographer or a colleague have an M. D. degree and a license to practice medicine. Activation by sleep can be performed by a technician or other non-medical person.

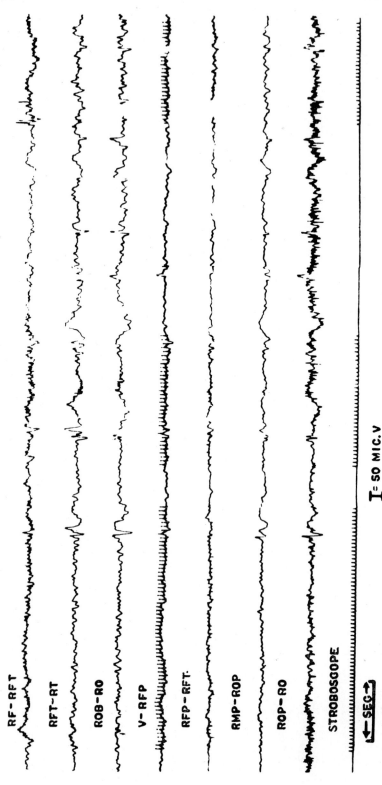

Fig. 51. The production of focal spikes in the right posterior temporal region by the intravenous injection of metrazol at a level of 300 mg. of the drug. The bottom line shows the stroboscope which has not any relation to the production of these spikes, which are due to the metrazol effect alone. The fourth line picks up the flashing light as an artifact which usually can be prevented.

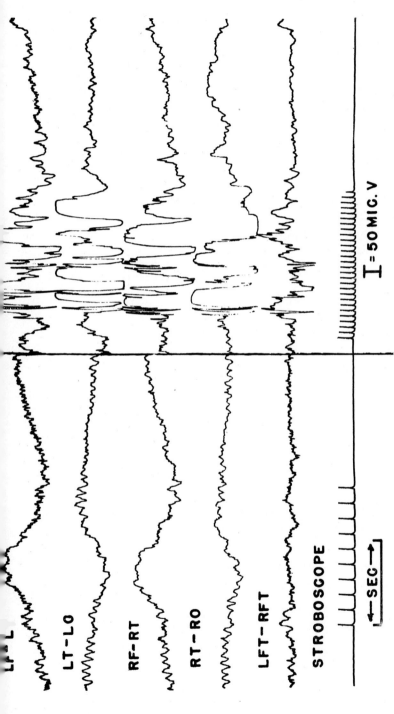

Fig. 52. The effect of stroboscopic and metrazol activation "Gastaut technique." Metrazol has been injected slowly until the level of 150 mg. has been reached. At the left of the picture the flashes are 6 per second and produce no change in the electroencephalogram. At 15 flashes per second characteristic myoclonic jerk was produced in the patient with the resulting bilateral frontal spikes shown in the picture. As soon as the light activation was discontinued the discharge stopped. (From Schwab and Abbott: EEG Clin. Neurophysiol., 2:262, 1950.)

or a generalized seizure occurs. This is particularly true in some auto-matisms. Some workers, therefore, have been disappointed with this technique. Gastaut[8] had the brilliant idea of combining photic stimu-lation and metrazol activation in order to overcome these objections and have better control of the activation. His technique, which he has thoroughly explored in normal controls, neurotics and child and adult epileptics, is as follows:

(a) A very bright source of light (stroboscope) is arranged an inch before the eyes of the patient so that the entire visual fields of both eyes will be intensely illuminated. An electronic switching device or mechanical shutter is arranged so that flashes of extreme brevity (1/10,-000 to 1/1,000,000 second) can be obtained. The flashes must also be ar-ranged so that the operator can produce them at will at rates of three per second to thirty per second. A photoelectric cell is placed by the subject's head and its output connected to one of the channels of the electroencephalograph machine. This will permit exact measurement of the flash frequency and the exact time of such activity on this photo-cell channel in relation to the electroencephalographic discharges being studied.

(b) The patient is examined first with the stroboscope flashes to see if they alone can activate abnormality. If nothing occurs at the various frequency flashes tried, injection of metrazol at 100 mg. per minute is started and the flashes at different frequencies tried for five to fifteen seconds at a time, with only five seconds of no light, until activation occurs. Voluntary opening and closing of the eyes during each flash of light is called for as well. As soon as a burst of metrazol-photo-combina-tion-activated waves appear, the light is turned off; this drops the level of activation to that of metrazol alone in a fraction of a second. A second or third burst may safely be produced, since the operator has the situa-tion under very delicate control by this means. Furthermore, the sud-den onset of the photic stimulation may produce specific epileptic dis-charge patterns in the electroencephalogram and also cause a larval or tiny clinical seizure to appear and be identified (Fig. 52).

A number of centers have confirmed Gastaut's observations and find this technique of activation the most reliable of any developed so far.

Supplementary Apparatus

There is a great deal of additional apparatus that has been used with electroencephalography. Some of these consist of specially tuned cir-cuits or "filters" which allow those frequencies that the workers are interested in to come through to the writing units and exclude those that are of no interest. For example, it is possible to have a tuned filter that will pass the 10-per-second alpha rhythm and attenuate the slower and faster rhythms on either side of it in the frequency band. Some workers have used these filters to measure the amount of any frequency present. However, these filters do not have much clinical application and therefore are mostly used for research purposes.

Further development of such tuned elements has been the construction of automatic frequency analyzers. These are very complicated electronic and mechanical pieces of equipment that can be connected to the ordinary electroencephalographic machine and give accurate frequency analysis of the record which has been taken. An excellent review of their characteristics and other properties with pictures and comments was published in 1948 by Boyd.[6] In this article the interested reader can find listed the more technical papers dealing with the specific types of equipment. The first automatic analyzer to be described was designed by Grass and Gibbs and essentially required that a sample of the electroencephalographic record to be studied was cut off after the recording had taken place. It was prepared so that it became a shadowgraph and then was put into a special automatic analyzer machine which after sometime produced a spectrum of the amount of the different frequencies of this particular sample of record. It was a very cumbersome and complicated piece of equipment and took several hours to give the distribution of frequencies in the small 30 cm. of record selected. It was found by the inventors to be of little use clinically and of questionable use in research.

Walter devised an automatic analyzer which obtains the frequency spectrum every 10 seconds of any particular channel that the operator wishes to examine and writes it out on the actual electroencephalographic paper under the appropriate electroencephalographic trace. It does this continuously as long as the apparatus is connected. This type of analyzer gives successive analyses of each 10-second-period of the record so that the entire record can be studied with the analysis before one at the time the recording was taken. This has many advantages over the Grass analyzer. On the other hand, the Walter analyzer is a very complicated piece of electronic equipment and is both large, cumbersome, and expensive. It requires considerable electronic knowledge to operate and a fairly constant maintenance to keep it accurate and functioning. It is in use in a number of laboratories in England and on the continent of Europe. There are also two or three in the United States. More recent models have overcome many of the mechanical and electronic difficulties of the original machine and the price has been reduced. It seems that this equipment may become common in the large research laboratories. Indeed several investigators in this country have built their own models and these operate efficiently. An American manufacturing company is producing a modified copy for sale in this country.

In our own experience with this type of analyzer, which we have had in our laboratory since 1947, we have found it extremely useful in clinical research and a very interesting supplementary piece of equipment to bring out and confirm the impressions obtained from ordinary inspection of the records. It is of more use in research than in clinical diagnosis and it is for this reason that it is not overemphasized in this book. However, there are a number of records that have been analyzed by this machine in the text so that the reader will get an idea as to what these tracings look like.

A number of other analyzers have been built and described but these are even more limited in their application or are more complicated than the ones mentioned. These are discussed in the review referred to previously.[6]

Other auxiliary equipment has been used in electroencephalography when special problems are required of the apparatus. For example, we have used the reaction time to a visual and auditory stimulus in the study and observation of the petit mal seizure.[20] Details of connecting this reaction time set-up to the electroencephalograph are covered in the article describing its application.

A number of workers have obtained simultaneous spirograms, electrocardiograms, skin temperature recordings and other physiological observations at the time the electroencephalogram was made. There is no particular complication to this except that the auxiliary apparatus must not radiate air-borne artifacts or interfere with the electroencephalogram. Some form of signalling or synchronization is necessary so that what happens with one piece of equipment can be accurately compared to what is occurring in the electroencephalogram.

A number of centers have tried successfully to photograph by motion pictures the subject during the recording of the electroencephalogram. In some cases the electroencephalographic tracing was included in the picture by means of lenses and mirrors. These are rather elaborate and complicated to adjust. In our own laboratory we have obtained the same results by covering one half of the moving picture film with a special steel diaphragm and taking the subject on the exposed half. Synchronization is obtained by means of a stroboscopic light which shows in the motion picture of the subject and indicates the exact time on the electroencephalographic recording through a photo-cell producing a discharge that moves one of the pens. After the subject has been photographed the film is wound back to its original position in the motion picture camera and the metal diaphragm is placed on the opposite side of the film. The brain wave recording, having been labelled appropriately and adjusted for photography, is placed back in its machine, the pens are elevated so that they do not write, the paper is fed through the writer and the motion picture is taken off this paper when it is moving by. When the film is developed this gives the "split frame" study of the patient as well as the electroencephalogram and the movements of the patient, and the discharges in the electroencephalogram are synchronized perfectly.

REFERENCES

1. Abbott, J. A.: Unpublished Data.
2. American Electroencephalographic Society: Recommendations for Minimum Requirements for Acceptable Direct Reading EEGs. J.A.M.A., *138*:958–960, 1948.

3. Arellano, A. P.: A Tympanic Lead. EEG Clin. Neurophysiol., *1*:112–113, 1949.
4. Arellano, A. P., Schwab, R. S., and Casby, J. U.: Sonic Activation. EEG Clin. Neurophysiol., *2*:215–217, 1950.
5. Berger, H.: Das Elektrenkephalogramm des Menschen. Nova Acta Leopoldina, *6*:173–309, 1938.
6. Boyd, W. E.: The Wave Analysis of Low Frequency Potentials of the Human Body. J. Brit. Inst. Radio Engineers, *8*:1–13, 1948.
7. Davis, H., and Wallace, W. M.: Factors Affecting Changes Produced in Electroencephalograms by Standardized Hyperventilation. Arch. Neurol. & Psychiat., *47*:606–625, 1942, and Tr. Am. Neurol. A., *67*:139–143, 1941.
8. Gastaut, H.: Combined Photic and Metrazol Activation of the Brain. EEG Clin. Neurophysiol., *2*:249, 261, 1950.
9. Gibbs, F. A., and Gibbs, E. L.: Atlas of Electroencephalography. 2nd Ed. Cambridge, Mass., Addison-Wesley Press, Inc., 1950.
10. Gibbs, E. L., and Gibbs. F. A.: Diagnostic and Localizing Value of Electroencephalographic Studies in Sleep. A. Research Nerv. & Ment. Dis., Proc., *26*:366–376, 1947.
11. Grass, A. M.: Electrical Characteristics of Some Types of Electrodes. EEG Clin. Neurophysiol., *1*:255, 1949.
12. Grinker, R. R., and Serota, H. M.: Studies on Corticohypothalamic Relations in the Cat and Man. J. Neurophysiol., *1*:573–589, 1938.
13. Grossman, C.: Sensory Stimulation During Sleep. Observations on the EEG Responses to Auditory Stimulation During Sleep with Brain Pathology. EEG Clin. Neurophysiol., *1*:487–490, 1949.
14. Jasper, H. H.: Electroencephalography. In W. Penfield and T. C. Erickson: Epilepsy and Cerebral Localization. Springfield, Charles C Thomas, 1941, pp. 380–454.
15. Jasper, H. H.: Electroencephalography in Epilepsy. In Hoch and Knight: Epilepsy. New York, Grune & Stratton, 1947, pp. 181–203.
16. Jasper, H. H.: Personal Communication, 1949.
17. Kaufman, I. C., Marshall, C., and Walker, A. E. Activated Electroencephalography. Arch. Neurol. & Psychiat., *58*:533–549, 1947.
18. MacLean, P. D.: A New Nasopharyngeal Lead. EEG Clin. Neurophysiol., *1*: 110–112, 1949.
19. Meyers, R., and Hayne, R.: Electrical Potentials of the Corpus Striatum and Cortex in Parkinsonism and Hemiballismus. Tr. Am. Neurol. A., *73*:10–14, 1948.
20. Schwab, R. S.: The Influence of Visual and Auditory Stimuli on the EEG tracing of Petit Mal. Am. J. Psychiat., *97*:1301–1312, 1941.
21. Schwab, R. S., Grunwald, A., and Sargant, W. W.: Regulation of the Treatment of Epilepsy by Synchronized Recording of Respiration and Brain Waves. Arch. Neurol. & Psychiat., *46*:1017–1034, 1941.
22. Walker, A. E., and Johnson, H. C.: Surgical Treatment of Epilepsy. Amer. J. Surg., *75*:200–218, 1948.
23. Walter, W. G.: In Electroencephalography—A Symposium on its Various Aspects. London, MacDonald & Co., Ltd., 1950
24. Walter, W. G., and Dovey, V. J.: Delimitation of Subcortical Tumours by Direct Electrography. Lancet, *2*:5–7, 1946.
25. Walter, W. G.: The Location of Cerebral Tumours by Electroencephalography. Lancet, *2*:305–308, 1936.
26. Walter, W. G., Walter, V. J., Gastaut, H., and Gastaut, Y.: Une forme électroencéphalographique nouvelle de l'épilepsie, l'épilepsie photogénique. Rev Neurol., *80*:613–614, 1948.

The Electroencephalogram in Epilepsy

IT IS APPROPRIATE to begin this chapter on epilepsy and the electroencephalogram with a clinical classification of this condition. This is done to emphasize the great importance of the clinical history and description of the seizure pattern in relation to the brain wave findings. Many electroencephalographers have lost sight of the former in their interest in the minutiae of the electroencephalographic records.

CLASSIFICATION

Petit Mal ("Lapse" or "Absence")

There is no aura. These are short spells lasting from one to twenty seconds (averaging seven to ten seconds). They are invariably associated with impairment of consciousness. This may vary from a dazed or blank feeling, in short lapses, to complete loss so that the subject does not respond to even a painful, loud whistle. During a mild petit mal the subject may have a "blank" look and stare into space with no motor movements. In others there is often blinking of the eyes. During longer or more severe ones, movements of the lips or face may occur, such as chewing or smacking of the lips with motion in the tongue. This usually indicates spread to the rhinencephalon and properly is part of an "automatism." If twitching of the facial muscles occurs for a few seconds, it indicates spread to the motor face area and is essentially a minor segment of the "convulsion." Therefore in petit mal sharp lines of demarcation are not possible. Respiration usually ceases during a lapse; *and* this can be seen graphically when a spirogram is recorded during such a spell (Fig. 54). These spells are most common in children from ten to eighteen years of age. Above that age they tend to disappear or are replaced by other types of seizures.[13]

During such seizures the electroencephalogram invariably shows some form of the classical 2- to 3-per-second "wave and spike," which should be called *spike and wave* as there is evidence that the slow component of this complex follows the fast.

This pattern of the "wave and spike" of petit mal has been extensively studied (Fig. 55).[5, 9, 17] They appear in the usual case as bilaterally synchronous discharges in the two hemispheres. This suggests at once that the source of such a bilateral disturbance is in a deep midline structure. Jasper[14] has produced such spikes and waves in the cat from stimulation of the intralaminar system of the thalamus. Such an origin would explain the frequency of the bilateral motor involvement such as eye blinking and chewing and smacking of lips, previously men-

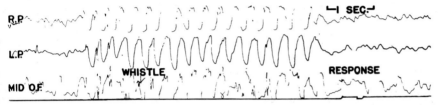

Fig. 53. The recording of a petit mal attack in a 17-year-old male during auditory stimulation. The line under the third electroencephalographic trace is the signal pen which is pulled down electrically at the time that the loud auditory signal (air whistle) is turned on. The patient had previously been instructed to respond to this signal immediately by pressing a key which will allow the signal pen to return to its previous position. It is seen in the diagram that the patient did not respond until after the seizure is over. The delay in the reaction time in this case is 4¼ seconds. The normal reaction time with this technique in an alert person is about ⅕ of a second. (From Schwab, R. S.: The Influence of Visual and Auditory Stimuli on the EEG tracing of petit mal. Am. J. Psychiat., 79:1301–1312, 1941.)

tioned. Unilateral involvement of either sensory skin areas or limb movements is rare indeed in petit mal, and this fact supports the concept of a midline deep source for the event.

There are four other types of short seizures that are infrequent in clinical practice. All are believed to have their origin in deep midline structures closely connected to the thalamus. They will, therefore, be briefly described and grouped for convenience under petit mal.

Pyknolepsy. This is a type of familial petit mal in female children clinically similar to ordinary petit mal and showing the same findings in the electroencephalogram.

Vasovagal or Mesencephalic Seizures. These are rare spells in which there occurs a sudden tachycardia, sweating, dilation or constriction of the pupil, paroxysmal alterations of blood pressure, and other signs of hypothalamic or midbrain discharges. Electroencephalograms during such spells are not at all specific, but usually show bilateral synchronous

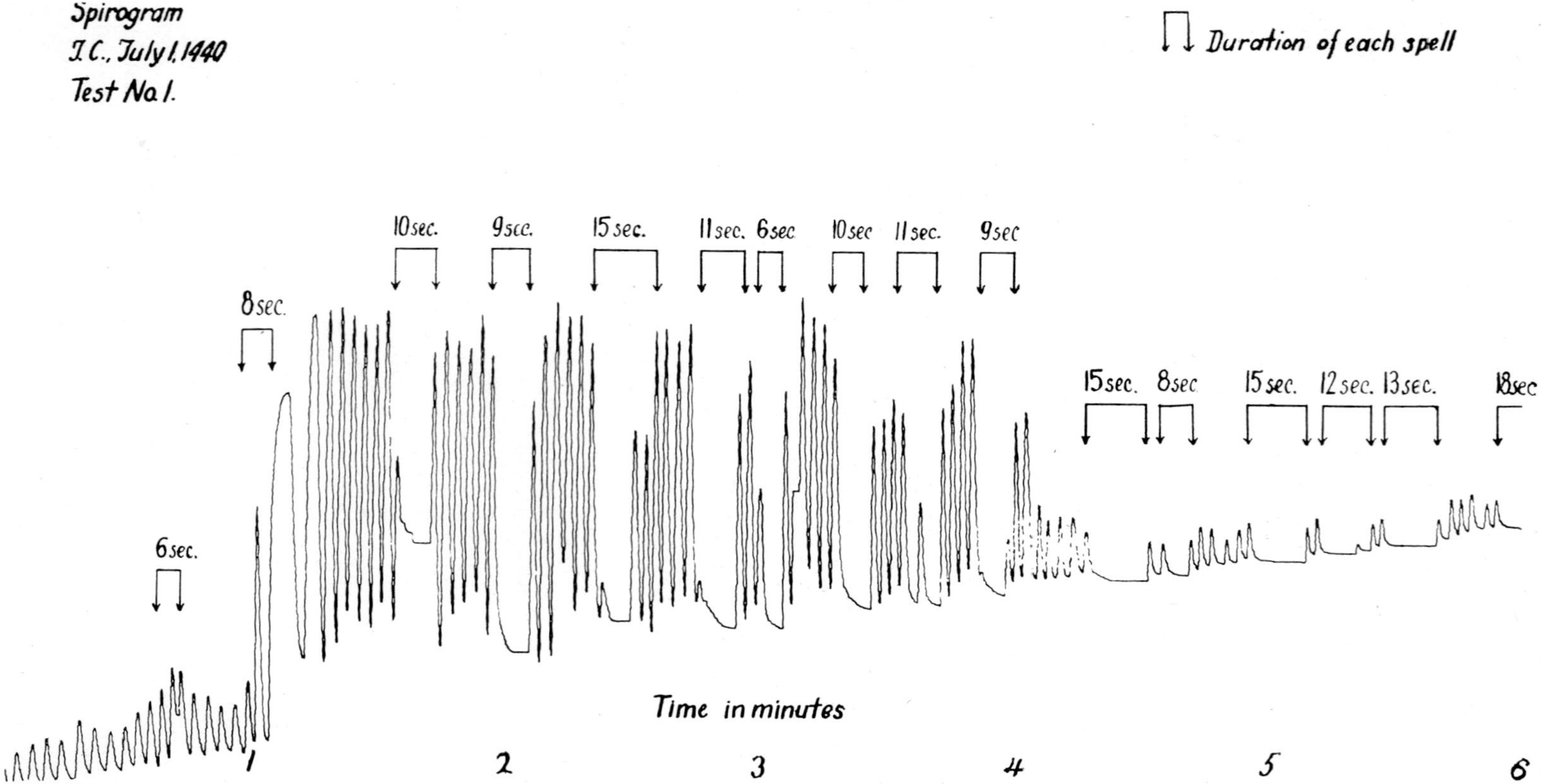

Fig. 54. A spirogram taken at the same time as the electroencephalogram and synchronized with this recording. Each petit mal seizure is illustrated on the spirogram by the double arrows and the duration of the attack. Note that nearly every seizure is accompanied by a cessation of respiration and that respiration starts again in its regular way at the end of the spell. (From Schwab, R. S., Grunwald, A., and Sargant, W. W.: Regulation of the Treatment of Epilepsy by Synchronized Recording of Respiration and Brain Waves. Arch. Neurol. & Psychiat., *46*:1017–1034, 1941.)

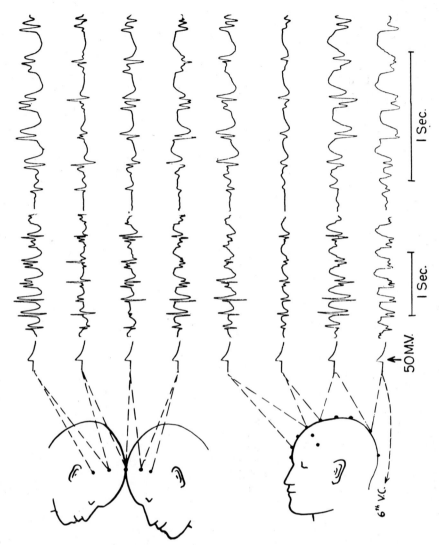

Fig. 55. A study of the voltage distribution and phase relationships during a short petit mal attack in a patient 19 years old. On the left part of the recording the paper speed is the usual one of 3 cm. per second, whereas on the right it has been doubled to 6 cm. per second. Note that both the spike and slow wave component have their scalp origin in the midline in the post frontal region but the phase reversals are best seen in the fast speed record. This agrees with the experimental work that this type of spell begins in the thalamus, but the cortical area involved is that of the projections of the dorsal medial nucleus and not the diffuse distribution of the intralaminar system. (From Arellano, A. P. −Z.: A preliminary report on the localization of some specific brain wave patterns in the cases of petit mal, automatisms and migraine. EEG Clin. Neurophysiol., 2:229, 1950.)

delta or theta waves over the temporal and frontal regions. Spikes are rare.

Akinetic Seizures. This form of short spell, lasting only one to four seconds, begins with a sudden loss of muscular tone, usually in midline muscle groups. The head falls forward, or, with more involvement, the patient may collapse to the floor. Consciousness seems to be impaired for only the briefest time, and the patient usually gets up or raises his head, again fully aware of his surroundings.

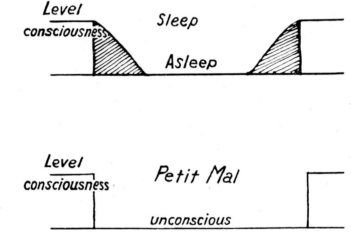

Fig. 56. A diagrammatic representation of the difference in the speed of loss of consciousness in patients with petit mal seizures and in the normal dropping off to sleep. Note that consciousness is gradually lost over perhaps one minute as one falls asleep and tends to return perhaps in seconds to ½ minute. This allows the memory of the transition from consciousness to full awakeness to be retained. In petit mal on the other hand deep unconsciousness occurs immediately from full awakeness and the return to consciousness is equally abrupt. This does not allow any transitory period where memory can work and therefore in many cases a patient having such a seizure is totally unaware of the lapse of consciousness.

The electroencephalogram shows 2- to 3-per-second delta waves, often with spikes during the event, and in the interseizure period runs of 2- to 3-per-second delta waves are not uncommon.

Myoclonic Seizures. The characteristic feature here is a short sudden movement in a limb, part of a limb, or synchronously in two limbs. When this occurs, the flexors in both arms contract simultaneously in a jerk, repeating two to three times in a second. This period of time is usually the longest of a myoclonic spell. The seizure may repeat itself many times a minute in a severe case. They are often the only clinical signs brought out by *sudden* types of activation by stroboscopic light or sudden noise (see Chap. III, p. 66). Consciousness is probably impaired during this short time (Fig. 56).

When present, either spontaneously or when activated, the electroencephalogram shows high voltage spikes, four to eight per second, bilaterally synchronous with some theta slow waves as well.[3]

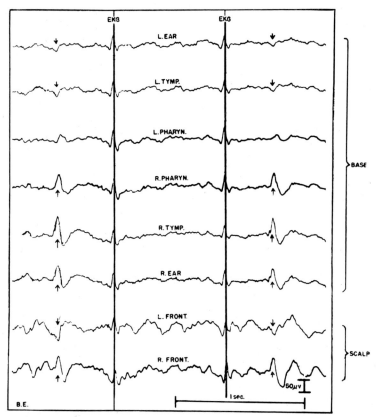

Fig. 57. The recording of a sharp wave or temporal spike in a patient with automatisms. This patient was a 28-year-old female who had had a head injury at the age of 3. This is a unipolar recording with the indifferent point over the 6th cervical vertebra. The electrocardiogram is indicated by the black line throughout. The recording speed is twice that usually used, namely 6 cm. per second. The greatest amplitude of the discharge is in the right tympanic electrode. This agreed with the clinical localization of a right deep temporal focus. (From MacLean, P. D. and Arellano, A. P. —Z.: Basal Lead Studies in Epileptic Automatisms. EEG Clin. Neurophysiol., 2:9, 1950.

Automatisms (Psychomotor Seizures)
(PSYCHIC EQUIVALENTS: RAGES, FUGUES)

Often an aura is referred to the gastro-intestinal tract. This group is larger and far more complex than petit mal. Short automatisms lasting ten to sixty seconds involve blank staring, chewing and smacking of lips, swallowing, blinking of eyes, and movement of the tongue, often with drooling of saliva. Various extensor phenomena can occur, from throwing back the head to extension of the arms and wrists. Short periods of vocalization may take place, such as, "Ah, Oh." Breathing continues normally or may be increased in rate. Longer periods from one minute to five minutes may begin as described and then include apparently purposeful movements such as reaching over and over again into the pocket or turning the hand on the floor as if a valve were there. Such movements may be more complex, such as buttoning or unbuttoning, scratching at the inside of the ear, or even trying to fill a pipe without tobacco. As such seizures become longer and more severe they involve more motor activity: moving about the room, throwing objects, urinating in a corner, seizing an observer by the throat, breaking furniture, throwing glassware, or even efforts to kill, maim and destroy. *The characteristic feature is the inappropriateness of the behavior to the surroundings.* Although some of these spells adhere to a specific behavior pattern over and over again, others change on each occasion. This unpredictability and this inappropriateness produce in the observer a strange feeling of fear which is not at all unreasonable. Behavior of this sort lacks the unconscious but often obvious motivation of hysterical action. The attack may end with the patient collapsing on the floor or in a chair and falling asleep, or it may swing into a generalized convulsion. On awakening, the patient is again fully conscious and oriented, but has a complete or nearly complete amnesia for the whole episode. Some automatisms follow a short motor seizure and are called post-ictal automatisms.

During automatisms the electroencephalogram usually shows abnormal electrical activity. Gibbs[11] felt that all of these consisted of 5- to 7-per-second "flat-topped waves" in chains or runs, but this has not been substantiated. Many show runs of 3-per-second high-voltage delta waves, some the 5- to 7-per-second "theta" waves of Gibbs; others show runs of sharp waves or actual spikes, especially from electrodes over the temporal lobes[4] or along the base, which may be more prominent or even localized on one side (Fig. 57). In some the record is a mixture of all kinds of abnormal waves and normal alpha. In a few, especially during the early part of the seizure, little abnormality at all is seen, and what appears is of low voltage and confined to the frontals. There is no specific pattern for automatisms, and in our opinion there is no justification to call any of the abnormal disturbances seen during these seizures "psychomotor waves."

Convulsions (Grand Mal, Focal Grand Mal, Jacksonian Seizures, Fits)

Aura is common and may consist of focal tingling or other sensory components. This type of seizure is more familiar to physicians and laymen. The shortest ones are the focal type, which involve motor twitching of a group of muscles, perhaps in the face or hand. Consciousness is usually intact, the seizure does not spread, and the duration is from twenty to sixty seconds (Fig. 58).

Longer spells of a focal character usually spread to involve other muscle groups (face to hand to shoulder, for example). Consciousness is often intact or only partially impaired, and the duration is from one to two minutes. Focal spells may be sensory, a burning or numb feeling replacing or supplementing the focal movements. Still longer focal spells spread further and often cross to involve the other side of the body (march of jacksonian seizure, which is what they are). Consciousness is usually lost at this point, and the convulsion is now a generalized one.

Generalized seizures usually begin bilaterally and are ushered in by a cry. Consciousness is lost, and bilateral, often synchronous, clonic movements of the limbs occur. Extensor tone is greatly increased. The

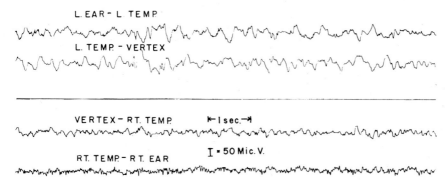

L. EAR - L TEMP.

L. TEMP. - VERTEX

VERTEX - RT. TEMP.   ⊢ I sec.→

I = 50 Mic. V.

RT. TEMP. - RT. EAR

Fig. 58. The electroencephalogram during a Jacksonian seizure in a young boy aged 6. The right arm and face are involved in the attack. The seizures were due to an abscess in the left temporal lobe which was subsequently removed. Note that the slow and fast discharges are localized by both phase reversal and amplitude to the left temporal lobe. On the right side of the head there is some reflection of the muscle components of the seizure. The patient was conscious at the time of this attack.

jaw closes and opens on the tongue ("bitten tongue"). The involved diaphragm drives air through the buccal saliva, producing "foaming," and tends to remain contracted. Intense cyanosis develops, and, to the uninitiated, death seems imminent. Urination often occurs. The spell lasts one to five minutes and is often followed by deep sleep or stupor lasting several hours.

During the recording of any of the spells by the electroencephalogram a variety of abnormalities may be found. In the short focal seizures the record may be normal unless the electrode placement is exactly over the discharging cortex. Longer ones, by their spread to adjacent cortex, show slow waves or sharp waves of increased voltage and localized to a particular area. Still more involvement may cover an entire side of the head with high-voltage abnormal waves. Spikes may be seen as well as slow waves, but, since so much muscular activity occurs, *muscle spikes* must be eliminated before calling any fast activity a "spike" of cerebral origin. In the generalized seizure this is most important (Fig. 59). During the period of loss of consciousness and stupor, slow waves are seen in all leads, and are not localized to any focus. In the so-called "grand mal" pattern of Gibbs,[14] trains or runs of high-voltage fast activity (twenty to thirty per second) are sometimes seen at the beginning of a seizure (Fig. 60), but they are often muscle spikes from the periodic contraction of facial muscles. Sharp waves, single spikes and slow waves, all of high voltage, are the usual components of the electroencephalogram during convulsions.

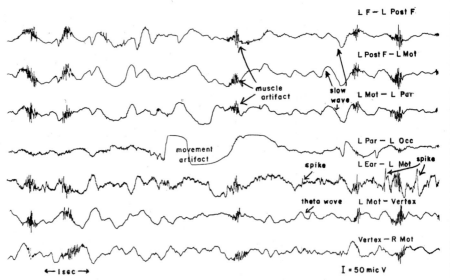

Fig. 59. A part of a generalized convulsion during a clonic phase in a 26-year-old male with generalized convulsions without localizing signs. Note the variety of electroencephalographic discharges as well as the presence of many different types of artifacts which are indicated in the figure.

The word "psychic equivalents" has been used by some as synonymous with automatisms, but it is a wretched use of this term. In a few patients with epilepsy, particularly if the disease is severe and of long standing, a true psychosis develops which may replace the seizures for a time. This is a far better state for the use of "equivalents." This form of insanity may be like schizophrenia or mania, or a paranoid delusional picture, or it may be a delirium with much confusion. It invariably requires commitment to a mental hospital. It is usually of short duration, weeks to months, and may end abruptly with the return of the seizures. The two may exist together for a short time.

Other so-called "equivalents," like gastric pain in paroxysms or bouts of aerophagia, are actually part of the *aura* of the usual seizure patterns. It is not unusual for *aura* to occur alone, especially under medication.

CLINICAL CORRELATION OF EPILEPSY WITH
ELECTROENCEPHOLOGRAPHIC ABNORMALITY

Since there are about 500,000 epileptics in the United States, the amount of material available for electroencephalographic research is tremendous. Many of the early papers, and those of today, deal with various aspects of the electroencephalogram in epilepsy. This field has been productive of clinical correlations with the electrical discharges, and there has been a certain amount of therapeutic value as well. As regards the correlation between an abnormal record and the history of

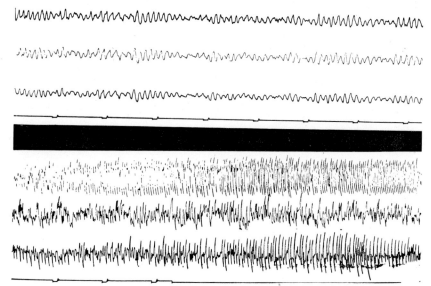

Fig. 60. The recording of the beginning of a generalized seizure in a deteriorated boy of 16. The electrodes were arranged on the right posterior part of the head. The upper tracing shows the record before the seizure, strong 10-per-second alpha coming from all three leads in this area. The bottom part of the tracing shows the beginning of the seizure discharge which lasted for one minute. It also shows the high voltage spikes appearing more marked in the anterior part. The main purpose of this figure is to show the remarkable difference in the same subject between the interseizure record and the seizure pattern. There is considerable muscle artifact in the lower tracing.

clinical epilepsy, at first it was felt from the early work of Gibbs and Lennox[5] that every epileptic would show enough electrical abnormalities for a diagnosis to be made, if examined for a long enough period. Furthermore, Gibbs and Lennox found that overventilation for two or three minutes often activated abnormal waves not seen with normal breathing (Fig. 61). If this test were used in addition to an ordinary run, the correlation between the history of clinical epilepsy and abnormal activity would be even higher. However, as their series of cases became larger, the high correlation, which at first was over 90 per cent,

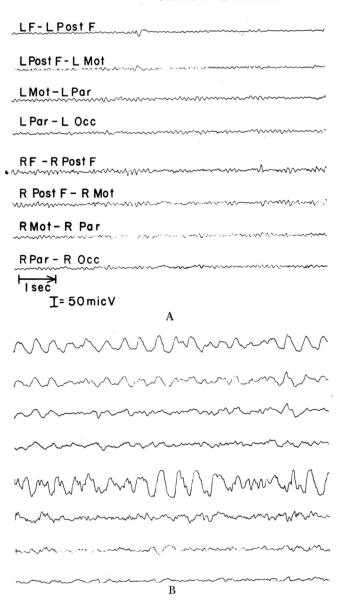

LF - L Post F

L Post F - L Mot

L Mot - L Par

L Par - L Occ

RF - R Post F

R Post F - R Mot

R Mot - R Par

R Par - R Occ

I sec

I = 50 micV

A

B

Fig. 61 *A*. Electroencephalogram of a 25-year-old male who nine years before had 20 grams of his right premotor and post frontal cortex removed as a treatment for a left-sided unilateral Parkinson's disease. The Parkinson's disease was greatly benefited by this but Jacksonian epilepsy occurred as a complication. The seizures were usually controlled by dilantin and phenobarbital. The patient was taking this medication at the time of the recording. Note that the interseizure record with normal breathing was very close to normal except for an occasional random sharp wave that is seen in the right post frontal region.

B. This shows the same electrode placements during the third minute of over-breathing. Note that slow waves have appeared but are more conspicuous on the right post frontal to right frontal lead.

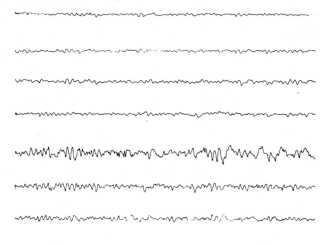

Fig. 61 *C*. Four minutes after overbreathing had stopped there was still a persistence of an activated focus in this area as shown in *B*. The rest of the record has become normal. Same electrode placement as in 61 *A*.

E.E.G. IN EPILEPSY

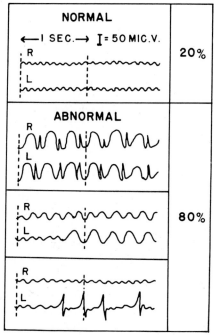

Fig. 62. A diagrammatic representation of the distribution of the normal and abnormal patterns in epilepsy.

began to drop. In 1945 and 1946[2] a number of papers appeared from different clinics, and it was found that about 80 per cent of epileptics had definitely abnormal electroencephalographic records or ones that could be specifically activated by overbreathing (Fig. 62). This leaves 15 to 25 per cent of patients with true clinical epilepsy whose inter-seizure electroencephalograms are normal and who fail to react to over-breathing. There is no other laboratory test in epilepsy with better cor-relations, but some physicians were disturbed when they received a report that the electroencephalogram of one of their patients, known to be an epileptic, was normal.

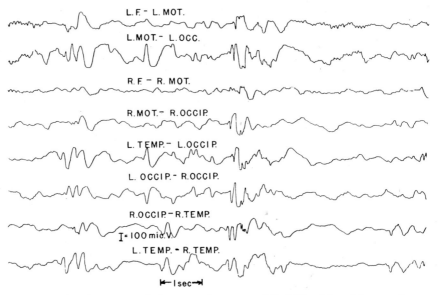

Fig. 63. The electroencephalogram of a 2-year-old child with a history of many convulsions and clinical evidence of deterioration. Note the bilateral character of the discharges and the absence of normal rhythms particularly any occipital alpha. This is a severely abnormal record in a patient with severe epilepsy.

Abbott and Schwab, in 1947,[1] published a paper in which this par-ticular sample of the epileptic population was closely scrutinized. They found that these patients who had normal electroencephalograms and proved epilepsy were different from those with abnormal tracings in several respects. They responded more favorably to anticonvulsive medication, tended to have their seizures mostly at night, preserved their intellectual faculties better, held their jobs longer and more effici-ently, and in general had a better prognosis than those with abnormal electroencephalograms. A higher percentage of this group were able to drop their anticonvulsant medication after a period of treatment and still remain seizure-free. This was a statistical study and could not be applied specifically with any degree of accuracy in an individual case.

Thus a discrepancy in correlation between the laboratory test and the clinical findings was made an indication of a better prognosis.

The 85 per cent incidence of abnormal activity in the electroencephalogram of epileptics in the interseizure period with hyperventilation as the only activation technique has not been high enough to satisfy most clinicians. One of the characteristics of abnormal records is instability over a period of time. By obtaining serial tests at weekly intervals over a period of several months this 85 per cent abnormal incidence

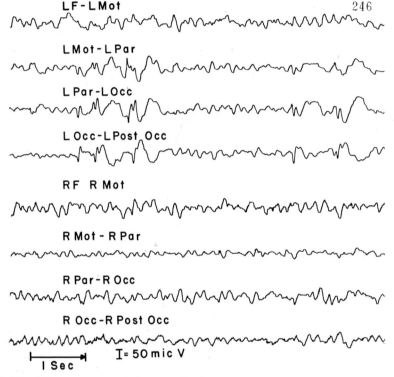

LF-LMot   246

LMot-LPar

L Par-LOcc

L Occ-L Post Occ

RF R Mot

R Mot - R Par

R Par-R Occ

R Occ-R Post Occ

I = 50 mic V

I Sec

Fig. 64. The electroencephalogram of a 6-year-old girl with marked mental deterioration and cortical atrophy confirmed by air studies. The electroencephalogram shows paroxysmal discharges more marked on the left side but there is a good deal of normal rhythm throughout the record and the right side is relatively normal. Here is a severe epilepsy with moderate abnormality in the electroencephalogram.

may be increased a few points. This is, of course, tedious and expensive. A better way is to use other forms of activation such as *sleep, metrazol* or *metrazol-photic* stimulation. If any individual case of true epilepsy is studied sufficiently, and a variety of activation techniques are used, the percentage of normal electroencephalographic records becomes so low that some authorities are willing to say it is nearly zero—i.e., 100 per cent of true clinical epilepsy can be shown to have an abnormal tracing by some technique short of producing a generalized seizure.

The next correlation between the clinical findings and that of the electroencephalogram that would interest the clinician is the severity of the epileptic state in relation to the degree of the abnormality in the electroencephalographic record. Some patients with grossly and diffusely abnormal records had few seizures and responded rather well to anti-

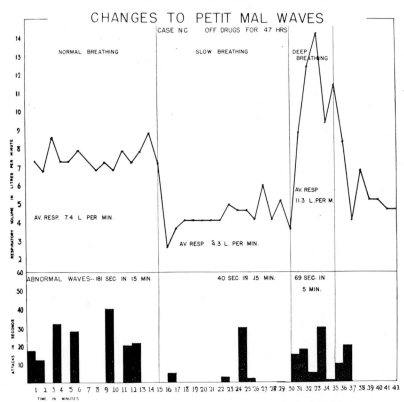

Fig. 65. The graphical summary of the duration in seconds of abnormal waves in the electroencephalogram of a 15-year-old girl off all medication. The spirogram taken at the same time is shown in the upper graph and represents the liters breathed per minute. Note that there is a direct relationship between the minute respiration volume and the amount of abnormal electrical activity in this subject. Chart prepared by W. W. Sargant.

convulsant medication; they showed little evidence of cerebral deterioration. Others, with the minimal amount of abnormality in the electroencephalogram, possibly only on hyperventilation, have many seizures, do poorly on anticonvulsant medication and, on pneumoencephalography, show indications of severe cortical atrophy. There is, however, a tendency in institutions caring for severe epileptics to find in this group more abnormal records than in those seen in clinics or office practice. No exact correlation of the degree of electroencephalographic abnormality with the clinical disability can be relied on in an individual case (Figs. 63, 64).

There are, however, some general relationships to the degree of abnormality of the interseizure electroencephalogram and the type of clinical seizure. There is also some difference between the child and adult as to the significance of a severe abnormality.

In general, patients with petit mal have some specific wave and spike pattern in the routine examination even without overbreathing activation. There may be only a small number of single wave and spike discharge during a three- to five-minute recording or a short five- to seven-second seizure during this time. A number may show only the slow 3-per-second waves in short paroxysmal bursts lasting one-half to one second. Overbreathing in such cases invariably brings out more short spells of wave and spike and usually of eight to twelve seconds in duration (Fig. 65). Children with petit mal are far more prone to have records like this than adults. Some adults with clinical petit mal may have a normal interseizure and normal hyperventilation record.

Patients with grand mal at frequent intervals usually show a variety of mild abnormalities which are non-specific during the interseizure examination. These consist of short paroxysms of 4- to 7-per-second waves, some 3- to 4-per-second waves, usually in the frontals, and sharp waves of seven to eight per second here and there.

Adults tend to show less abnormality than children in this type of clinical seizure. There is a parallel improvement in the abnormality of many children with epilepsy to the maturation of the electroencephalogram in the same age group if the records are compared year to year. Therefore, the degree of abnormality of a child of six with seizures three times a week cannot be compared to one of twelve with the same number of fits.[11]

The automatisms have the most difficult clinical correlations with abnormality in the electroencephalogram. Some show no abnormality unless basal leads are used. Others show normal tracings except in sleep. Some show temporal abnormality at all times. A few have normal records for one examination and a clear-cut disturbance on the next. Nearly all can be activated by one of the techniques described in Chapter IV.

In general, the child shows far more abnormality than the adult, the form and number of seizures being the same.

The usual favorable prognosis in a child is the improvement in the electroencephalogram as he grows older. A record that becomes more abnormal with the years indicates a poor outcome. In an adult, too, an electroencephalographic record that shows less abnormality through the years, greater stability to activation, and constancy of form and pattern is of far better prognosis than one that slowly develops more and more abnormality.[11]

It was felt early in the study of a patient with epilepsy that if the anticonvulsant drugs would stop the clinical seizures, the electroencephalogram would show a concomitant return to normal level.[12] This is not always so. In some individual subjects, however, close correlations with the amount of anticonvulsive protection from medication and the electroencephalogram is possible, and this is discussed in detail in a paper

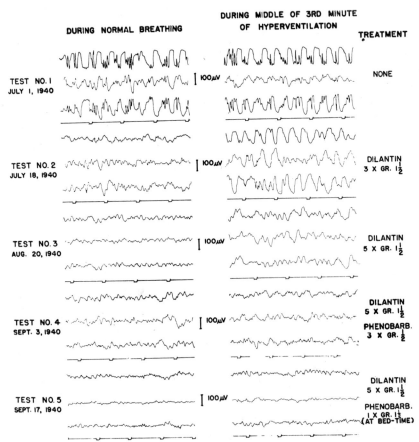

Fig. 66. A composite pattern of the electroencephalogram during normal breathing and during the third minute of overbreathing in a 21-year-old male who had an excellent clinical response to dilantin and phenobarbital. In this case the clinical and electroencephalographic improvement under medication were directly related as is shown in the chart. (From Schwab, R. S., Grunwald, A., and Sargant, W.W.: Regulation of the treatment of epilepsy by synchronized recording of respiration and brain waves. Arch. Neurol. & Psychiat., 46:1017–1034, 1941.)

by Schwab and Sargant[16] in which the respiratory volume was quantitated by using a basal metabolism machine. It could be seen that the patient's response to overventilation in abnormality in the electroencephalogram could be improved by the administration of an increasing amount of anticonvulsant medication, and in an example of one of the subjects examined the record was kept completely normal during the entire period of overventilation on four 100 mg. doses per day of dilantin and four 30 mg. tablets of phenobarbital (Fig. 66). Other patients, although they were free from seizures, showed abnormal waves during the overbreathing. The new drug, tridione, which is specific against the wave and spike discharge of petit mal, does definitely improve the electroencephalogram in a number of ways as well as help the patient's clinical condition. In a patient subject to frequent petit mal seizures the number of seizures and length of each during a five or ten minute period on the electroencephalograph can be measured. In addition, the increase in the number and duration during hyperventilation can be noted. Then the drug can be administered for a few days and the test repeated. When this is done, it is usually found that the number of spontaneous seizures in normal breathing is greatly reduced or eliminated entirely, that the response to overbreathing is greatly improved as well, and that in some cases there is no evidence of the wave and spike component at all. This is the best drug from the standpoint of correlation with the beneficial effects of anticonvulsive medication on the electroencephalogram.[8]

VALUE OF ELECTROENCEPHALOGRAM IN DIFFERENTIAL DIAGNOSIS

The previous pages show clearly that the electroencephalogram confirms the diagnosis of clinical epilepsy in ordinary recording in 85 per cent and with activation techniques in 95 to 100 per cent of cases. The value of a confirming laboratory test is indisputable in the practice of medicine. There are, however, numerous occasions when the electroencephalogram can be the key to the actual diagnosis in patients suspected of having epilepsy. As is well known, some patients with rare seizures are over them before the doctor arrives. Others, who have both epilepsy and hysteria or other neurosis, have such a bizarre seizure pattern that the physician who sees one is not at all clear about the diagnosis. In such cases the wrong clinical guess may be extremely unfortunate for the patient. If it is hysteria and called epilepsy, a protracted period of useless anticonvulsant therapy must be endured and the necessary psychotherapy withheld. The reverse situation is even more disastrous. The true epileptic in such a case is compelled to have seizure after seizure, and proper medication is withheld, while the therapist wastes both his own time and the patient's resources in useless psychiatric explorations and techniques. The electroencephalogram in such cases is particularly useful in giving the physician a guide to the correct assessment.[10]

Furthermore, we know that many persons react to stresses in their lives with a variety of neurotic behavior patterns, such as different sorts of anxiety attacks, exaggeration of somatic complaints, tension states,

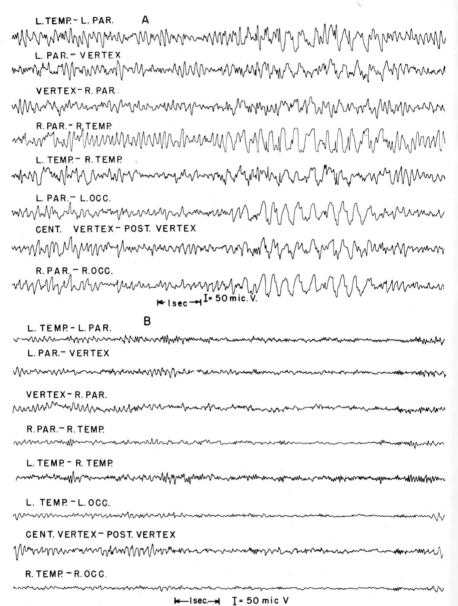

Fig. 67. The electroencephalogram of a 25-year-old woman who had generalized seizures for the past seven years. (*A*) shows the record taken when she was off medication. (*B*) is the record taken on this same subject one week later when she was taking 2 gr. phenobarbital each day. This very dramatic alteration in the electroencephalogram by this drug is not the usual finding but it illustrates the type of recording before and after medication that can be found in a variety of different drugs, particularly in some patients.

conversion hysterical pictures, and sometimes bizarre and acute personality deviations resembling schizophrenia. Children and adolescents are particularly prone to such reactions, particularly if their familial and environmental situation is favorable for their development. The mature facing of the reality situations in stresses cannot be developed in many people.

Epileptic seizures of one sort or another are terrifying and emotionally disturbing stresses when they occur without warning in a vulnerable personality. It is no wonder that they often produce or are associated with various forms of psychoneurosis.

There is an illogical tendency on the part of some clinicians to limit the diagnosis to one category which, when clearly established, excludes the presence of another diagnosis. This is often the case in the group just described. If the psychiatric interview specifically identifies the psychoneurosis, then the findings of an abnormal electroencephalogram are regarded as a misleading or irrelevant laboratory complication. It is more intelligent to accept the presence of two diagnoses and to direct therapy on these two fronts. The electroencephalogram, therefore, is most valuable in suggesting the presence of epilepsy in such patients if seizure patterns are observed. Further history or observation usually brings out in such cases the clinical confirmation of seizures.

For example: a divorced woman forty-four years old was referred to the hospital during a course of psychotherapy for anxiety attacks and insomnia. The psychiatrist was properly disturbed because the patient had a prolonged syncopal attack following a stormy interview with her ex-husband. The routine electroencephalogram showed mild, non-specific abnormalities in both temporal and frontal areas and, when activated by metrazol and photic stimulation, showed a low threshold with myoclonic jerks. Subsequent history brought out by the subjective symptoms of the patient during activation revealed the following data not known to the psychiatrist: In high school she had had a number of short spells at the time of her menses which were then termed "nervousness." During her first pregnancy she had had similar spells on four occasions which she was told were due to pressure of the uterus and to albuminuria. During the divorce proceedings a few more spells occurred. All the spells resembled her subjective sensations during activation with metrazol and flicker and were thus recalled in the subsequent interview. The diagnosis of clinical epilepsy was thus clearly established in addition to the obvious neurosis under treatment. Anticonvulsant drugs were therefore added to the successful psychotherapy already under way.

A number of papers appeared during World War II proving the value of the electroencephalogram in helping to establish the diagnosis of epilepsy and allowing prompt discharge from the service of such poor military risks. On the other hand, patients who wished to get out of the service and who, therefore, gave their medical officers fantastic stories of frequent convulsions could be quickly examined; if a normal electrical tracing was found, it was highly unlikely that their stories were true. In other words, this objective test was of great value in disproving or substantiating the history of seizures.[15, 18]

The motivation of a civilian with convulsions is to give the physician his history as honestly as he can, and the relatives concur in this because both desire proper treatment and help. In the military service, on the other hand, the problem is often different. Under pressure of war and patriotic fervor, a young man with seizures may intentionally hide the history from the recruiting officer and during his medical examination in order to get into the service. His home may be far away, and a social service investigation by such an agency as the Red Cross involves delays and is often impractical (Fig. 68). As a result, patients with epilepsy

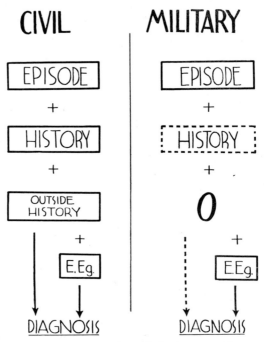

Fig. 68. A diagrammatic representation of the increased importance of the electroencephalogram in leading to the diagnosis of epilepsy in patients under a military setting as opposed to those in a civilian setting. (From Schwab, R. S.: Application of Electroencephalography in the Navy in War Time. War Med., 4:404–409, 1943.)

entered the service. During their early training they were often unable to continue their anticonvulsant medicines and therefore had convulsions. Sometimes these were observed by medically trained personnel, but often were not. If an electroencephalogram were available, an abnormal record could be obtained and a diagnosis made in spite of any denial of the patient. Separation from the service or at least removal from the dangers of combat or other duties could be promptly secured.

Example 1. An officer had a convulsion during class at a training station. After he had arrived at the Naval hospital he showed perfectly normal responses on neurological examination. Furthermore, he was firm and consistent in denying all episodes remotely or directly suggesting epilepsy in any of its forms. There was no family history. The electroencephalogram showed a typical burst of wave and spikes running about one second in length and occurring several times each minute (Fig. 69). Overbreathing brought out a five-second burst during which the patient failed to respond to a signal (command). The subject denied any feeling or loss of awareness during the test. When the problem was discussed with him, he was firm in objecting to discharge and insisted on a repetition of the examination. In all, four tests were done, with similar results. Furthermore, an air encephalogram was done which was normal in every way. The Board of Medical Survey felt, however, in spite of the man's consistent denial, that he was suffering from epilepsy and were satisfied with the electroencephalographic findings as the most important evidence.

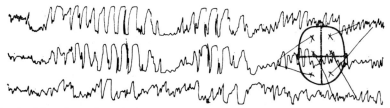

Fig. 69. The electroencephalogram in a naval officer (Example No. 1.) This is one of the 7 records taken and shows the characteristic seizure discharge of wave and spikes occurring during ordinary breathing in this subject and of which he was unaware.

Example 2. A candidate from the Air Force fainted during an examination. An overconcerned hospital corpsman thought he saw movements of the hand suggesting a convulsion. Neurological examination gave negative results. It was brought out on questioning that the candidate had not had breakfast; this was his first faint, and while on the floor he had tried to rise by moving his hand. He was passed and did well. The electroencephalogram was normal in all respects (Fig. 70).

The relationship of an abnormal electroencephalogram to the diagnosis of epilepsy is a critical point. We have shown that, except for the

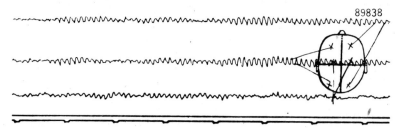

Fig. 70. The normal electroencephalogram in Example No. 2. Note that there is no trace of abnormality in this record.

runs of 3-per-second wave and spikes that accompany petit mal seizures, there is no specific pattern of the electroencephalogram for epilepsy. Unless the electroencephalographer can record the tracing during a spell of some sort so that he can specifically relate abnormal activity in the electroencephalogram with clinical symptoms of epilepsy, he has no ground to make a *diagnosis*. If he does make a diagnosis of epilepsy after seeing, for example, a few short spells in a patient, produced by an activating agent such as metrazol, each accompanied by a localized discharge in the electroencephalogram, he is acting as a physician. He has taken clinical signs and combined them with laboratory findings to make a clinical diagnosis. He is both an electroencephalographer and a clinician when he does this. It is no different if he takes the history of fainting spells from the patient or from the referring physician and, with an abnormal tracing in the electroencephalogram, establishes the diagnosis (see Chap. IX, p. 165).

The diagnosis of epilepsy in any person is serious enough with its employment restrictions, social handicaps, medication requirements and other burdens, that responsibility for making it must be left to a properly qualified physician.

In conclusion, it must be repeated that the first and most important criterion in the establishment of the diagnosis of epilepsy should be an adequate and careful clinical history and a detailed neurological examination. The second criterion should be evidence of a clinical epileptic convulsion, petit mal seizure or paroxysmal automatic behavior, preferably observed by a clinician and not a nurse or relative, although their account is also of value. The third criterion for the making of the diagnosis of epilepsy should be the presence of abnormal paroxysmal seizure patterns in the electroencephalogram, and it should be restricted to this third place in importance.

REFERENCES

1. Abbott, J. A.. and Schwab, R. S.: Some Clinical Aspects of the Normal Electroencephalogram in Epilepsy. New Eng. J. Med., *238*:457–461, 1948.
2. Baudouin, A., Fischgold, H., and Rémond, A.: Diagnostique Electroencéphalographique de l'épilepsie. Semaine d. hôp. Paris, *22*:1217–1221, 1946.
3. Dawson, G. D.: Investigations on a Patient Subject to Myoclonic Seizures after Sensory Stimulation. J. Neurol., Neurosurg. & Psychiat., *10*:141–162, 1947.
4. Fuster, B., Gibbs, E. L., and Gibbs, F. A.: Pentothal Sleep and Localization of Seizure Discharges of Psychomotor Type. Dis. Nerv. System, *9*:199–202, 1948.
5. Gibbs, F. A., Gibbs, E. L., and Lennox, W. G.: Epilepsy; a Paroxysmal Cerebral Dysrhythmia. Brain, *60*:377–388, 1937.
6. Gibbs, F. A., Gibbs, E. L., and Lennox, W. G.: The Likeness of Dysrhythmia of Schizophrenia and Psychomotor Epilepsy. Amer. J. Psychiat., *95*:255–269, 1938.
7. Gibbs, F. A., Gibbs, E. L., and Lennox, W. G.: EGG Classification of Epileptic Patients and Control Subjects. Arch. Neurol. & Psychiat., *50*:111–128, 1943.
8. Hoefer, P. F. A., Hoff, H. H., and Pluvinage, R. I. L.: The Effect of Anticonvulsant Therapy on the Electroencephalogram of Patients with Idiopathic Epilepsy. Tr. A. Neurol. A., *72*:185–188, 1947.
9. Jasper. H. H., and Kershman, J.: Electroencephalographic Classification of the Epilepsies. Arch. Neurol. & Psychiat., *45*:905–943, 1941.
10. Kershman, J.: Syncope and Seizures. J. Neurol., Neurosurg. Psychiat., *12*:25–33, 1949.
11. Laplane, R., Fischgold, H., and Brisac, C.: L'électroencéphalographie chez l'enfant: difficultés techniques et interprétation du tracé. Le Nourrisson, *35*: 59–63, 1947.

12. Lennox, W. G., Gibbs, F. A., and Gibbs, E. L.: Effect on the Electroencephalo-
    gram of Drugs and Conditions Which Influence Seizures. Arch. Neurol. & Psy-
    chiat., 36:1236–1245, 1936.
13. Lennox, W. G.: Science and Seizures. 2nd ed. New York, Harper & Bros., 1946.
    258 pp.
14. Penfield, W., and Jasper, H. H.: Electroencephalography in Focal Epilepsy.
    Tr. A. Neurol. A., 66:209–211, 1940.
15. Rossen, R.: A Critical Analysis Obtained from 873 Electro-encephalographic
    Findings with Admission Diagnosis and Final Discharge Diagnosis of Patients
    with Various Neuropsychiatric Disorders at a U. S. Naval Hospital. U. S.
    Nav. M. Bull., 47:494–503, 1947.
16. Schwab, R. S., Grunwald, A., and Sargant, W. W.: Regulation of the Treatment
    of Epilepsy by Synchronized Recording of Respiration and Brain Waves.
    Arch. Neurol. & Psychiat., 46:1017–1034, 1941.
17. Walter, W. G.: Analytical Means of Studying the Nature and Origin of Epileptic
    Disturbances. A. Research Nerv. & Ment. Dis., Proc., 26:237–251, 1946.
18. Williams, D.: The Significance of an Abnormal Electro-encephalogram. J. Neu-
    rol. & Psychiat., 4:257–286, 1941.

CHAPTER VI

The Electroencephalogram in Neurological and Neurosurgical Problems

ELECTROENCEPHALOGRAPHY, since it deals with the electrical activity of the brain, should be of interest and importance to the clinical neurologist. Many neurologists in the United States and Europe have not only been skeptical, but have been rather cold and contemptuous of this new diagnostic test. This attitude is in sharp contrast to the friendly and enthusiastic support shown by their neurosurgical and psychiatric colleagues. The reason for this attitude probably lies in the failure of the routine electroencephalographic examination to localize sharply every area of pathology within the central nervous system. For many neurosurgeons the additional electroencephalographic evidence of something abnormal within the skull encourages them to go ahead with the more precise localization techniques of the ventriculogram or arteriography. To the psychiatrist who sees a patient with an abnormal electroencephalogram there is (or should be) the immediate need of a neurological or neurosurgical consultation. He is usually satisfied to await the result of this move. But for the neurologist who is trying by his detailed study of visual fields, cranial nerves, reflex, sensory and motor examination to obtain a precise localization, a generalized confirmation that something is wrong is of little interest and rather an obvious anticlimax. No doubt, as the newer and more exact electroencephalographic localization techniques develop, greater interest on the part of the neurologist will follow.

The electroencephalographic abnormalities in the various neurological conditions to be described are in *no way specific* for these states. The electroencephalogram can never be a diagnostic flag like the Wassermann test for syphilis. We *cannot* match the tracing found, for example, in a left parietal meningioma to a similar record in a case to be diagnosed and call it a meningioma. To do this would be as stupid as making a clinical diagnosis alone from a leucocytosis of 18,000 cells per cubic millimeter.

The electroencephalogram can tell us if the record is normal or abnormal, if the abnormality is localized, lateralized, diffuse, deep, paroxysmal or continuous. We can deduce various types of physiological impairment from the tracings by correlations with *other* laboratory and clinical data. By serial records days or weeks apart we can state whether the abnormality is static, regressing or progressing. Armed with this information correlated with the clinical findings, a physician should be able to make a more accurate diagnosis, and make it more promptly and with fewer reservations and errors.

Recently, in an effort to see if our own reports were of value to the referring physicians, we sent out with each report a postcard questionnaire. Ninety-five per cent of the 100 replies stated that the reports were clear and understandable to them. Eighty-seven per cent found that the data on the report fitted in with the other clinical findings and the final diagnosis. Fifty-one per cent found that the electroencephalographic material was an essential factor in making this diagnosis, whereas 33 per cent noted that it was only of confirming value. Thirteen per cent reported the electroencephalogram of no value whatsoever or misleading if taken seriously.

The electroencephalographic findings in the progressive mental deteriorating conditions will be discussed in the chapter on Psychiatry. The findings in epilepsy have been covered in the preceding chapter.

Trauma to the brain usually brings the patient to a neurosurgeon, but the clinical signs and sequelae are of general neurological interest. The electroencephalographic findings in such cases have the best correlative data with the clinical findings of any condition except epilepsy.

In the experimental animal[9, 30, 31] a blow on the head sufficient to disturb consciousness always alters the normal electroencephalogram. There is first a disappearance for a few seconds of the normal activity in the area of the blow, followed ten to twenty seconds later by slow waves. Return of the electroencephalogram to normal levels in unanesthetized dogs occurs after several minutes and precedes the recovery of lost conditioned reflexes by several minutes.

In the human being such early studies are not possible, but there are an adequate number of records of brain injuries one-half to several hours after their occurrence.[10] Slow waves are usually encountered locally in the area injured if the blow is mild enough. A severe brain injury may show very slow waves in all regions. As recovery takes place there is usually a steady improvement in the electroencephalogram, but this is nearly always behind the clinical recovery. The diffuse type of slow wave activity may disappear first and leave the focal area of trauma as a residual abnormality that may take weeks or months to return to

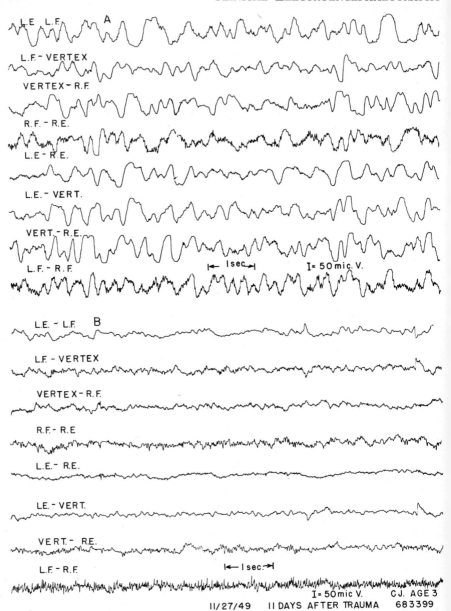

Fig. 71 *A*. The electroencephalogram of a 3-year-old child who was brought into the hospital unconscious with a compound fractured skull as the result of an automobile accident. The electroencephalogram was done the day following admission and it shows high voltage slow waves in all leads. Recovery was rapid and the patient was sitting up in bed eight days after admission.

B. The electroencephalogram was made eleven days after the injury. The high voltage slow waves have disappeared and the recording is very close to normal for a person of this age. The remarkable change in this period of time closely paralleled the excellent clinical improvement.

normal. In a mild head injury with only a short period of unconscious-ness and no residual neurological signs, the electroencephalogram may be normal if it is taken several days after the accident. In such cases a normal record is excellent evidence that recovery has taken place and that late sequelae are unlikely (Fig. 71).

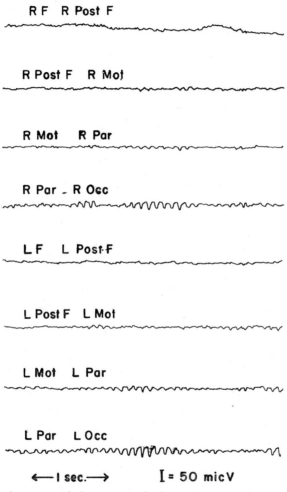

Fig. 72. The electroencephalogram on the baseball player described in Example No. 1. Note the completely normal occipital alpha rhythm and total absence of any abnormal activity.

Example 1. A thirty-five year old professional ball player was knocked unconscious by a batted ball. He recovered his senses on the field and was kept overnight at a hospital. Neurological studies, roentgenogram of the skull and lumbar puncture were normal. He was kept out of the line-up for three days and, before joining his teammates, had an electroencephalographic examination which was obviously nor-mal (see Fig. 72). He had no further trouble during the season.

This may even be the case in spite of roentgenographic evidence of fracture.

Example 2. A young naval officer fell 30 feet down an open hatch on a battleship, striking his head on the steel deck below. He was limp and unconscious when he reached a nearby naval hospital. Roentgenograms of the skull showed numerous linear fractures over the entire vault. There was slight bleeding from both ears. Full consciousness was recovered in three hours. There were no neurological signs, and

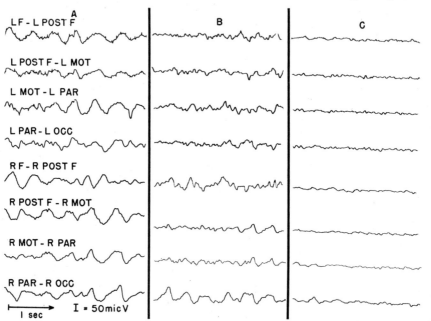

Fig. 73 *A.* The electroencephalogram of a 21-year-old male college student who was struck in the back of the head in a fall from a truck. He was unconscious but there were no focal signs or fracture of the skull. The patient recovered consciousness but was "groggy" and slept a good deal. The first record shows slow waves in all leads and was taken four days after the injury.

B. The second record shows the same patient two days later (six days after the accident). There was clinical improvement but the patient complained of lassitude and some slight headache. Neurological signs were absent.

C. This shows the record taken two days later (eight days after the accident). The patient was up in a chair and about to be sent home for further convalescence. Note the steady even improvement in the record as indicated by the electroencephalographic tracings.

much to our surprise the electroencephalogram the next day showed normal 10-per-second alpha waves on both sides and no abnormalities. A ten-day period of close observation followed during which *no* neurological, psychiatric, spinal fluid or further electroencephalographic abnormalities were encountered. He returned to his ship, which was about to sail overseas, with no headache, but with a copy of his extraordinary skull film as a souvenir. No residual symptoms, signs or complications were reported in a check-up fourteen months later.

In both examples the normal electroencephalogram was of great value in making the clinical decision to send the injured men back to their jobs. The outcome justifies the reliance that can be placed on a normal electroencephalogram in such situations.

A severe head injury with electroencephalographic abnormalities is described next.

Example 3. A marine was struck on the head by a horse and knocked unconscious. He was brought to a naval hospital, suffering from a compound fracture of the skull. He recovered consciousness after three days and during the next month made an excellent clinical recovery without neurological signs or symptoms. The first electro-

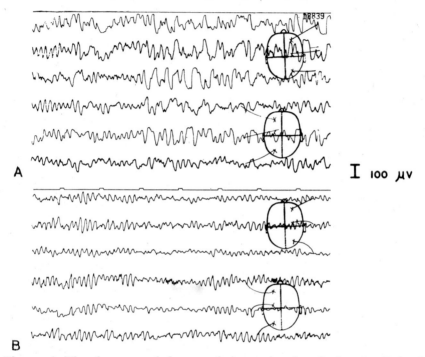

Fig. 74 *A*. The electroencephalogram of the marine described under Example No. 3. This record was taken one month after the injury and still shows large amplitude and slow waves particularly on the right side and both frontal regions. However, the clinical neurological examination was normal.

B. This shows the record of the same marine two months later when full clinical recovery had taken place and he was able to go to duty without difficulty.

encephalogram was taken on the day he was sent to duty. It was grossly abnormal with delta waves on both sides (see Fig. 74 A). After a month of guard duty, because of many dizzy spells and headaches, he was returned to the hospital. The electroencephalogram was still abnormal, but showed some improvement. Further electroencephalograms were taken several times a month until the record was almost normal (see Fig. 74 B). He was not heard from again, but in this case the outcome is by no means certain.

This example, however, does show the value of the test in preventing premature return to normal activity of patients with severe head injuries, in spite of the absence of clinical signs. It also shows the use of serial tracings during convalescence in such cases.

The fourth case illustrates that the electroencephalogram should be considered seriously, but not followed blindly, when it is at variance with clinical judgment.

Example 4. In April, 1949, a child of eight fell backward into an excavation, striking his head. He was unconscious when admitted to the hospital and the roentgenogram showed linear fractures on both parietal bones. When seen next day by the neurological consultant, the youngster was alert and showed no neurological signs. The lumbar puncture showed pinkish fluid at normal pressure. Three weeks later he was sent for an electroencephalogram. This showed slow waves in both occipital areas. There were still no neurological or mental deficits, nor was there any headache, history of seizures or syncopal attacks. Because of the electroencephalographic

EEG IN SUBDURAL HEMATOMA

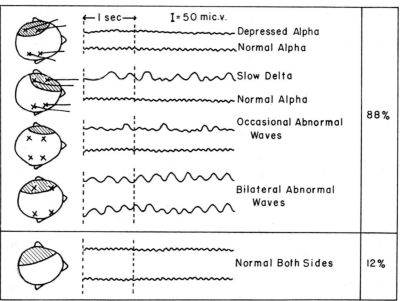

Fig. 75. A diagrammatic representation of the type of electroencephalograms seen in subdural hematoma.

findings the child was kept quiet at home during the summer. In September, 1949, a second electroencephalogram was done which was slightly improved but still abnormal. Since nothing else could be found, the child was allowed to go back to school. He made up his lost work and otherwise did well. In January, 1950, he was checked a third time, and the electroencephalogram was still bilaterally abnormal in the occipital areas, and not as good as before. Intelligence quotient, neurological examination and performance tests were all normal. He will be followed as a matter of interest at intervals of six months. The persistence of this electroencephalographic abnormality without any clinical correlates should call for follow-up tests, but no medication or restrictions in life or habits.

The electroencephalogram not only correlates well with the reversible changes that occur in edema, contusion and laceration of the brain, but is also useful in the lateralization and localization of 80 per cent of subdural hematomas (Fig. 75).[27] The usual pattern of the course of the electroencephalographic abnormalities in simple brain trauma is one of slow but steady improvement in the records. The reverse is usually

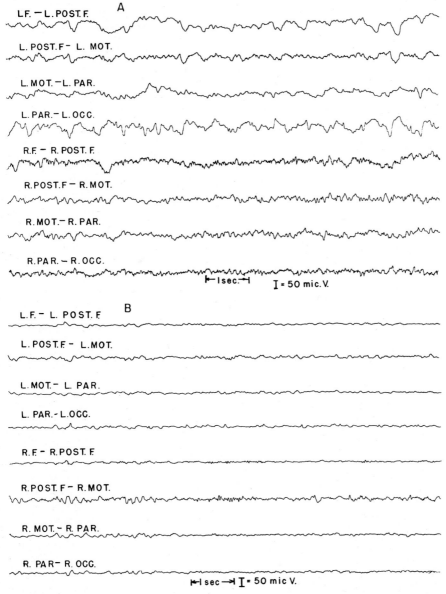

Fig. 76 *A*. The electroencephalogram in Example No. 5. This shows the preoperative recording with activity more marked in the left parieto-occipital region.

B. Eleven days later the electroencephalogram was repeated and shows the absence of the slow delta activity. This recording is close to normal.

true in the presence of a subdural hematoma. The clot may act as a tumor producing a focus of delta waves that persists and often increases from record to record. Or it may, if it is thin and flat, by pushing the cortex away from the skull, depress and attenuate the normal scalp rhythms so that they show a clear voltage asymmetry or even a flat line of no activity.

Example 5. A seventy-nine year old man was admitted to the hospital, having been found unconscious at home. The patient showed, on examination, bilateral extensor plantar responses. He was completely unresponsive and in a deep stupor. The fundi showed no choking, and the lumbar puncture showed normal pressure with a slight increase of protein. There was no history obtainable as to the cause of this coma. His housekeeper had found him unresponsive in bed when she brought him his breakfast one morning. The electroencephalogram showed some abnormal activity in the frontal and post-frontal regions on both sides. There was, however, on the left side in the parietal and occipital regions continuous delta activity (Fig. 76 A). The

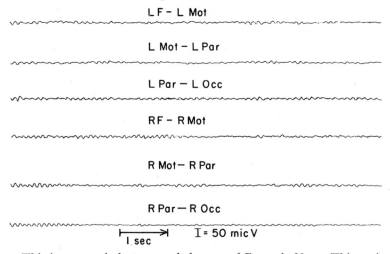

Fig. 77. This is a normal electroencephalogram of Example No. 7. This patient actually had a subdural hematoma that was quite thin in the right parietal region.

electroencephalographic report suggested the possibility of a lesion in the left posterior quadrant of the head, such as a subdural hematoma. The patient was taken to the operating room a few hours after the electroencephalogram, and bilateral burr holes were made. Nothing was found on the right side, as would be expected, but on the left side a subdural hematoma was encountered, running from the Rolandic fissure as far back as the occipital pole. It was completely evacuated by suction. The patient recovered consciousness during this procedure and made a complete recovery. The electroencephalogram after the operation showed a return to normal level 11 days later (Fig. 7 B).

In our study of the electroencephalogram in subdural hematomas, a normal recording occurred in only 10 per cent of the cases (fifty verified). This means that, in a patient who is suspected of having this lesion, a normal electroencephalogram reduces the chances of its being present to nine to one. When the statistical evidence is *combined* with the neurological evidence of a normal clinical examination, there is little chance of missing the condition.

Example 6. A fifty-one year old truck driver was struck on the head in a collision. He was taken to hospital, and all studies, including an electroencephalogram, were within normal limits. After discharge he continued to complain of chronic headache. Investigation revealed he had had three previous accidents and was fearful of being maimed in the next. A shift to a position in the shipping room so reassured him that his headache subsided.

On the other hand, a normal electroencephalogram does not *exclude* a hematoma, even a large one.

Example 7. A fifty-eight year old male farmer, with a history of a number of minor falls associated with drinking, was brought to a hospital because of awkwardness of the left side and a slowly progressing loss of memory and alertness. The spinal fluid showed a protein of 80 mg. The electroencephalogram was normal. A pneumo-encephalogram showed slight displacement of the ventricular system to the left. A large, thin subdural hematoma was evacuated from the right parietal region (Fig. 77).

The value of the electroencephalogram in head injuries is threefold. (*a*) It is an excellent aid in prognosis when it is normal. (*b*) It may localize a co-existing subdural clot or scar not evident from the clinical signs. (*c*) It may show, by the persistence of the electrical abnormality beyond the disappearance of all clinical signs, that recovery is delayed and that further precaution, rest or treatment is indicated. In 40 per cent of patients with symptoms and residuals one year after head injury there is abnormality in the electroencephalogram which makes an emotional or compensatory cause for all these symptoms unlikely in such cases.[17]

VASCULAR LESIONS

In vascular lesions of the brain, such as cerebral thrombosis or subarachnoid hemorrhage, 80 per cent of patients have normal electroencephalographic records taken four or five days after the episode. This is disturbing to the neurologist, who cannot see how the hemiplegic could have normal activity from the involved motor area in the brain. It is, however, of some clinical value in special cases when a tumor is suspected.

Abbott[1] and also Strauss[26] have shown that a person with a hemiplegia and a normal electroencephalogram has a one to ten chance of having a tumor. Directly after the onset of a cerebrovascular accident the electroencephalogram may show mild focal disturbance over the area involved. In a few days this usually clears up, even if no return of motor function occurs, and such rapid disappearance of a focus in the electroencephalogram is never seen in tumor cases (Fig. 78).

Example 8. A seventy-seven year old woman had progressive headache for six months and loss of memory with peculiar notions of her assets. One week prior to admission she showed marked speech defects and awkwardness of her right side. She was sent sixty miles to a hospital as a brain tumor suspect. Her electroencephalogram was mildly abnormal. The blood pressure on admission was 180/110. Lumbar puncture was entirely normal. Air studies at her age carried some risks. She was kept quiet under mild sedation for two weeks. A second electroencephalogram taken ten days later was again normal. Her blood pressure had dropped to 150/90, and her speech had improved. She was sent home as a case of vascular accident (Fig. 79).

Example 9. A sixty-three year old woman had a sudden loss of speech and paralysis of her right arm. One observer described a focal facial seizure at this time. Bed rest

E.E.G. IN CEREBRAL FAT EMBOLISM

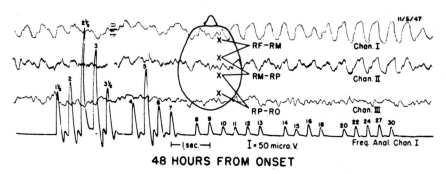

48 HOURS FROM ONSET

10 DAYS FROM ONSET

Fig. 78. The grossly abnormal electroencephalogram forty-eight hours after a fat embolism from a fractured right tibia. The patient was a 20-year-old athlete. Large slow delta waves are seen in both frontal and postfrontal regions with no sharp focus. The occipital area was relatively normal. The upper part of the tracing shows the record from the right side and the analysis of the recording from the first channel. Note that the analysis (fourth line in the figure) shows slow waves in abundance, the frequency running from 2 to 3½ with a peak at 2½. There is also a peak at 5 per second. There is no normal activity present in this channel according to the analysis.

Ten days after the injury when clinical recovery was complete and the embolism had been absorbed, the patient was up and around on crutches and free of neurological signs or symptoms. At this time the electroencephalogram showed a normal trace and the analysis of the same channel recording showed no abnormalities present. There is a normal peak at 11 per second with a secondary one at 10 per second. (From Bourne, G. C., and Schwab, R. S.: Cerebral fat embolism. Arch. Neurol. & Psychiat., 62:355–357, 1949.)

at a local hospital was followed by clear improvement in speech and function of her arm. After her return home a second episode of the same nature brought her back to the hospital. Her electroencephalogram showed a delta wave focus in the left anterior temporal region extending to the left frontal region. Lumbar puncture was normal. Blood pressure was 190/110. After three days the aphasia again improved.

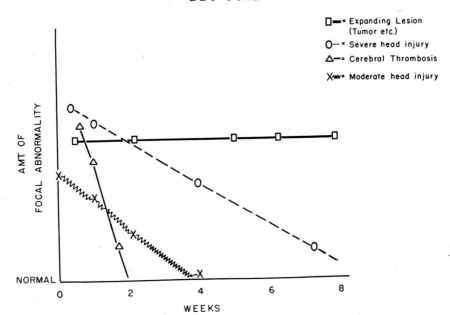

Fig. 78 *A*. Diagrammatic plot of the use of consecutive electroencephalograms in differentiating between an expanding lesion such as a tumor and a focus due to an injury or vascular thrombosis. The latter tend to disappear with the passage of time, whereas the focus due to a tumor or abscess persists or becomes worse.

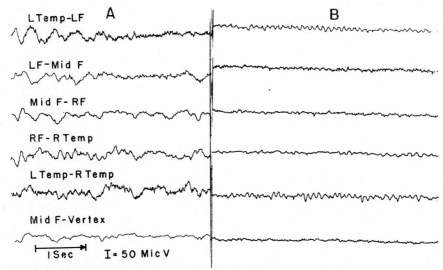

Fig. 79 *A*. The moderately abnormal electroencephalogram of Example No. 8 is shown. There are more slow waves in the left side than on the right.

B. Ten days after her admission to the hospital—just before her discharge home, there was marked clinical improvement in this case and the electroencephalogram essentially is within normal limits.

A second electroencephalogram on the sixth day showed the same delta wave focus. An air encephalogram showed normal ventricles without displacement. She was sent home as a case of vascular accident, but the electroencephalographer still felt that a tumor was more likely. Three weeks later the electroencephalogram still showed the same focus, which had become a little more prominent. Clinically, she was improved. Ten days later a routine visual field examination showed a right homonomous defect. This patient was most carefully followed every few days by her physician, who was concerned about the electroencephalographic focus. Her speech began to fail again. When she was readmitted to the hospital, the electroencephalogram showed for the fifth time this left anterior temporal focus. This time an arteriogram showed a clear defect in the left anterior cerebral artery. Exploration showed a rapidly growing astrocytoma in the left temporal lobe, and the patient died about one month later.

In this case the persistent electroencephalographic focus correctly indicated an expanding lesion in spite of contrary clinical and laboratory findings.

In tumors or abscesses of the brain the electroencephalogram is abnormal in 85 per cent of all cases.[6, 19] Most of the interest in such findings is the accuracy of lateralization or localization of such abnormality.

It was Hans Berger who first found, in his study of the electroencephalograms in human beings, that a patient with a brain tumor has an abnormal tracing.[4] He noted, furthermore, in 1930, that the tumor tissue itself shows no electrical activity. These early findings of this distinguished pioneer have since been confirmed many times and are fully accepted by all workers in this field. Around the tumor, Berger found that there are slow waves that are definitely abnormal with increased voltage. He believed that these slow waves are the result of interference by the tumor of the normal metabolic requirements of the brain cells in the vicinity of the tumor. Pressure resulting from the growing neoplasm on blood vessels produces ischemia, congestion, stasis or even extravasation of blood cells, any of which interferes with normal exchanges of oxygen and glucose and thus disturbs the normal electrical activity of these brain cells. The other factor to be considered is the interruption of connections by the tumor from midline deep cell stations in the thalamus or from other cortical centers. This would facilitate abnormal synchronization of cellular electrical activity producing the slow waves of increased amplitude. But, as we have previously stated, vascular lesions in the white matter sufficient to produce hemiplegia usually show normal electroencephalograms after the initial edema has subsided. A striking corroboration of this is the experimental injection of a non-irritating wax into the subcortical regions of dogs. In this work Ulett[28] showed that after three to four days the delta activity presumably due to the initial pressure and edema all disappeared, leaving a normal electroencephalogram in his animals.

Outside the area immediately around the tumor, where the circulation and metabolism of the brain cells are not interfered with, the electroencephalogram is normal. It is quite obvious that this state of affairs could be caused by a brain abscess or even by an expanding clot of blood, both electrically inactive like tumors. If the tumor is large and on the surface of the hemisphere, this picture of no electrical activity over a small area, surrounded by an area of slow waves with increased voltage, would then be found. Beyond this slow wave activity the brain rhythm would gradually approach the normal level, so that 6 or 7 cm. from the tumor normal waves would be seen. On the other hand, every neurologist knows that a large percentage of intracranial tumors are not on the surface of the hemisphere. If the tumor is deep, there will be no area of electrical inactivity seen from electrodes on the scalp, and only the slow wave activity around the tumor in the electroencephalogram. If the tumor, such as a pinealoma, is still deeper, abnormal electrical activity may be so far away that it is not detected from surface leads. From this we may have some notion of the depth of a growth from the amount of electroencephalographic disturbance seen. If the tumor is small and slow-growing and has not obliterated blood vessels or caused edema of the cerebral substance, its presence might not interfere at all with the electrical activity of the brain cells and no slow waves would be seen. On the other hand, if the tumor is rapidly growing, or happens to be growing in the vicinity of an important blood vessel, either artery or vein, with resulting interference of the blood supply to the brain cells in this area, there might be a large disturbance of the electrical activity of the electroencephalogram. As already stated, dead brain cells produce no electric current. Some tumors infiltrate evenly, and slowly destroy the cells in their path, but do not exert pressure or interfere with circulation to any extent, at least during the early stages. Metastatic carcinomas, such as melanomas, and some rapidly growing gliomas (glioblastoma multiforme) may act this way for a time. The electroencephalogram, therefore, may show nothing abnormal in the tracing during these early stages of the tumor growth even though the destroyed cortical cells are represented clinically by weakness or anesthesia of part of a limb. It can well be seen that the use of this technique in the localization of intracranial lesions, particularly tumors, is not going to be 100 per cent accurate as was hoped at one time. The percentage of accurate localizations by the electroencephalogram will vary with the type of clinical material examined by the laboratory.

In a survey[24] made in 1941 of 200 verified brain tumors of *all* types and locations, the electroencephalographic localization was 73 per cent correct, the neurological opinion 71 per cent correct and the air studies 90 per cent correct. If only deep or posterior fossa tumors are considered, the electroencephalogram localizes and lateralizes correctly in 45 per cent. On the other hand, 90 per cent of *all* brain tumors have abnormal electroencephalograms, even though 15 per cent do not localize or lateralize. This alone is of obvious value to the clinician. In a recent combined study of 200 patients who had electroencephalograms because they were suspected of having brain tumors, Culbreth[7] at Baltimore and the present author[25] at Boston found excellent agreement in their follow-up figures; 25 per cent of such cases had tumors of the brain, and the electroencephalogram was abnormal in 92 per cent and correctly localized it in 85 per cent. In the 75 per cent who were shown to have other disease or no organic difficulty, the electroencephalogram was normal in 90 per cent. In only two cases did the electroencephalogram falsely localize a focus in this negative group.

In assessing the clinical value of the electroencephalogram in the case of tumors of the brain, four questions may be asked:

1. How often does it localize when other methods fail?—Five per cent.

2. How often does it confirm the localization of other techniques?— Eighty per cent.

3. How often does it aid in eliminating the possibility of neoplasm when the tracing is normal?—Ninety per cent.

4. How often does it mislead in *1, 2,* or *3*?—Five per cent.

These percentages are gathered from several series and represent a composite value and opinion of many experts. The accuracy of the localization of the electroencephalogram in brain tumors depends also on the experience and skill of *both* technician and interpreter and is greatly increased if the interpretation can be fully discussed with the clinician in charge of the case (correlative interpretation instead of absolute interpretation: see Chap. IX).

The following examples will illustrate some of these points:

Example 10. A forty-eight year old man was admitted to the neurological service complaining of progressive headaches over the past six months and some awkwardness of the right hand. The neurological examination showed increased reflexes in the right arm, one degree of papilledema in both eyes, roentgenograms within normal limits; the lumbar puncture showed increased pressure of 180 mm. of water and a moderate increase in the total protein of the spinal fluid of 70 mg. per cent.

The electroencephalogram showed waves of three to four cycles per second, with increased voltages that came mostly from the left parietal region, both by phase shift and direct inspection. A few of them were seen in the left frontal area, but there was no doubt in inspecting the record that the majority of the slow waves were seen in the left frontal area and that the voltage of these slow waves was more promiment in this area. The occipital rhythm and voltage on the right were within normal limits. The localization was clear and definite, and further placements were not used at that time. The patient had, within 48 hours, a ventriculogram which showed a displacement of the left ventricle and an exploratory craniotomy was then done. A meningioma, about 3 cm. in diameter, was found on the surface of the left parietal lobe just posterior to the motor area and was removed *in toto* without damage to the rest of the cerebral substance (Fig. 80).

In this case the electroencephalogram was accurate in localizing the site of the tumor, *although the clinical findings also pointed to the localization in this area.* The use of air confirmed the electroencephalographic localization, which was verified by surgical exploration.

On the other hand, the following case should be cited to show that errors can occur, especially in posterior fossa lesions.

Example 11. An eleven year old child was admitted to the children's service of the hospital with vomiting and headache of six weeks' duration. There were three diopters of choking in both eyes but otherwise the neurological examination showed nothing localizing. Roentgenograms of the skull were within normal limits. A lumbar puncture was considered inadvisable because of the choked disks. The electroencephalogram showed a great many slow waves, three to four per cent, coming from the left frontal region. There were a few in the right frontal region and in

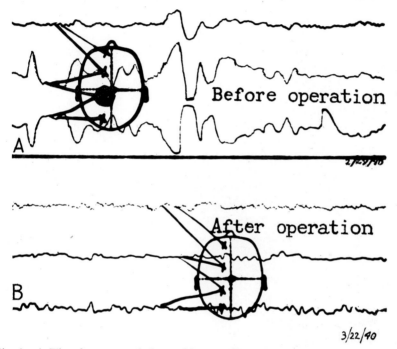

Fig. 80 *A*. The electroencephalographic recording of the focus in the left parietal region just before operation in Example No. 10.
B. The same patient one month after the removal of the meningioma. (From Schwab, R. S.: The clinical application of electroencephalography. Med. Clinics North America, 1477–1489, Sept. 1941.)

both occipital regions but the strongest disturbance of electrical abnormality was in the left frontal region under the left frontal electrode connected to the left ear electrode. Therefore, at this point, a diagnosis of a localized lesion in the left frontal area was made. However, the ventriculogram which was done the same afternoon showed an enlarged fourth ventricle and no displacement or alteration in either of the anterior horns of the ventricular system. From the air studies, a posterior fossa lesion was diagnosed and a posterior fossa bone flap was turned down. A right cerebellar tumor was found and removed.

In this case the electroencephalographic findings were about as far away from the actual lesion as could be possible and *still remain in the cranial cavity*. One might surmise that the abnormal electrical activity that appeared under the left frontal electrode could have arrived there through the commissural fibers that go from the cerebellar hemispheres to the frontal lobe on the opposite side. On the other hand, there was no evidence that the disturbance was not under the left frontal electrode. From clinical considerations, posterior fossa lesions in patients of this age are more likely than frontal tumors, but this would not concern the straight interpretation of the electroencephalogram.

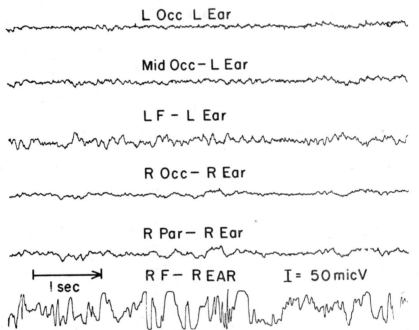

Fig. 81. Electroencephalogram in a 76-year-old male who five years before had a small epithelioma removed from his right frontal skin area. Intensive x-ray treatment was given for one year in this region. One year later the skin broke down and left a small area of exposed bone which never healed. The patient had no clinical symptoms and there was no evidence of recurrence of the tumor. Rather suddenly three days before the electroencephalogram was taken in January 1948, this patient had a series of left-sided Jacksonian seizures. The electroencephalogram shows the continuous spiking discharge between the right frontal and right ear leads and implicates the right frontal region rather strongly. The patient continued to get worse and died one month later. Postmortem examination revealed a small 3 cm. abscess presenting on the surface of the frontal lobe in the area of the exposed bone and sharply agreeing with the electroencephalographic focus.

In the localization of intracranial abscesses the same problems are present as with tumors. Abscesses are like expanding tumors, as far as the electroencephalogram goes. Ninety per cent of the patients who have verified brain abscesses have some abnormality in the electroencephalogram, even when they are in the posterior fossa. Therefore, a normal electroencephalogram in a patient suspected of having a brain abscess is against this finding nine-to-one. The accuracy of localization of brain abscesses is not as good as that in tumors. Abscesses are mostly found in the cerebellum or temporal lobe. Both of these situations are more difficult to localize electroencephalographically than on the convexity.

Examination of a frontal abscess that was sharply localized is shown in Figure 81.

Sometimes further confirmation of the electroencephalographic focus can be obtained from direct cortical recording in the operating room, and this was first done in the United States by us in March, 1938.

Example 12. A thirty-seven year old woman was admitted to hospital because of convulsions which in some cases involved her right arm. There was no aphasia. The neurological examination showed a questionable increase in reflexes in the right leg, but this was not accepted by all the consultants. The lumbar puncture showed

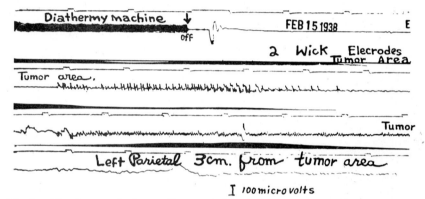

Fig. 82. The first cortical recording made in this laboratory in 1938 as described in Example No. 12. Only a single channel of the electroencephalogram was used. The interference from the diathermy machine connected to the line is shown in the beginning of the tracing and the difference between the normal cortex and the tumor area is shown in the figure.

normal pressure and protein, and the roentgenogram of the skull showed no abnormality. The ventriculogram was within normal limits and showed normal ventricles on both sides *without any displacement* or deformity of the ventricular system. The electroencephalogram showed normal activity from all areas except from a small circumscribed region in the left temporal region (3 cm. in diameter), just above the ear, where two electrodes had been placed. From this area, high-voltage, fast activity of around thirty cycles per second appeared continuously during the examination. Nowhere else was this fast abnormal discharge seen. Because of the similarity in certain respects to muscle discharges, successful efforts were made to rule this out by relaxation of the jaw, neck and facial muscles in a number of different examinations. No slow delta activity was seen in any of the leads, and this fast discharge was sharply circumscribed to the area mentioned. Two days later a bone flap was turned down over the area of the abnormal electrical activity. After the pia had been reflected, there was an area of 3 cm. which was discolored, but did not look grossly like a tumor.

The electroencephalographic apparatus was brought up to the operating room, set up and attached to two cotton pledgets soaked in saline which were laid over the abnormal area. The same fast discharge previously described from the scalp was seen. When these electrodes were removed 3 cm. away from the discolored area, a normal electroencephalogram was obtained (Fig. 82). A frozen section biopsy taken from the discolored area revealed an infiltrating glioblastoma. Because the neoplasm was near the speech area and was probably infiltrating and of large extent, only a subtemporal decompression was done and the tumor was not removed. The patient subsequently died in a month's time, and at the autopsy an infiltrating tumor was found in the area described.

Further use of the electroencephalograph in the operating room by direct recording from the exposed brain is shown by the following example.

Example 13. A fifty-eight year old man with a right hemiplegia and evidence of increased pressure, both by lumbar puncture (350 mm. of water) and two diopters' choking in the optic fundi, showed on the ordinary electroencephalogram a rather diffuse left temporal, parietal slow wave focus. The ventriculogram was not entirely satisfactory, showing some deformity of the left temporal bone. After the large left parietal bone flap was turned down no visible or palpable evidence of a neoplasm was seen. Needling the brain substance in a search for the tumor was considered too risky in this area of the dominant hemisphere. The direct corticogram showed slow waves over most of the exposed cortex with no sharp phase reversal. A small 2 cm. oval area in the post-parietal lobe just above the Sylvian fissure showed consistently depressed to no electrical activity. By inserting a needle here a hard mass was encountered 2 cm. below the surface and an osteocystoma was dissected out.

SOURCES OF ERROR

Sources of error commonly encountered in the localization of intracranial tumors or abscesses discussed in this chapter will be limited to phenomena not associated with poor function of the apparatus or faulty attachment of the electrodes. Such artifacts are usually readily identifiable by experienced workers and do not normally complicate the problem of cerebral localization by the electroencephalogram. The most common source of error in localization of intracranial lesions is localization of the disturbance on the wrong side of the hemisphere. This is possible when the lesion is near the midline and the electrode recording the abnormal disturbance is near the midline on the opposite side; thus a right central pair of leads near the midline might record a maximum disturbance from a tumor in the opposite ventricle. Usually such errors are easily picked up because of the inconsistency of the electroencephalographic findings with the neurological picture. In the same way a posterior fossa tumor may cause an abnormal disturbance of electrical activity in the occipital lobe above it, either on the same side or on the opposite side from pressure against the tentorium causing an interference in the circulation in the occiput alone. Again, the clinical findings must be correlated with the electroencephalographic localization and marked or glaring inconsistencies identified as a possible error. Lesions in the cerebral substance around the thalamus, in particular, are sometimes causes of error because the thalamus or basal structures near the supply through the commissures are identical parts of both hemispheres.

Example 14. A patient with a brain abscess in the right occipital cortex and a clear and sharp left homonymous hemianopsia always showed a focus of 3-per-second delta waves in the left occipital lobe, his right field was normal, and his vision was 20/20. Over the pathological area where the brain abscess had been found, there was little activity of this sort and a rather irregular low-voltage 6- to 7-per-second activity. At the time of operation five years later and after seven electroencephalograms with these findings, direct cortical recording over the whole scarred abscess was done and many spikes were seen.

The explanation for this erroneous focus of 3-per-second waves is that the old abscess cavity extended down into the thalamus, producing enough edema and defective circulation so that this structure was firing off bilateral synchronous 3-per-second waves into both occipital lobes. The one on the right, which was the area of the brain abscess, was so deteriorated and damaged that these waves did not arrive, whereas the healthy, intact left occipital lobe received them in abundance. Again the careful correlation of the clinical and neurological findings with the electroencephalographic recording would have straightened us out in this situation.

THE ELECTROENCEPHALOGRAM IN THE SURGICAL TREATMENT OF EPILEPSY

The most important group of workers in this field are at Montreal at Dr. Penfield's Neurological Institute, where the electroencephalographic department is under the direction of Dr. Herbert Jasper. It is an active neurosurgical unit that has been specializing in the surgical treatment of epilepsy since 1934. In 1937 they began to make plans to incorporate the removal of epileptogenic scars they could see in the operating room with direct electrocortical examination. In 1938, when the electroencephalographic laboratory was formally opened, apparatus and plans were available to carry on an extensive mapping of the electrical activity of the cerebral cortex in human beings on the operating table. This work has gone on fruitfully under able and industrious leadership.[18] Not only do the patients who pass through this clinic receive careful neurological studies, but the electroencephalograms are done with measured placements of the electrodes. This provides exact identification of the electrocorticographic finding at operation with the data obtained from previous scalp recording.

Localization on the exposed cerebral hemisphere is obtained in two ways. The first involves stimulation by subconvulsive threshold currents so that the motor strip and sensory areas are identified. After this is done, the cortical electrodes are put in place and recordings on the electroencephalographic machine are made. The investigators are looking for spike discharges and localized slow wave foci, and they correlate the data with visible scars or atrophy. If no electrical abnormality is seen by this first method, a low-voltage stimulating current (3 volts at 60 cycles, for example) is applied for five seconds to a likely area in the operative field. The electroencephalographic record is obtained during and after this stimulation. Since the patient in such procedures is fully conscious (the operation is done under local anesthesia), a detailed description of all he feels, thinks and does during such stimulation is obtained at the time. Particular interest is paid to any feelings or thoughts

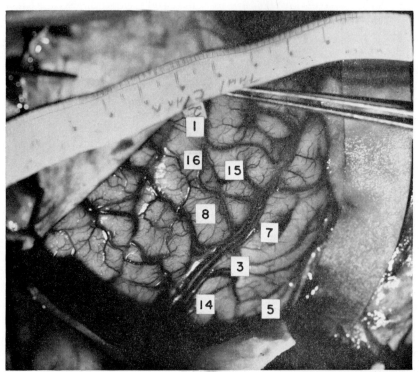

Fig. 83. The electrocorticogram of a 24-year-old male who had a head injury eight years before, and for the past four years had frequent automatisms with drooling, blank staring, twitching of the eyes and occasional movement of the right face with some slight involvement at times of the other side as well. Neurological examination showed slight increase of the reflexes on the right side. The ordinary electroencephalogram on three occasions was normal and the patient was able to tolerate 500 mg. Metrazol intravenously with a stroboscopic light activation stimulus without producing a seizure. Basal lead recording, however, showed occasional spikes from the left tympanic electrode. Exposure of the brain in the operating room shown in photograph in the figure revealed no gross abnormality. The photograph shows the left temporal lobe below the Sylvian vessels and on which the Nos. 14, 3, 7, and 5 have been placed. Nos. 1, 16 and 8 are anterior to the Rolandic fissure and No. 15 is posterior to it. The cortical electrode holder has been removed in this photograph so that it will not interfere with the visualization of the numbers and the topography.

produced at this time that may be associated with aura or beginning of the seizure pattern. The low-intensity electric stimulation often triggers off a short seizure discharge that shows up clearly in the electroencephalogram and can be localized to a particular electrode, since twelve of them are in place within the operative field. When such areas are local-

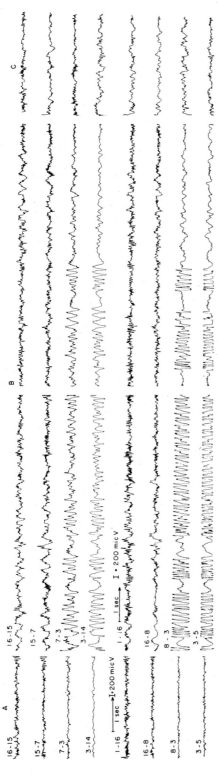

Fig. 83. *A.* Shows the electrocorticogram from these 8 electrodes according to the numbers in the figure. Note the beta activity from the motor area and the absence of spikes or slow waves.

B. This was taken directly after the application of a 5 second electrical stimulation at 4 volts 1 millisecond in duration at 30-per-second between electrodes 3 and 14. A long seizure discharge lasting 12 seconds was evoked. This was localized quite sharply in the area of electrode No. 3. Note that the electrode placements in the first 4 channels showed the phase reversals and seizure pattern in one direction at electrode 3 and the bottom 4 channels shows the same discharge localized at 3 in another direction. Stimulation in other areas produced either no response or a seizure discharge lasting only a second or two. The area around electrode 3 was removed and stimulation carried out in the same manner and the same general electrode placements.

C. No long seizure discharges were found after the resection of this area. This is shown in C of this figure. The patient made an excellent clinical recovery. He was seizure-free for 6 months and then had a few milder spells at rare intervals.

ized, they are removed surgically and the recording continued until the abnormal discharges have been eliminated. In this way about 50 per cent of the patients are restored to a seizure-free state after operation.

Gibbs,[12] at the University of Illinois, has concentrated on the temporal lobe in cases of automatism (psychomotor epilepsy). With Fuster of Uruguay, he found evidence of temporal lobe spikes in such cases. When these were in the non-dominant temporal lobe, Dr. Bailey, the neurosurgeon, removed portions of this lobe where the spikes were found at operation. About 40 to 50 per cent of such operated cases have been clearly improved.

A number of other centers are taking up this technique,[29] and the future is encouraging for the surgical removal of electrically located epileptic foci. Many epileptics are, however, not suitable for such procedures. The foci may be bilateral, or the focus may shift from one side to the other. There may be serious concomitant disease such as tuberculosis which makes a brain operation inadvisable. The focus may be in an area such as the speech center where removal would produce aphasia. It may be so deep that exploration or removal would be too hazardous.

It is generally agreed by those experienced in this field that such resection should be limited to special cases and done only after a thorough and adequate trial on *all* the anticonvulsant drugs available. The technique is a complicated one which requires not only experience, but a good deal of technical knowledge and mutual understanding on the part of the surgeon and the electroencephalographer together in the operating room. This, however, is not beyond the scope of any good neurosurgical clinic if the apparatus can be wheeled into the operating room and if the electroencephalographer and his technicians can maintain a reasonable degree of surgical and operating room technique. An example of this procedure is presented.

A twenty-eight year old man with left-sided seizures for sixteen years was explored in 1935 (he was then seventeen years old), and a normal cortex seen. He continued to have seizures, not controlled with large and varied anticonvulsant therapy. In 1946 he was re-admitted, and the usual electroencephalogram showed diffuse abnormality of the slow wave type, much more marked on the right temporal parietal area. Air studies showed a large right ventricle. The second bone flap again showed an apparently normal brain. The corticogram showed slow waves from all the surface examined, with some spikes in the temporal lobe. When this area was stimulated by a 4-volt current, three separate spike foci were brought out. These were all dissected out, and after this procedure (four hours) no further spikes could be produced, but the slow wave activity persisted. After the patient left the hospital he had one convulsion, but since then (one year) he has been free of spells. He has taken dilantin, however, which he was taking before, and the success here is not in any way considered as a cure at this date (Fig. 83).

ELECTROENCEPHALOGRAPHY IN NEUROLOGIC DIAGNOSIS

Disseminated sclerosis (multiple sclerosis) and other forms of chronic demyelinating diseases encountered in neurological practice have little that is specific in electroencephalograms.[39] In multiple sclerosis in particular, cerebral involvement as indicated by intelligence tests, and history is minimal. On the other hand, some euphoria in the mood is common and is suggestive of frontal lobe involvement. The electroencephalographic tracings in multiple sclerosis usually do not fit in too well with clinical findings, but in over half of the cases examined in this laboratory the records show a mild abnormality that may be diffuse or, in some cases, limited to one side of the head. In still fewer these may

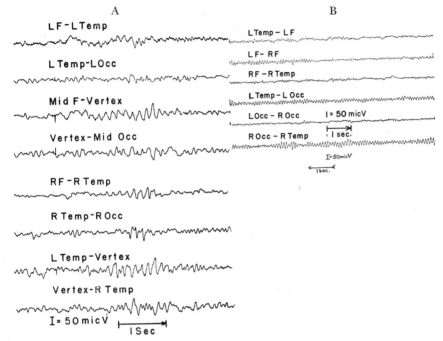

Fig. 84 *A*. The electroencephalogram of a patient 19 years old with some spasticity, central scotoma and ataxia. There was a definite diagnosis of multiple sclerosis. Clinically he is not very much different from the patient in Fig. 84 *B* but the electroencephalogram shows an abundance of 5–6 per second activity and some theta activity in the left temporal region.

B. The electroencephalogram of a 32-year-old male with early and rather marked multiple sclerosis of approximately four years' duration with involvement of vision and slight ataxia as symptoms. The record is essentially normal.

be focal, although the focus may not fit the neurological signs. The usual abnormality is in the 5-, 6- and 7-per-second or theta band with voltages within normal limits. Abnormal activity is not continuous, nor is it paroxysmal, but it is random and irregular in occurrence.

There is some value in such mild disturbances in the electroencephalogram in the differential diagnosis between a localized spinal lesion due to trauma, tumor or infection and that of multiple sclerosis. The presence of such abnormal rhythm points to involvement of some cerebral structures which pure spinal disease would not show. On the other hand, in the presence of inflamed optic disks (retrobulbar neuritis) and cerebellar signs, a nearly normal electroencephalogram would

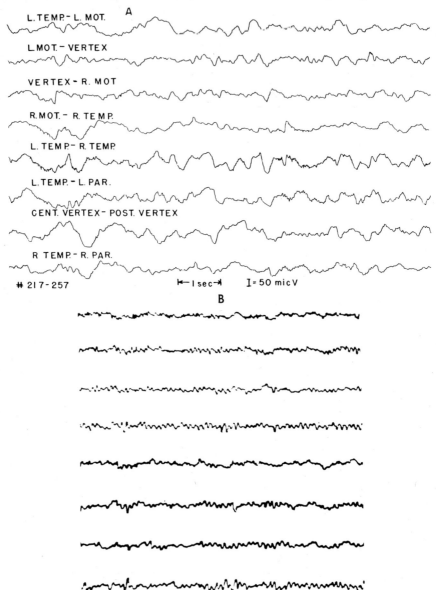

Fig. 85 *A*. Electroencephalogram in Example No. 15 taken three days after his admission to the hospital and showing the high voltage slow activity in all leads.

B. This shows the same case after complete clinical recovery when the boy returned to the laboratory for a check-up. This record is entirely within normal limits. Same electrode placements as in Figure 85 *A*.

make a posterior fossa tumor unlikely. Unnecessary ventriculograms and posterior fossa explorations may thus be prevented now and then in cases of multiple sclerosis by paying more attention to the electro-encephalographic findings.

In acute encephalitis[22] in which the infection is chiefly in the basal ganglia, thalamus and other midline structures, the electroencephalogram shows high-voltage delta and theta activity that is diffuse in both hemispheres or even bilaterally synchronous. In milder forms, early in the disease in some and in the convalescence of others, the rhythm is chiefly in the theta band. Some indications as to prognosis or the extent of the process may be inferred from the study of several electroencephalograms in such cases.

In Sydenham's chorea there is usually a non-specific diffuse abnormality, sometimes mild. In others, slow activity may be conspicuous in both frontal leads and much theta in the motor areas.

In Huntington's chorea, on the other hand, all cases show diffuse irregular and multiple types of abnormality, indicating rather gross disturbances in both structure and function, a finding in agreement with the clinical and pathological findings. Furthermore, Bagchi[20] finds that 75 per cent of the offspring of patients with Huntington's chorea have diffuse abnormal records, half of which show paroxysmal types of discharges and yet do not have clinical epilepsy. They bring out some evidence that the worst of these (50 per cent) may eventually have the disease.

In poliomyelitis, on the other hand, the electroencephalographic changes are minimal[13] after the first few days and may be normal within a week, whereas in encephalitis the electroencephalogram is far more abnormal.

Example 15. A twelve year old boy was accidentally bitten in the hand while feeding a stray cocker spaniel on July 8, 1949. His parents became alarmed when the dog disappeared, and on August 1, two injections of antirabies vaccine were given. Within forty-eight hours the lad had a severe chill, headache, nausea and some stiff neck. There was a moderate epidemic of poliomyelitis that summer with a good number of cases from the patient's locality. When admitted to the hospital, he showed photophobia, a temperature of 104° F., 60 cells in his spinal fluid, but no paralysis. Some thought that it might well be an atypical poliomyelitis; others, an acute encephalitis from the vaccine. The electroencephalogram showed diffuse high-voltage delta waves all over the scalp and an abundance of theta waves in addition. No other case of infantile paralysis, even of the bulbar type, showed this degree of electroencephalographic abnormality. This pushed the diagnosis into encephalitis, and the type of treatment and isolation was guided by this decision. In two weeks the electroencephalogram was markedly improved and showed only the theta activity. The boy had then recovered clinically with no residuals of any kind. Two months later the electroencephalogram was entirely normal (Fig. 85).

A neurological disease common in North American and north European countries is Parkinson's disease. The etiological factors in this disease are not clear in many cases, and vascular diseases in the brain may be minimal on post-mortem examination. Often there is no history of encephalitis. However, lesions are usually found in the basal ganglia and reticular formation of the midbrain, and in some there is cortical atrophy. The electroencephalogram in these patients is usually normal. A few workers in the past reported in this disease a 4- to 5-per-second discharge from electrodes on the scalp over the motor region synchronous with the characteristic tremor of the limb. When these are carefully examined, they are usually found to be artifacts due to head movement from the tremor that was shaking the electrodes and producing a non-cerebral origin for the electrical disturbances. A report of this in 1938 by Schwab and Stanley Cobb[24] settled this clearly, and the report has been confirmed by others. Russell Myers has introduced electrodes into the thalamus and basal ganglia directly through ventricular tre-

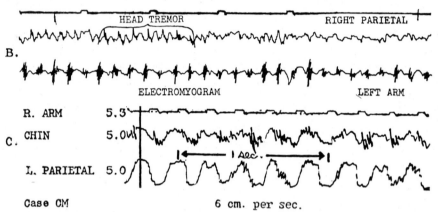

Fig. 86. This is a patient with a normal electroencephalogram but showing the tremor artifact described previously by us which has misled some to believe that the artifact was a brain rhythm. The figure shows the electromyogram of the left arm at the same time the electroencephalogram on the right side is being taken with the tremor artifact in the electroencephalogram. The bottom part of the picture shows the gross tremor artifact in the left side of the electroencephalogram and it is obviously synchronizing with leads from the chin and the right arm. (From Cobb, S., and Schwab, R. S.: Simultaneous Electromyograms and Electroencephalograms in Paralysis Agitans. J. Neurophysiol., 2:36–41, 1939.)

phines in cases of Parkinson's disease and failed to find any activity related to the actual tremor. In a number of these cases, however, there is evidence of cortical atrophy by pneumoencephalogram, and in a small percentage, less than 10 per cent in the group we have examined, one can see in the electroencephalogram random sporadic runs of 5-, 6- and 7-per-second low voltage activity bearing no relation whatsoever to the tremor, but indicating mild generalized cerebral abnormality. Study from the basal leads indicates that these abnormal waves may originate in this area and that they are found more often when the examination includes this type of recording.

An interesting neurological disorder associated with emotional problems is narcolepsy.[14] This condition with its episodes of sleep and sleepiness at inappropriate times has been studied with the electroencephalogram by different workers. In most of them the waking electroencephalogram is perfectly normal, and, when patients fall asleep, the record shows the characteristic pattern that one sees in normal sleep. The electroencephalographic pattern is perfectly normal in spite of the fact that there is definite evidence of hypothalamic disturbances causing the excessive drowsiness.

The electroencephalogram is usually normal in Wilson's disease, familial mental backwardness, hemiatrophies, progressive muscular atrophies and dystrophies, myotonia congenita, myasthenia gravis, mongolism, neuritis, syringomyelia and stammering.

The effect of poisons and chemicals on the electroencephalogram is of great physiological and clinical interest, and here we have some correlations that may be of use to the clinician. Some work done by Davis[8] and Greenblatt[15] in this field shows that, when alcohol is ingested in large enough amounts to produce intoxication, there are alterations in the electroencephalogram. When the patient becomes dull and drowsy, there are slow waves first in the 5-, 6- and 7-per-second cycle band occurring mostly in the frontal areas at random with low voltage. Later on, as the person becomes more intoxicated and is intellectually retarded, the slower waves, as slow as three per second occurring in longer bursts that are symmetrical on both sides, are found. After the alcohol has been eliminated from the system by the next day, the electroencephalographic pattern is in the fast group of beta waves with some increase in voltage. This is associated with the familiar tension, headache, "hangover," irritability, and the like that are found in post-alcoholic states.

There has been no large series of studies in delirium tremens, but those that have been done show that the predominant rhythm is the fast beta activity that one gets in other tension states in which there is increased motor activity and that this is often associated with low-voltage, 5- and 6-per-second activity on both sides of the head. The other conspicuous finding is the absence of a smooth, regular, normal alpha rhythm pattern, which may not develop until the entire episode has subsided.

Another chemical which produces profound changes in the electroencephalogram is carbon monoxide. When poisoning from this gas occurs, it produces a degeneration in the thalamus and the basal ganglia as well as in the cortex, and often is followed by postencephalitic symptoms similar to those seen in Parkinsonism. In an acute case of such poisoning there is an asymmetrical, irregular, sporadic appearance of very slow waves, sometimes as slow as one per second, with voltages mildly or greatly increased, depending upon the state of coma and unconsciousness. There is a close correlation between the degree of unconsciousness and the abnormalities in the electroencephalogram. The total absence of normal activity in the occipital and parietal areas is a bad sign in carbon monoxide poisoning, but there are not enough data to use it as an accurate prognosis. If the cases are mild, the electroencephalographic disturbance may be minimal, and, with return of consciousness and the disappearance of the gas from the blood stream, the electrical record may be normal in three or four days. In fatal cases there is a progressive increase in abnormality in the electroencephalogram. There is no normal activity, and the abnormal record begins to show evidences of activity as slow as one-half wave per second of low voltage. Finally no electrical activity at all is seen, and shortly afterwards the patient dies.

There are many drugs that can disturb consciousness, and sedatives are the most commonly experienced in clinical practice. There is a good deal of literature on the effect of barbiturates on the electroencephalogram. From the work of Alexander,[2] Brazier[5] and others, it has been shown that small amounts of barbiturates injected intravenously produce fast activity in the frontal leads and that only as drowsiness and sleep are produced do slow waves appear. If the intoxication is severe, very slow, low-voltage waves are found.

THE ELECTROENCEPHALOGRAM IN METABOLIC DISORDERS

Metabolic correlations with the electroencephalogram are chiefly changes in the rate of the alpha rhythm. Hoagland[16] showed, in subjects who were receiving fever treatment, that the alpha activity increased in rate as the temperature of the body rose. This followed the formula of thermodynamic action, indicating that the alpha rhythm is a function of metabolic activity of the brain cells. Ross and Schwab[21] showed that there was a correlation with the alpha rate in myxedema and hyperthyroidism. For example, a patient with a basal metabolic rate of minus 40 might have an alpha rate of about 12. In a series of some forty patients reported in 1939 the coefficient of correlation was good enough to be shown in a graph that approached a straight line. There were many exceptions, and it was quite obvious that the alpha rate itself is of no value in determining the basal metabolic state. On the other hand, it is sometimes of value to the physician to know that a normal-appearing alpha rhythm that is slower than normal, say seven to eight per second, might well be due to a depressed metabolic rate. Patients who have depressed metabolic rates with slow alpha rates of six and a half or seven, who are given thyroxin or other thyroid preparations which return their basal metabolism rates to normal, show a slow return of the alpha rhythm to normal limits after a delay of some five to twelve days.

In a variety of pituitary disorders the electroencephalogram is normal. When the disturbance is associated with depressed metabolism or when a tumor of the pituitary or neighboring structures causes pressure on the brain, the electroencephalogram is abnormal. The abnormality is not severe with 5-, 6- or 7-cycle waves which are of normal voltage and are difficult to localize because of the central position of the gland and the tumor around it. It can be said that mild bilateral abnormalities

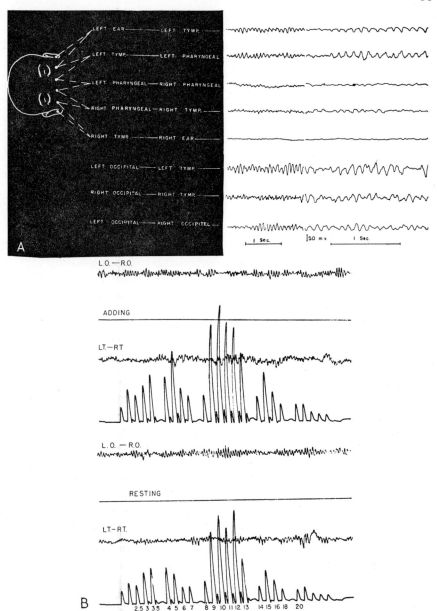

Fig. 87 *A*. The basal electroencephalogram in a 25-year-old female subject to migraine attacks. The electroencephalogram shows normal activity at the base.

B. Electroencephalogram of the same subject when doing some mental work consisting of adding figures. The electroencephalographic tracing is shown from 3 leads and the analysis of the temporal leads is shown in the middle of the figure. The analysis shows the presence of a peak at 5 per second as well as the strong 9 to 10, 11 and 12 alpha and a secondary peak in the intermediate fast band at 15 per second. The bottom tracing shows the same subject when she is at rest with the theta and intermediate fast activity not in evidence and the normal alpha components shown in the analysis in the figure.

in the midline near the vertex may be consistent with the central lesion around the pituitary gland or fossa. There have been a number of electroencephalographic studies of diabetics which are within normal limits, although the blood sugar may be over 200 or 300.

HEADACHE

The subject of headache is a complex one and involves a diffuse psychosomatic classification of disorders in which one would not expect any specific findings. Patients who complain of headaches, anxieties or other psychosomatic symptoms usually have normal electroencephalograms. Headaches that are due to vascular disease, such as hypertension, have normal electroencephalograms. There may be a few mild abnormal waves on both sides associated with vascular thrombosis of a minor sort, but usually the electroencephalogram is normal. Patients with migraine have more abnormal electroencephalograms (30 per cent) than do normal controls. However, Arellano,[3] working in my laboratory, has shown with recording from basal leads during the headache that 5-, 6- and 7-per-second activity is found (Fig. 87).

The true value of the strong chance of the ordinary headache having a normal electroencephalogram is obvious. In tumors, abscesses or subdural hematomas one of the chief complaints is a severe, persistent, often progressive, headache. Such symptoms, when they fail to disappear with usual analgesics, bring up at once the possibility of an expanding cerebral lesion (tumor suspect).

In 90 per cent of such intracranial growths the electroencephalogram is abnormal. Therefore a normal tracing is ten to one against a tumor. This is of great value and reassurance to both patient and physician.

REFERENCES

1. Abbott, J. A., and Bautista, P. C.: Electroencephalographic Findings in Various Types of Intracerebral Vascular Accidents. EEG Clin. Neurophysiol., *1*:252, 1949.
2. Alexander, L., Winston, M. R., and Berman, H.: The Electroencephalogram During Sodium Amytal and Sodium Pentothal Narcosis and During Resuscitation with Benzedrine Sulfate in Normal and Schizophrenic Subjects. EEG Clin. Neurophysiol., *1*:255, 1949.
3. Arellano, A. P. —Z.:Unpublished Data.
4. Berger, H.: Das Elektrenkephalogramm des Menschen. Nova Acta Leopoldina, *6*:173–309, 1938.
5. Brazier, M. A. B., and Finesinger, J. E.: Action of Barbiturates on the Cerebral Cortex. Arch. Neurol. & Psychiat., *53*:51–58, 1945.
6. Cobb, W. A.: The Electro-encephalographic Localization of Intracranial Neoplasms. J. Neurol., Neurosurg. & Psychiat., *7*:96–102, 1944.
7. Culbreth, G. C.: Electroencephalograms in Brain Tumor Suspects. EEG Clin. Neurophysiol., *2*:115, 1950.
8. Davis, P. A., Gibbs, F. A., Davis, H., Jetter, W. W., and Trowbridge, E. H.: The Effects of Alcohol upon the Electroencephalogram. Quart. J. Studies on Alcohol, *1*:626–637, 1941.

9. Dow, R. S., Ulett, G., and Tunturi, A.: Electroencephalographic Changes Following Head Injuries in Dogs. J. Neurophysiol., 8:161–172, 1945.

10. Dow, R. S., Ulett, G., and Raaf, J.: EEG Studies Immediately Following Head Injury. Am. J. Psychiat., 101:174–183, 1944.

11. Dow, R. S., Ulett, G., and Raaf, J.: Electroencephalographic Studies in Head Injuries. J. Neurosurg., 2:154–169, 1945.

12. Gibbs, E. L., and Gibbs, F. A.: Diagnostic and Localizing Value of Electroencephalographic Studies in Sleep. A. Research Nerv. & Ment. Dis., Proc., 26:366–376, 1947.

13. Goldbloom, A., Jasper, H. H., and Brickman, H. F.: EEG Studies in Poliomyelitis. J.A.M.A., 137:690–696, 1948.

14. Gozzano, M. e Colombati, S.: Osservazioni Elettroencefalografiche in un Caso di Narcolessia. Riv. di. Neurol., 18:578–582, 1948.

15. Greenblatt, M., Levin, S., and Cori, F. di.: The EEG Associated with Chronic Alcoholism, Alcoholic Psychosis and Alcoholic Convulsions. Arch. Neurol. & Psychiat., 52:290–295, 1944.

16. Hoagland, H.: Brain Metabolism and Brain Wave Frequencies. Am. J. Physiol., 123:102P, 1938.

17. Hoefer, P. F. A.: The EEG in Cases of Head Injury. In Injuries of the Skull, Brain and Spinal Cord. Baltimore, Williams and Wilkins, 1943, pp. 576–605.

18. Jasper, H. H.: Electroencephalography in Epilepsy. From Epilepsy, Hoch and Knight. New York, Grune & Stratton, 1947, pp. 181–203.

19. Paillas, J. E., Gastaut, H., Tamalet, J. et Verspik: Intérêt de l'électroencéphalographie pour le diagnostic et la localisation des tumeurs cérébrales. Rev. Neurol., 79:688–692, 1947.

20. Patterson, R. M., Bagchi, B. K., and Test, A.: The Prediction of Huntington's Chorea; an Electroencephalographic and Genetic Study. Am. J. Psychiat., 104:786–797, 1948.

21. Ross, D. A., and Schwab, R. S.: The Cortical Alpha Rhythm in Thyroid Disorders. Endocrinol., 25:75–79, 1939.

22. Ross, I. S.: Electroencephalographic Findings During and After Acute Encephalitis and Meningoencephalitis. J. Nerv. Ment. Dis., 102:172–182, 1945.

23. Schwab, R. S., and Carter, R.: EEG in Relation to Otology. Laryngoscope, 52:757–767, 1942.

24. Schwab, R. S., and Cobb, S.: Simultaneous EMG's and EEG's in Paralysis Agitans. J. Neurophysiol., 2:36–41, 1939.

25. Schwab, R. S.: Unpublished Data.

26. Strauss, H., and Greenstein, L.: The Electroencephalogram in Cerebrovascular Disease. Arch. Neurol. & Psychiat., 59:395–403, 1948.

27. Sullivan, J. F., and Abbott, J. A.: EEG in Cases of Subdural Hematoma. Proc. EEG Clin. Neurophysiol., 1:517, 1949.

28. Ulett, G. A.: EEG of Dog with Experimental Space Occupying Intracranial Lesions. Arch. Neurol. & Psychiat., 54:141–149, 1945.

29. Walker, A. E., Johnson, H. C., and Marshall, C.: Electrocortigraphy. Bull. Johns Hopkins Hosp., 84:583, 1949.

30. Ward, J. W., and Clark, S. L.: The Electroencephalogram in Experimental Concussion and Related Conditions. J. Neurophysiol., 11:59–74, 1948.

31. Williams, D., and Denny-Brown, D.: Cerebral Electrical Changes in Experimental Concussion. Brain, 64:223–238, 1941.

32. Zeifert, M.: The Electroencephalogram of Multiple Sclerosis; Review of the Literature and Analysis of 34 Cases. Arch. Neurol. & Psychiat., 60:376–387, 1948.

CHAPTER VII

Electroencephalography in Psychiatry

THE FIRST clinician to use electroencephalography was its founder, Hans Berger, a psychiatrist. The various electroencephalographic laboratories in the United States and Europe are located for the most part in psychiatric hospitals or in general hospitals associated with the department of psychiatry. Thus psychiatry has given far more support and encouragement to electroencephalography than has either neurosurgery or neurology. These specialties apparently feel satisfied and confident enough with air studies and the patella hammer to disregard this new diagnostic technique. In spite of this backing by psychiatry, the clinical value of electroencephalography in the diagnosis of mental disease has been, on the whole, less helpful than in neurology and neurosurgery.

TYPES OF NORMAL PERSONALITY AND ELECTROENCEPHALOGRAMS

Before discussing the abnormal type of psychiatric disorders studied by means of electroencephalography, brief comment should be made on attempts to correlate various personality types in normals with the electroencephalographic pattern. In 1937 Liberson[13] made a study in Paris of a number of railroad employees to see if the amount of occipital alpha activity could be correlated with the aptitude and job stability of these workers. In general, he found that the most reliable locomotive engineers had the most alpha activity and the more unstable and unsatisfactory employees the least. The correlations were far from exact, and there were so many exceptions that practical use of these data was not recommended.

In 1937 Saul and Davis[16] reported some observation on correlations of personality with electroencephalographic findings in reference to the amount of alpha present. In their small series they showed that the person with a large amount of 10-per-second normal occipital alpha tended to be methodical, dependent, trustworthy, sensitive and, on the whole, a bit slower and more cautious than other people. Conversely, they had some evidence to show that the normal person with little or no alpha activity in the occipital lobe tended to be somewhat erratic and unstable, jumping from this to that with excessive dynamic drive and enthusiasm, was usually dissatisfied with routine tasks and duties, and more visionary and creative than his colleague with the high alpha index. Other observers, however, showed that this was not always the case and that there were many persons with high alpha indexes who were dynamic, creative, temperamental, and so forth. In spite of the interesting implications of this preliminary work, no very careful statistical analysis of personality types in normals in relation to their alpha activity has followed this preliminary work of Davis and Saul. In 1949, at the third annual meeting of the American Electroencephalographic Society, Davis[17] reviewed this work with more data. He showed further that, after successful psychoanalysis, patients had the same type of brain wave pattern as before. He still found that there is a general division of normals into those with high alpha indexes who are more passive, dependent, placid and reliable, and those with little or no alpha who are tense, driving, independent and restless. These "pure" types are found in about 30 per cent of the population. Various mixtures of alpha and beta rhythms do not correlate at all with mixed personality patterns.

PSYCHONEUROSIS

There have been papers on the alpha index in various psychosomatic disorders such as gastric ulcers, anxiety neurosis and hysteria. There is slight evidence that patients who have ulcers have more alpha than those who are free from this disease. Anxiety neurosis is usually associated with more rapid activity in the beta band (eighteen to twenty-four) than is found in a comparable normal group. For example, Brazier and Finesinger[1] have shown that, if one examines an accurately diagnosed group of psychoneurotics with the electroencephalograph by means of a careful analysis of the frequencies in the record, this group tends to have a faster frequency than in the normal control group. In a group of relaxed normals the mean frequency would be around ten per second, whereas this same group alerted and tense would have a frequency of about sixteen to twenty per second. Thus psychoneurotics essentially show the faster rate of the normal. This has also been found by Jasper[10] and others. These findings in the normal and the psychoneurotic group were both *within normal limits,* and it is only by a careful analytical count of the various frequencies present that this difference between the normals and psychoneurotics can be shown. The mechanical or electronic analyzers such as those of Grass or Walter show this graphically and confirm manual analysis.

Hysterics, on the other hand, show records with more alpha. All this information is, however, of little clinical value, and the interpretation and selection of the clinical material varies in different series.

Gastaut[5] has found that certain hysterics and other neurotics have occipital rhythms that drive readily with photic stimulation and show temporal theta waves when the stroboscope flashes are five to seven per second. This group, like epileptics, have in many instances a low threshold to metrazol activation. In some of these there is either a definite history of familial seizures or a past history of spells, syncopal attacks or peculiar paroxysmal behavior. Clinically, to some observers, their spells are typically hysterical, to others epileptic, and to the more open-minded physician a complicated mixture of both. To Gastaut, their spells suggest disturbances in the autonomic centers in the hypothalamus and thalamus. Hence he feels that they are related to the petit mal group of epileptics. Kershman,[12] using Gower's term "borderlands of epilepsy," has shown that a large percentage have interseizure abnormal electroencephalograms. In no other group is it more essential to withhold a hasty diagnosis. The most careful clinical examination and history should be obtained. The electroencephalographic studies in these patients should include a number of tests, with particular attention to such physiological variables as blood sugar, respiration in liters per minute, and assessment of their sensitivity to several different types of activating agents. By such means it may be possible, in the near future, to explain a large segment of neurotic personalities on physiological and anatomical peculiarities instead of only in the terms of stereotyped dynamic concepts. In such cases we can have a sound basis for combining medical remedies with the psychotherapy that these patients need so badly. An example of such a case illustrates the complexity of the problem.

A thirty-four year old woman was sent to an internist because of a history of bizarre seizures. Nothing was found in the physical or neurological examination. Her past history revealed many typical hysterical symptoms, and there were a number of emotional conflicts she could not cope with. The routine electroencephalogram was close to normal except for some unilateral theta activity in the left temporal region, intensified with overbreathing. Activation with metrazol and photic stimulation produced at only 200 mg. of metrazol typical myoclonic jerks and spikes in the electroencephalogram at flashes of sixteen per second. This upset this vulnerable patient enough so that she overbreathed vigorously and had a short generalized seizure. The focus implicated the left temporal region. Because of her many hysterical and neurotic symptoms she was admitted to the psychiatric service. A combination of psychotherapy and anticonvulsant drugs improved her greatly. When she left the hospital, her seizures were under control and her emotional problems reduced by better insight and understanding.

BEHAVIOR DISORDERS

One of the first types of abnormal behavior examined with the electroencephalogram was that found in children. This work began in 1936 at the Bradley Home in Providence, Rhode Island, under Jasper[19] and was continued by Lindsley.[14] Since these pioneer observations, papers and communications have appeared all over the world on this subject. They found that children in the age group between eight and fourteen who were enough of a behavior problem so that psychiatric help was sought, tended to show abnormal electroencephalograms (Fig. 88). The abnormality was bilateral and diffuse, and consisted of intermediate abnormal slow waves between four, five, six and seven per second that came in runs sometimes as long as four or five seconds. There was a suggestion that these wave patterns were similar to some of those seen in epilepsy. On the other hand, many children with severe behavior disorders did not show this pattern in any way. Those that did show it often did not give a history of head injury or infection of the nervous system, such as encephalitis, which might account on a

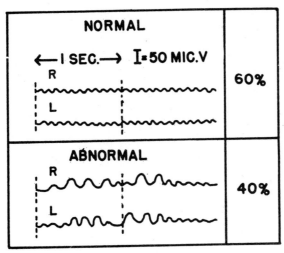

Fig. 88. A diagrammatic illustration of the percentage of abnormality in behavior disorders in children.

structural basis for the electroencephalographic abnormality. A certain number had hereditary taints, such as familial epilepsy or other abnormal neurological conditions which might have accounted for the abnormal discharges. The best that can be said of this amount of correlation with juvenile behavior disorders is that, in a large series of children with such conditions, the percentage of abnormal records runs rather high, anywhere from 40 to 50 per cent. Therefore, since this is only a statistical correlation, it is not of specific value in an individual case. However, if a personality disorder in a child is brought to the attenton of a neuropsychiatric clinic and the electroencephalogram is diffusely abnormal and there is no evidence of organic brain disease or epilepsy, the abnormal electroencephalogram may be called consistent with the behavior disorder. The fact that abnormal waves are present suggests the use of a drug such as benzedrine or phenobarbital in handling these patients. A number of reports show good results in improving the behavior of these children with abnormal brain waves by using these drugs in small amounts over a protracted period of time.

Turning now to the adult group in the same general category, namely, psychopathic personality, we again run into conflicting data and statistical correlations rather than individual characteristics. A number of papers have shown that psychopaths in general have a tendency to have abnormal electroencephalograms (Hill[9]). These abnormalities are similar to those seen in the behavior disorders previously mentioned, namely, diffuse bilateral abnormalities in the intermediate slow group of 5, 6 and 7 per second coming in runs and not showing the characteristics suggestive of an epileptic disorder. Often this theta activity is most marked in the temporal regions. However, there have been some reports by O'Leary[18] and others in a series of military psychopaths which showed the incidence of abnormal electroencephalograms to be as low as 20 per cent, which is close to the percentage of mildly abnormal records in a normal control group. On the other hand, there have been papers indicating that the percentage is as high as 65 per cent in other groups examined.

The conflict between such percentages probably lies in the definition of what constitutes psychopathic behavior. In the eyes of certain clinicians, any repetitive antisocial behavior that is out of line with the demand and needs of the person would be regarded as psychopathic. There is also a tendency on the part of psychiatrists, particularly those without broad experience, to regard the behavior of people they do not understand as psychopathic. For example, a conservative old New England psychiatrist might regard the shooting sprees and wild behavior of a west Texas rancher as psychopathic because it is totally incongruous to his method of living. On the other hand, a psychiatrist living in the Far West might regard some of the conservative and overmeticulous attitudes of some of his New England brethren as psychopathic in themselves. This prejudice and lack of understanding of the environmental and regional differences of human beings has certainly led to the erroneous diagnosis of psychopathic personality in numbers of instances. There are, however, enough data to show in a large series of true psychopathic persons without psychosis and without demonstrable organic diseases of the brain that the percentage of abnormal records is higher than in a normal control group, varying anywhere from 25 to 45 per cent.

An interesting question might arise here. Is this abnormal electrical activity simply a delayed maturation of the cerebral cortex in certain people? Stearns[21] in Massachusetts has shown that most psychopaths, when they reach the fourth and fifth decades, settle down, become decent citizens, stay out of trouble and out of jail, begin to earn their living efficiently and drop out of the attention of both the social services and the law. If one follows the electroencephalograms—and this has been done in a number of instances (Kennard[11]) —these psychopaths gradually lose these electroencephalographic abnormalities over a period of years, so that in the third, fourth and fifth decades the records may be normal. In other words, there is some evidence that the maturation process in these persons whose behavior is antisocial or amoral is simply a delayed development, and the electroencephalograph bears this out.

We must conclude, then, that in behavior disorders, in spite of a higher incidence of abnormal waves compared to normals, in any individual case one cannot make a diagnosis from the electroencephalographic records alone.

The electroencephalogram may play a critical role in court in helping a judge or jury to decide whether the perpetrator of a particular crime is fully responsible or not for his acts. Much, of course, depends on the type of the crime and the circumstances of its occurrence. A murder with clear motivation, during the interseizure period, by an epileptic is one thing. The killing of a stranger in an unnecessary, violent way without motivation during an attack of automatism by an epileptic is another. The electroencephalogram that is normal or nearly so between seizures in the first situation carries with it responsibility for the deed. An abnormal tracing during violent or aggressive behavior in automatism is excellent corroboration that the person did not know what he was doing. The electroencephalogram has been introduced into court as evidence numerous times in this country and abroad. The electroencephalographer who, as an expert witness, introduces such data must be thoroughly familiar with its limitations and statistical correlations or he will be made to look ridiculous by a clever and well-informed attorney. Gibbs[6] has written a useful and informative article on the general subject of this examination in a court of law.

Stafford-Clark[20] found that the successful criminal who has a purpose and motives for his crimes usually has a normal electroencephalogram. The psychopathic character who seems to blunder into unnecessary and purposeless violations of the law and often is an aggressive psychopath has a high incidence of abnormal tracings. Details of the electroencephalogram in epileptics have been covered already. The best advice to the electroencephalographer on the witness stand is to be exceedingly cautious and conservative in his statements and opinions and to be able to substantiate these by references to the literature that may cover the particular phase of his testimony.

PSYCHOSES

The more serious types of mental disorder, such as manic depressive psychosis, schizophrenia and paranoid states, have been carefully studied by means of the electroencephalograph,[4] and there is definitely no specific pattern. Some schizophrenics have an abnormally persistent and stable alpha in the occipital regions that is little affected by mental effort. Others, according to Gastaut,[5] show 5- to 6-per-second theta in their temporal regions, especially when driven by a stroboscope at that frequency. He feels, too, that a few have a low threshold to metrazol-stroboscopic activation and in that way resemble epileptics. Schizophrenics who have been ill for many years may show diffuse slow activity in the frontals. Others have perfectly normal records. The variable electroencephalographic findings in schizophrenia are no more variable than the clinical concepts of this disease and the dynamics of its etiology.

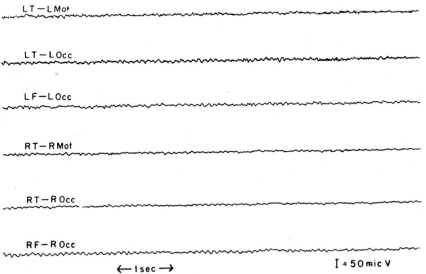

Fig. 89. The electroencephalogram of a 50-year-old male with recurring depressions. Physical and neurological examinations were normal and although the patient complained of being slowed down, apathetic and indifferent, the general clinical picture was that of depression and not of a tumor of the brain. The electroencephalogram as shown in the figure is normal and this aided in the decision not to have air studies. The patient was given electric shock treatment and there was a rather prompt disappearance of the depression.

However, there are some statistical correlations indicating that in a population of psychotics taken in a state hospital, for example, the number of abnormal records is higher than any control group.[7] It runs anywhere from 30 to 50 per cent, depending upon the institution and type and age of the patient. In such cases the abnormality is usually mild and bilateral and suggests that we still have a great deal to learn about the cause of these conditions. One would suppose that the presence of an abnormal electroencephalographic tracing in an adult with a mental disease such as schizophrenia would indicate that there is some underlying structural abnormality that defies the usual neurological examination, even pneumoencephalography. This should be a challenge to psychiatrists working in this field and certainly to neurologists who are called in from time to time for consultation to see such patients.

The burden of proof, if there is an abnormal electroencephalogram, should be on the psychiatrist to show that organic disease is not the cause of the picture. Sometimes when this situation is carefully investigated, it is found that the psychiatric pattern of the patient which has been called, for example, a depression, is due to an organic lesion of the brain, such as a tumor. The electroencephalogram can be helpful to the psychiatrist in avoiding such errors and lead in some cases to the patient's cure and release from the hospital.

A normal electroencephalogram in a psychiatric disorder is strong evidence (nine to one) against a structural (organic) cause for the condition (Fig. 89). The most important application of this test in psychiatry is to assist the psychiatrist in identifying the few patients under his care who may have an *unsuspected neurological* or neurosurgical condition that demands special treatment by the consultants in these fields.

The following case report is a typical example of such an application of the routine use of electroencephalography.

During World War II an officer in the supply department of the Navy with a tremendous load of responsibility was referred to a psychiatrist because of irritability, difficulty in concentrating on his tasks, and such severe discouragement that a diagnosis of reactive depression was made. In addition, he complained of intermittent headaches. Physically and neurologically he showed nothing. After four weeks of failure to help him by psychiatric interviews, he was admitted to a naval hospital. A routine electroencephalogram showed a clear-cut slow wave focus in the left post-frontal region. There were no reflex or motor abnormalities. A careful aphasia study (the patient was right-handed) did show slight hesitancy with certain words. Air studies revealed a tumor in the left frontal lobe which was completely removed. The patient recovered and went back to duty in one month.

MENTAL DETERIORATION

There is a rather good correlation between psychiatric patients who are deteriorated mentally and the electroencephalographic record. About 85 per cent of such patients show mild, diffuse frontal abnormality, usually symmetrical. The rhythm is from three to seven per second, and the amplitude low. In severe cases such abnormality involves the temporal and occipital areas as well. The occipital alpha in some cases looks normal, but is slowed to seven or eight per second.

There are four groups of deteriorated patients in the average mental institution. The largest group is associated with advancing years and vascular disease, called senile or arteriosclerotic dementia. The brain, post mortem, shows conspicuous and gross vascular disease, convolutional atrophy, especially in the frontal lobes, and enlargement of the ventricles.[3] The mental deterioration may be extreme, with severe memory loss, confusion, soiling or other antisocial behavior. There is often abundant neurological evidence of structural disease of the brain, such as pyramidal tract signs, tremors, incoordination of movements, and so forth. The electroencephalogram may be within normal limits, but usually shows the findings described above. An example of one of these is shown in Figure 90, where there is evidence of low slow activity, symmetrical on both sides, more marked in the frontal and post-frontal areas.

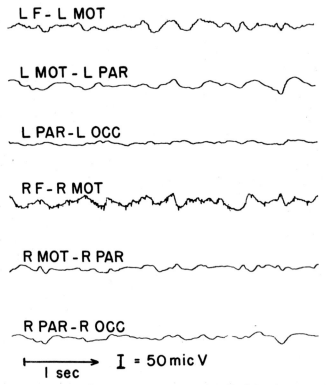

Fig. 90. The electroencephalogram of patient described in the text who showed progressive deterioration during the past five years. The electroencephalogram shows abnormality in both frontal regions. The degree of electroencephalographic abnormality and the marked loss of mental and cerebral function were related in this case.

A fifty-eight year old woman had borne two children and reached the age of fifty-three without any evidence of mental impairment. At that time, very slowly and insidiously, she became increasingly vague and dull, lost interest in her usual hobbies and home, became absentminded and careless about her affairs and was unable to take on the full responsibility of her household. She was, however, not violent in any way and was easily cared for at home by her husband. Her children, who were adults, lived elsewhere.

She was seen by a number of physicians during the first two years of this decline, and no neurological abnormalities had been found. There was nothing noted in the nature of malignancy, endocrine or vascular disease. Her family history revealed that a brother was somewhat neurotic and unstable, and had been in a hospital with a depression for a month. However, he had made a satisfactory and full remission without the use of shock or other physical methods. During the third year of her illness her memory became increasingly deficient, with periods of confusion. Because of the possibility that this might be a slow-growing meningioma in the frontal area, her family physician sent her into the hospital for neurological study.

The neurological examination showed brisk and hyperactive tendon reflexes bilaterally, but no extension response of the great toe. Sensory and motor power were normal. There was no evidence of defect in the cranial nerves. The patient showed gross evidence of mental deterioration, was confused, disoriented, and in conversation used only the simplest of sentences and words. Lumbar puncture showed normal pressure and protein. The Wassermann test was negative both in blood and spinal fluid. Pneumoencephalogram showed enlargement of the ventricular system on both sides and of the third ventricle as well. The convexity showed definite evidence of cortical atrophy, rather extreme in the frontal regions and extending as far back as the parietal region, with some atrophy even in the occipital lobes, where lakes of air were seen. There was considerable air under the tentorium, indicating that the cerebellar hemispheres were atrophied as well. There was no displacement of the ventricular system from the midline, and the radiological and neurosurgical consultants felt that neoplasm was definitely ruled out.

Diagnosis of progressive cerebral atrophy was made, and she was sent to a state hospital for terminal care and protection.

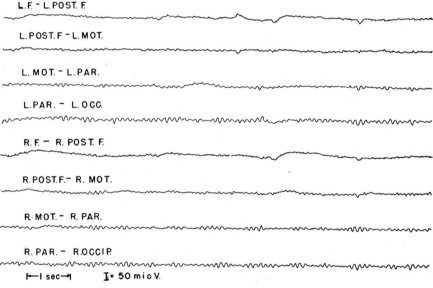

Fig. 91. A 63-year-old male who was a chronic alcoholic with very definite mental deterioration for the past ten years. The electroencephalogram shown is normal and in no way indicative of the degree of mental deterioration.

The second group of deteriorated patients consists of general paretics, those with post-encephalitic diseases from virus and other organisms, and those with heredito-familial syndromes with cerebral degeneration. In this group, too, the electroencephalogram may be normal or close to normal levels in spite of severe loss of mental function. Usually diffuse, mild, slow activity is found similar to that in the first group. In none is there a specific pattern or any hint that the amount of mental deterioration can be quantitated with the electroencephalographic abnormality.

The third group consists of deterioration due to previous brain trauma. In this group there is a high percentage of electroencephalo-

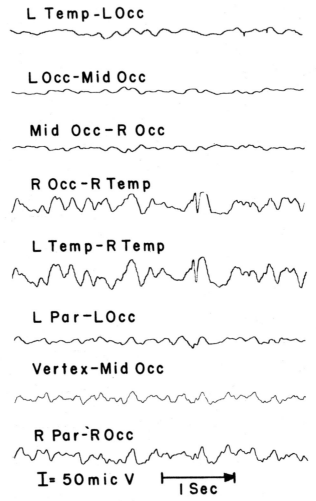

Fig. 92. An abnormal electroencephalogram in a patient with mental deterioration as a result of a severe brain injury from which he did not recover. Slow waves are seen on both sides and there is little normal activity present. Most of the abnormality is localized in the right temporal region and a fast and slow wave component is seen. The patient never had any convulsions.

graphic abnormality. The pattern usually shows 3- to 6-per-second slow waves of increased voltage in all leads. There is usually more abnormality on the side of the original injury, and in a few a residual focus of the abnormal waves can be found by electroencephalography. In rare instances such a focus may be due to a residual clot or subdural hydroma, and further brain surgery is indicated. Sometimes this may partially restore such a chronic head injury patient to a better state of health, particularly if there are focal seizures. Often, however, such late surgery does nothing for the patient, since the whole brain has been affected. When an electroencephalographic focus is found in the chronic deteriorated patient, it should be carefully discussed with the consult-

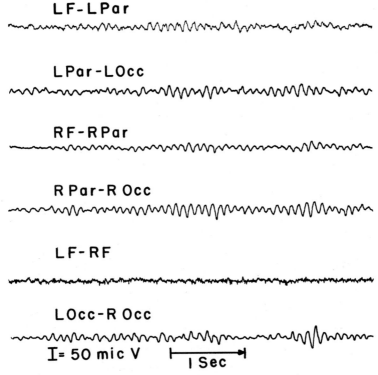

LF-LPar

LPar-LOcc

RF-RPar

RPar-ROcc

LF-RF

LOcc-ROcc

I= 50 mic V 1 Sec

Fig. 93. The electroencephalogram of a boxer 25 years old who had been knocked out seventeen times in his professional work during the past three years. His manager felt that he was showing signs of awkwardness and poor concentration and brought up the question of the effects of multiple head injuries. The electroencephalogram shows a normal record. Air studies were done and they were also within normal limits. The final conclusion was that the subject probably showed signs of inaptitude and most of his difficulties were psychological rather than due to brain injury. He was advised to take up some other form of occupation.

ing neurosurgeon, since occasionally a surgically removable meningi-oma may be uncovered and a brain tumor death avoided.

The fourth group consists of unexplained progressive brain deteri-oration such as presenile dementia (Alzheimer's disease) occurring in the fourth and fifth decades without demonstrable vascular disease, and a number of demyelinating disorders with mental deterioration such as Schilder's disease. In such patients the electroencephalographic examination may be normal, or, more usually, mild to moderately abnormal, with the more anterior leads most involved. It is rare to encounter

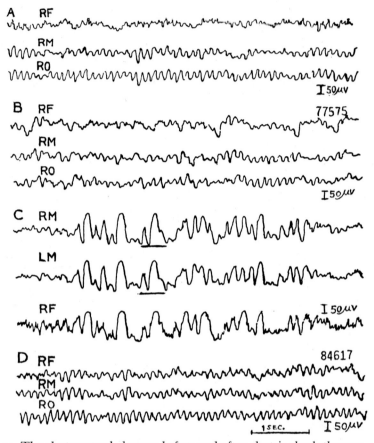

Fig. 94. The electroencephalogram before and after electric shock therapy.

A. Normal recording of the electroencephalogram before the series of shocks.

B. Electroencephalogram two days after the second shock treatment.

C. This is a diffusely abnormal electroencephalogram taken three days after the end of the series of shock treatments.

D. Electroencephalogram again normal one week after the shock therapy had been concluded. (From Bagchi, B. K., Howell, R. W., and Schmale, H. T.: The Electroencephalographic and Clinical Effects of Electrically Induced Convulsions in the Treatment of Mental Disorders. Am. J. Psychiat., *102*:49–61, 1945.)

any focus or lateralizing electroencephalographic abnormality in this group.

In summary, it can be stated that the majority of patients with mental deterioration have non-specific, non-focal, mild to moderately abnormal electroencephalograms.

ELECTRIC SHOCK AND LEUCOTOMY

Since electrical shock, lobotomy and insulin coma have become standard treatment in many mental hospitals for institutionalized patients and even for neurotics, the electroencephalogram has had an important part in the pre-shock and post-shock examination of these patients. It has been shown over and over again that, after a series of ten to twelve electric shock treatments, the electroencephalograph may change from a normal stable record to one with irregular frequencies[15] and even discharges suggesting an epileptic state and that this may persist for several months. Therefore it is important, in using electric shock on a patient, to do a pre-shock electroencephalography examina-

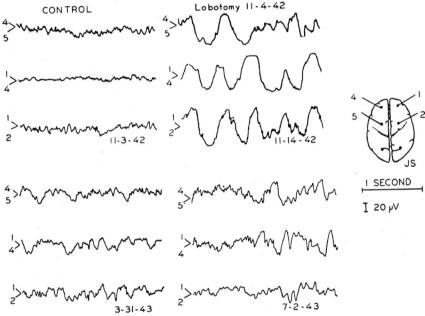

Fig. 95. The electroencephalograms before and after lobotomy showing the mild abnormalities that result from such a procedure. The first record shows the normal tracing one day before the operation. At the right is the record ten days after the operation showing diffuse slow waves. At the bottom on the left is the record five months after the procedure with still some evidence of abnormal activity on both sides, and the same patient four months later (nine months after operation) still showing an abnormal record. (From Cohn, R.: Electroencephalographic study of prefrontal lobotomy. Arch. Neurol. & Psychiat., 53:283–288, 1945.)

tion to be sure that the changes that occur after the treatment have not been present before.[22]

The use of surgery in the treatment of psychiatric conditions is becoming more and more important and common. Again, with the introduction of leucotomy, lobotomy, gyrectomy, and so on, the importance of the pre-operative electroencephalogram as well as the post-operative one is essential in enabling one to understand what has taken place and to follow the patient satisfactorily. After lobotomy it is usual to find abnormalities in the areas involved by the surgery.[2] These abnormalities persist sometimes for as long as six months before they gradually subside. The presence of a normal electroencephalogram prior to this lobotomy is an important guide as to whether this operative procedure should be carried out.

If the abnormality as a result of the leucotomy persists in an intense form for a long period, it may indicate that a scar has formed or that subdural blood or fluid may be present and re-exploration may be necessary. This is particularly important if the patient's recovery is delayed or obscured by loss of mental function.[8]

REFERENCES

1. Brazier, M. A. B., Finesinger, J. E., and Cobb, S.: The Electroencephalogram in Psychoneurotic Patients. Am. J. Psychiat., *101*:443–448, 1945.
2. Cohn, R.: EEG Study of Prefrontal Lobotomy. Arch. Neurol. & Psychiat., *53*: 283–288, 1945.
3. Delay, J., Neveu, P. et Deschaux, P.: Sur Quelques Résultats Concordants de la Pneumo-encéphalographie et de l'électroencéphalographie dans le diagnostic des atrophies cérébrales. Rev. Neurol., *76*:263–264, 1944.
4. Finley, K. H., and Campbell, C. M.: EEG in Schizophrenia. Am. J. Psychiat., *98*:374–379, 1941.
5. Gastaut, H.:: Combined Photic and Metrazol Activation of the Brain. EEG Clin. Neurophysiol., *2*:249–261, 1950.
6. Gibbs, F. A.: Medicolegal Aspects of Electroencephalography. Canadian Bar Review, *24*:359–388, 1946.
7. Greenblatt, M., Healey, M., and Jones, G. A.: Age and Electroencephalographic Abnormality in Psychiatric Patients; a Study of 1593 Cases. Am. J. Psychiat., *101*:82–90, 1944.
8. Greville, G. D., and Last, S. L.: Leucotomy as an Instrument of Research; Electroencephalographic Studies. Proc. Roy. Soc. Med., *40*:145–147, 1947.
9. Hill, D., and Watterson, D.: Electroencephalographic Studies of Psychopathic Personalities. J. Neurol. & Psychiat., *5*:47–65, 1942.
10. Jasper, H. H.: Personal communication.
11. Kennard, M. A.: Factors Affecting the Electroencephalogram in Children and Adolescents. J. Nerv. Ment. Dis., *108*:442–448, 1948.
12. Kershman, J.: Syncope and Seizures. J. Neurol., Neurosurg. & Psychiat., *12*: 25–33, 1949.
13. Liberson, W. T.: Recherches sur les Electroencéphalogrammes Transcrâniens de l'homme. Travail hum., *5*:431–463, 1937.
14. Lindsley, D. B., and Cutts, K. K.: Electroencephalograms of "Constitutionally Inferior" and Behavior Problem Children; Comparison with those of Normal Children and Adults. Arch. Neurol. & Psychiat., *44*:1199–1212, 1940.
15. Moriarty, J. D., and Siemens, J. C.: Electroencephalographic Study of Electric Shock Therapy; Psychotic Patients Treated in a U. S. Naval Hospital. Arch. Neurol. & Psychiat., *57*:712–718, 1947.
16. Saul, L. J., Davis, H., and Davis, P. A.: Correlations between Electroencephalograms and the Psychological Organization of the Individual. Tr. A. Neurol. A., *63*:167–169, 1937.

17. Saul, L. J., Davis, H., and Davis, P. A.: Psychological Correlations with the Electroencephalogram. EEG Clin. Neurophysiol., *1*:515, 1949.
18. Simons, B., O'Leary, J. L., and Ryan, J. L.: Cerebral Dysrhythmia and Psychopathic Personalities. Arch. Neurol. & Psychiat., *56*:677–685, 1946.
19. Solomon, P., Jasper, H. H., and Bradley, C.: Studies in Behavior Problem Children. Arch. Neurol. & Psychiat., *38*:1350–1351, 1937.
20. Stafford-Clark, D., and Taylor, F. H.: Clinical and Electroencephalographic Studies of Prisoners Charged with Murder. J. Neurol., Neurosurg. & Psychiat., *12*:325–330, 1949.
21. Stearns, A. W.: Personal communication.
22. Weil, A. A.: Neurophysiological Disturbances following Electric Shock Therapy (Electroencephalographic Observations). Ohio State M. J., *44*:10, 1948.

The Electroencephalogram in Research

Some clinicians feel that electroencephalographic records in the various neurological and psychiatric disorders for which the test is used do no more than confirm an obvious clinical diagnosis. They do not regard it with the same respect shown toward the Wassermann test or the roentgen examination. On the other hand, these friendly skeptics—and they are friendly, since they keep sending their patients in for electroencephalographic examinations year after year—agree that the technique is a valuable one for research.

The application of electroencephalography to the study of physiological function of the brain in the human being as well as in animals has opened up many new vistas and has proved a most valuable tool in the hands of neurophysiologists and clinical investigators.* Here we have a technique of examination that does nothing to the subject, causes no pain, and requires no anesthesia, and which will record the electrical pulsations of the brain as it exists intact and functioning in the subject. Since the test is not distressing in any way, it can be repeated day after day on the same person or run for long periods of time, as during sleep. The subject can be exposed to the usual stimuli of ordinary life or can be examined while breathing low oxygen mixtures or air under reduced pressure. His blood sugar may be reduced by insulin to low levels without introducing any other artifacts, and he can be stimulated by various forms of visual, auditory or tactile signals during the recording of the electroencephalogram.

Further physiological functions such as reaction time, skin resistance, electrocardiogram, skin temperature, and so on can all be recorded[4] while the electroencephalogram is being taken. The electroencephalo-

---

* The second half of the excellent little book, The Physical Background of Perception by Adrian,[1] covers some interesting examples and the whole volume is recommended.

gram can be applied and the patient be allowed to go off into natural sleep and be observed continuously for many hours—in fact, the whole night. Furthermore, by applying electrodes in the usual areas of the scalp and behind the pharynx and in the auditory canal, recordings can be secured from the entire surface of the intact brain without undue discomfort or complication.[10] Therefore it is not surprising that in the hands of investigators who are physiologists, psychologists, as well as clinically trained research workers, tremendous amounts of data have been gathered in the last ten years which throw considerable light on the functioning of the human brain without injuring any part of it by the experimental procedure. In spite of the careful and painstaking work of the neuropathologist with all their silver and gold stains on tissue, it is clear that they are examining structures that have been permanently altered by the application of such chemicals, and it is not easy to deduce facts about function, structure and relationships from changes that these chemicals produce. Much knowledge, of course, has been gained, particularly by the use of the Weigert stain showing myelin degeneration of damaged tracts. Little new knowledge about function and the interrelationship of the various parts of the brain, particularly in relation to patterns of behavior, was brought out by this careful type of neuropathological studies.

The first observation of Berger that the normal 10-per-second alpha rhythm in the occipital area could be abolished by opening the eyes introduced new concepts into physiology. Walter[12] showed that a flickering light could alter the 10-per-second alpha rhythm in the occipital area and drive it at nine per second. There is a considerable amount of experimental evidence at present that, by means of different frequencies and intensities, new components of the occipital rhythm may be brought out and studied. Such stimulation has brought out a number of different responses in normals and some pathological ones in patients with epilepsy. This has been described in Chapter V.

Since the introduction of the quantitative methods of measuring both frequency and voltage, and some localization of the various components in the record by phase reversals, it is possible to study the effect of subclinical anoxia or hypoglycemia on the normal person. Before the electroencephalograph was available a subject breathing low oxygen was followed along by rather crude signs such as cyanosis, slowness in response, blood pressure levels, and so forth, until he lapsed into unconsciousness. The crudity of the clinical observations here indicated that a severe degree of anoxia was necessary before consciousness was lost. By means of the electroencephalogram and either manual or electronic analysis of the resulting pattern, Finesinger[6] has shown that reducing the oxygen in the inspired air to as little as 15 per cent from the normal 20 produces a definite shift of the alpha rhythm from ten per second to nine or even eight. This amount of shift or slowing of the brain frequency by mild anoxia would be most difficult to parallel with any psychological test and neurological signs. The electroencephalogram is exquisitely accurate in determining slight loss of alertness and impairment of consciousness during such mild anoxia. The same is true when the sugar in the blood is lowered by means of insulin.[9] A normal person whose blood sugar is reduced from 100 to 60 or 70 shows no clinical observable objective neurological signs. He may describe a sensation of irritability or mild apprehension, his pulse may go a little faster, and there may be a slight tendency to perspire. These are not easy to quantitate and correlate with what is going on. It depends so much on the environment and other factors that are hard to control. By means of the electroencephalogram it is possible to follow accurately the shift of the alpha rhythm, from ten per second down to nine to eight and a half and eight, and so on, as the blood sugar slowly falls.

Observations on the effect of small doses of anesthetic or sedative drugs on a person is of most interest to the clinician and physiologist. It is difficult by means of ordinary neurological examinations or psychological studies to assess mild degrees of impairment after the ingestion, for example, of 100 mg. of nembutal or a small amount of an alcoholic beverage.

By means of the electroencephalogram, when small amounts of intravenous barbiturates are given, it is possible to follow quantitatively through frequency changes in the dominant rhythm of ten cycles per second in the occipital area. As the occipital alpha slows, there is seen in the frontal region an increase in voltage of the fast beta activity.[7] It is well known that subjects who are given such drugs in small amounts tend to become overtalkative, unburden themselves of repressed emotional material and psychological data that would otherwise be difficult to obtain. The method of narcosynthesis in World War II has amply proved the clinical value of this type of psychiatric exploration. It is not easy to follow accurately the level of such a subanesthetic dose by ordinary clinical means, and the usual experience was that the drug would be injected and the patient would become drowsier and even fall asleep, which required a delay until the drug began to wear off before psychiatric exploration could be undertaken. With the electroencephalogram a more accurate background for the amount of drug affecting the patient can be ascertained. It is well known that there are individual sensitivities to these drugs, and variations in the effect from day to day are considerable. If the electroencephalogram, including the frequency pattern, the voltage, and the distribution of the waves in relation to occipital, motor and frontal regions is carefully followed, accurate levels of dosage can be controlled and states of subclinical analgesia can be studied and followed accurately. All this opens new methods for the investigation of anesthesia, narcotics and sedatives. We may find, for example, that it is not necessary to produce insensibility to pain in order to perform minor surgery, but only an indifference to the painful sensation so that it will not disturb the patient, and that these levels can best be explored by the electroencephalographic technique.

The study of the sleeping subject by means of the electroencephalogram has many applications. It has always been assumed, of course, that every person needs about eight hours of sleep a night, but it is well known that there are persons who are quite healthy, yet get only four hours of sleep, and that others are miserable unless they get ten or even twelve hours. All this can be studied by means of continual recording during the night by means of the electroencephalogram. In sleep, normal alpha rhythm disappears and is replaced by a 14-per-second rhythm in the post-frontal regions, and this is followed later on as sleep progresses by disappearance of this rhythm and the presence of 6- or 5-per-second activity in the same area, and later on low-voltage slow waves as slow as one per second appear on both sides.[8]

By studying the pattern of sleep from the time the patient first goes to bed to the time he awakens, evidence has been brought out that the deeper sleep occurs earlier in the night. During the early morning the patient is more restless and moves about more.[2] The application of this in the life of a human being is hard to assess at the moment. We may learn that certain drugs that induce heavy sleep during the early part of the night are more advantageous than longer-acting drugs which extend their influence over the entire eight or nine hour period. For example, a person such as a master of a vessel at sea may be suddenly awakened to render an important decision, or a surgeon called in the middle of the night may have to rush out to do delicate surgery. Both may require at times a sleeping tablet. Knowledge of the rate of return of all the highest faculties such as judgment or manual dexterity may well come from electroencephalographic correlations during the various stages and periods of sleep with the time and type of the drug ingested. In situations in which a person is likely to be awakened to take on a task, certain drugs which only have a quick action are better than the longer-acting ones. The whole subject extends the application of this examination into numbers of unexplored channels and problems.

It has been possible with the more accurate recording equipment now available to measure the effect of peripheral stimuli on the appearance of the electroencephalogram; also to study the latency of these stimuli in arriving at the cortex. At the moment it is difficult to detect the arrival of the sensory impulse, say from the hand, to the appropriate sensory area by means of electrodes placed on the scalp. But Dawson[5] has shown by means of a cathode-ray oscillograph and repeated electrical stimuli to a peripheral nerve that he can, by summation of the feeble potentials coming from scalp leads, measure the latency of the peripheral stimulus, and he has determined that this is in a number of peripheral nerves in normal persons. Monnier[11] has worked out the same thing for visual stimuli in the human being. Its application may be of value in determining various degrees of adaptability and aptitudes in people.

In all sorts of pathological states, when a patient is slowed down or does not seem to respond normally, electroencephalographic investigation of the time of the stimulus and its arrival in the cerebral cortex may shed light on the deficiencies and the nature of the pathological processes involved. Since we are entering or have already entered on an age in which the airplane is commonplace and people travel at high altitudes, even though the planes are not pressurized, and fighting in war occurs at between 30,000 and 40,000 feet, laboratory studies of the function of the cerebral cortex by means of the electroencephalogram is of extreme importance. The subjective report of a pilot who is diving

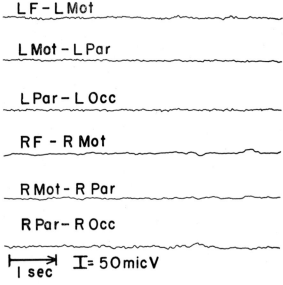

Fig. 96. Electroencephalogram of a 42-year-old male who had the entire right hemisphere removed because of an infiltrating brain tumor. The puzzling part is the appearance in the right parietal region of better alpha activity than on the intact side. This is undoubtedly a spread of the electrical activity from the normal left occipital lobe through the fluid spaces on the operated side.

on a target as to his state of alertness is valueless, because he may lose consciousness for many seconds and be totally unaware of it. The electroencephalogram can be recorded during such maneuvers and even be broadcast by shortwave[3] to a recording unit on the ground, and the presence of slow delta waves or other abnormalities be recorded. It may be possible to shed a good deal of light on some of the accidents in perplexing situations that occur in high speed aircraft and the various unknown factors in too rapid acceleration rates.

In clinical investigation electroencephalography allows access to the brain in spite of its being enclosed in a heavy skull. It has already been mentioned that patients with lower basal metabolism rates have slower alpha rhythms than normal, and that when the basal metabolism rate is brought up to normal with thyroxin the electroencephalographic rhythm follows, but with considerable latency. The large field of endocrinology may well be investigated along such lines. The minor alterations found in the brains of patients with hyperthyroidism or hypothyroidism are imperfectly understood, and there is some indication that electroencephalographic investigations may aid such studies.

In the case of epilepsy the effect of anticonvulsants on the electroencephalographic pattern when it is abnormal is important enough and may tell us more of the origin of the epileptic discharge. Some anticonvulsant drugs seem to have no effect on the abnormal electroencephalogram in spite of the fact that the patient's seizures are reduced. Other drugs, namely, tridione, seem to have a specific reduction in the abnormal wave and spike appearance both in the number and in the duration of attacks. Therefore, in the study of new drugs to be used as anticonvulsants in epilepsy, the correlation of the electroencephalographic pattern with the type, duration and severity of the seizures may be of real clinical help.

The amount and appearance of a dominant rhythm such as the alpha rhythm varies in each person from time to time and seems to be correlated with the amount of cerebral activity going on. It would seem possible in some of the dynamic approaches of psychiatry, such as psychoanalysis, and the like, that if recorded electroencephalograms were taken at the same time as that of the interview, we might learn something about the effect of the material that is highly charged with emotional problems on the brain wave patterns.

Surgical intervention in psychiatric conditions, psychosurgery, affords many opportunities to study the state of the brain on the operating table by means of cortical or subcortical electroencephalography. What this will show in the future is uncertain. Encouraging results seem to be coming out of those laboratories using this technique.

Some of the problems that are not yet solved in any way that may be aided by means of electroencephalography include the relationship of the living brain cell to the amount and form of the electrical activity. An example of one of the problems investigated by the electroencephalogram is described in Figure 97. The meaning of changes in the electroencephalogram in an alert or a relaxed state which has been previously described in the earlier chapter dealing with the alpha activity may be extended to include the slower rhythms. An example is shown in Figure 98 where the alpha type of response to opening and closing the eyes was clearly shown in the appearance and disappearance of the delta rhythm.

Figure 99 shows the change in the electroencephalogram as a result of inhaling a small amount of amyl nitrate. The amount of delta activity which was produced by overventilation disappeared when the patient inhaled the vapor. As far as could be told, there was no clinical change obvious in this subject. The response of the brain rhythms to various

Human E.E.G. and E.K.G. During Death

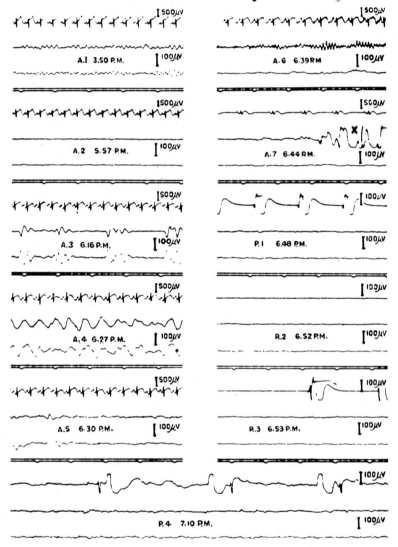

Fig. 97. Samples of the electroencephalogram and electrocardiogram recorded during a 7-hour period before death. The top left hand sample shows a relatively normal brain rhythm and a normal electrocardiogram. The patient was dying from a fatal injury to the cervical cord.

The second sample shows the sudden disappearance of all electroencephalographic activity without affecting the electrocardiogram.

The third sample—about one-half hour before death—shows the appearance of paroxysmal 5-per-second activity with no activity in between for 1 or 2 seconds.

The fourth sample—17 minutes before death—shows bilateral delta activity.

Fourteen minutes before death the record showed very little activity on either side.

Five minutes before death the right side showed no electrical activity at all but there was a single burst of rather normal appearing alpha activity on the left side. Respiration ceased at 6:44 as is shown by the movement artifact produced by the

physical and chemical changes, such as the last two described, may well be reflected in different levels of alertness or possibly in different states of highly integrated cerebral activity. Work is under way in several

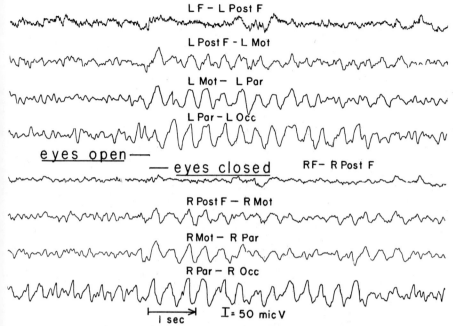

Fig. 98. A study of the effect of opening and closing the eyes on the delta activity in a subject with fainting attacks and rare convulsions. Note that when the eyes are open the delta activity is at a minimum but as soon as they are closed large slow waves appear immediately in the electroencephalogram in all leads.

centers using these responses to indicate the amount of emotional activity precipitated by a stimulus or even whether the reply to a question is true or false.

---

doctor placing the stethoscope on the chest. The amplitude of the electrocardiogram became very low. Although there was no pulse discernible the amplifier recorded the electrocardiogram when the amplitude was raised. This is shown in the third sample on the right. There was no electroencephalographic recording from this point on.

All electrical activity ceased both in the electrocardiogram and in the electroencephalogram in the fourth sample eight minutes after death but the heart resumed spontaneous activity one minute later. Twenty-six minutes after death moving the chest produced three abnormal electrocardiographic beats. There was nothing in the electroencephalogram.

This type of investigation of the changes occurring when a person dies was done in cooperation with the office of the Medical Examiner to see if the electroencephalogram could be used in medicolegal problems concerned with the exact time of death. It was obvious from this example that the electrocardiogram is a better indicator. (From Schwab, R. S.: The measurement of body currents. Trans. Am. Inst. Elec. Eng. 60:1–5, 1941.)

EFFECT OF AMYL NITRITE ON DELTA WAVES

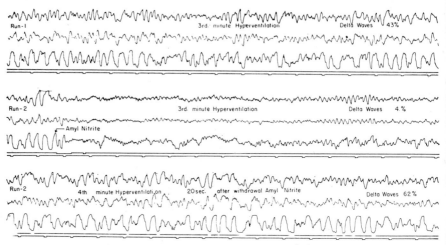

Fig. 99. A similar study of the effects of a vasodilator on delta activity. Delta activity was produced by overbreathing in a subject 19 years old who had a history of fainting attacks and rare seizures. At the arrow the patient was allowed without his knowledge to inhale from a piece of cotton soaked in amyl nitrite. Note the immediate disappearance of the delta waves which returned after the nitrite was withdrawn. The patient noted the sweet smell of the chemical and it is not absolutely certain that all of this effect is due to the chemical as a vasodilator. However, the possibility is present that drawing his attention olfactorily to the smell may have affected the rhythm.

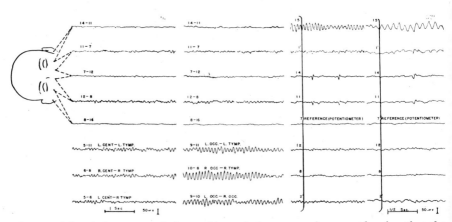

Fig. 100. A basal electroencephalographic study in a normal person showing that the activity from this region is similar to the waves picked up in the scalp.

Figure 100 shows the distribution of the normal rhythms in different parts of the scalp and in the basal leads so that these normal brain potentials may be studied in different places and representing different localizations in the brain.

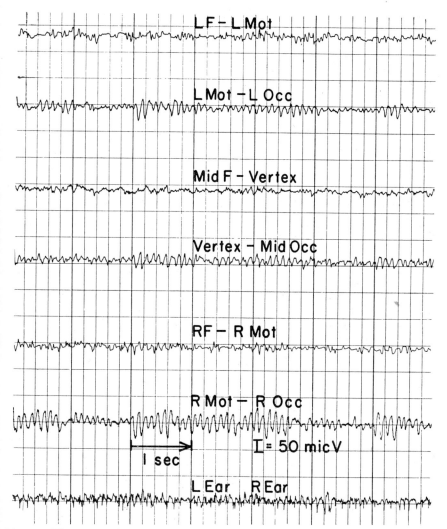

Fig. 101. Electroencephalogram in a normal person who is left-handed, showing definitely more alpha activity on the right side than on the left.

The asymmetry of the normal rhythm is encountered regularly in a mild form, and as shown in Figure 101 the right occipital alpha is much more prominent than that on the left. This particular subject was left-handed; and in some future projects something about dominance may be learned from investigations of the human electroencephalogram.

REFERENCES

1. Adrian, E. D.: The Physical Background of Perception. Oxford, Clarendon Press, 1947, 95 pp.
2. Blake, H., Gerard, R. W., and Kleitman, N.: Factors Influencing Brain Potentials during Sleep. J. Neurophysiol., 2:48–60, 1939.
3. Breakell, C. C., Manc, A. M., Parker, C. S., and Christopherson, F.: Radio Transmission of the Human Electroencephalogram and other Electrophysiological Data. EEG Clin. Neurophysiol., 1:243–244, 1949.
4. Darrow, C. W.: The Electroencephalogram and Psychophysiological Regulation in the Brain. Am. J. Psychiat., 102:791–798, 1946.
5. Dawson, G. D.: Cerebral Responses to Electrical Stimulation of Peripheral Nerve in Man. J. Neurol., Neurosurg. & Psychiat., 10:137–140, 1947.
6. Finesinger, J. E., Lindemann, E., Brazier, M. A. B., and Chapple, E. D.: The Effect of Anoxia as Measured by the EEG and the Interaction Chronogram on Psychoneurotic Patients. Am. J. Psychiat., 103:738–747, 1947.
7. Gottlieb, J. S., Knott, J. R., and Kimble, L. L.: Pharmacologic Studies of Schizophrenia and Depression, IV; the Influence of Electric Convulsive Therapy on the Sodium Amytal Response of the Electroencephalogram. Am. J. Psychiat., 104:686–696, 1948.
8. Harvey, E. N., Loomis, A. L., and Hobart, G. A.: Cerebral States During Sleep as Studied by Human Brain Potentials. Scient. Monthly, 45:191–192, 1937.
9. Heppenstall, M. E.: Relation between the Effects of Blood Sugar Levels and Hyperventilation on the EEG. J. Neurol., Neurosurg. & Psychiat., 7:112–118, 1944.
10. MacLean, P. D., Arellano, A. P. –Z., and Schwab, R. S.: Basal Electroencephalogram with Pharyngeal, Tympanic and Ear-Lobe Electrodes. EEG Clin. Neurophysiol., 2:108, 1950.
11. Monnier, M.: L'Electro-Rétinogramme de l'Homme. EEG Clin. Neurophysiol., 1:87–108, 1949.
12. Walter, W. G., Dovey, V. J., and Shipton, H.: Analysis of the Electrical Response of the Human Cortex to Photic Stimulation. Nature, 158:540–541, 1946.

CHAPTER IX

Laboratory Organization, Training of Staff, and Interpretation of Records

To MANY hospital directors the addition of an electroencephalographic laboratory to his institution requires only the purchase of the equipment and the assignment of a physician with time on his hands to run it. We hope that those who have followed this book will agree that electroencephalography is far too complex and intricate to be taken so lightly.

The organization of a laboratory that is clinically efficient in a general hospital requires time and thoughtful planning. The type of apparatus and space requirements have already been discussed, including shielding of the room. The selection and training of the personnel are of *far greater importance*. The minimum staff requirements seem to be:

1. Director of laboratory (responsible to the hospital for the clinical interpretation of the records, the organization and operation of the equipment, and the safety and comfort of the patients). He should be a physician, preferably a neurologist, psychiatrist or neurosurgeon, who can devote at least *half* of his time to electroencephalography. He should be properly trained. This will be taken up in more detail later.

2. A full time technician with at least six months' special training in electroencephalography at a recognized laboratory in this field.

3. A part-time secretary.

4. In addition to these three essential staff members, it is highly advisable to have available for consultation and help (*a*) an electronic engineer, (*b*) a physiologist, (*c*) a senior electroencephalographer.

As the work of a laboratory increases in both scope and volume, additional personnel will be necessary. A second technician, either part or full time, greatly increases the efficiency of the recording. Some cases such as a disturbed adult or a frightened child require someone to stand by in the room while one technician operates the machine. A full-time laboratory director or two part-time physicians may be necessary if complicated clinical studies (activation, and so forth) are undertaken or if electrocorticography in the operating room is done. If research is undertaken on any scale, the cooperation, either full time or part time, of a physiologist or other scientist specially trained in investigative problems is almost essential. If modification of the equipment or additions to it are planned, a part-time electronic engineer with a small, well-equipped workshop in the laboratory area is of great help.

The best routine clinical work as well as the soundest research in this field stems from laboratories whose staff and consultants are well oriented in both clinical and basic scientific spheres. Efficient and well-trained technicians usually receive from 1800 to 3000 dollars a year. A part-time electroencephalographer with adequate clinical and special training should be paid not less than 5000 dollars a year. A part-time electronic engineer usually asks and gets 2000 to 3000 dollars a year. The total salary budget, including a half-time secretary, would be 10,000 dollars (as a minimum figure).

The usual fee for electroencephalography is from 10 to 25 dollars per examination. The efficient daily load of the usual laboratory should be five to eight cases per day, or roughly from 1200 to 2000 examinations a year. With an average collection of 15 dollars per test, the income would be 18,000 dollars annually. This would allow a comfortable margin of 8000 dollars for apparatus, depreciation, equipment, overhead, stationery, and so forth. Therefore it is reasonable to estimate that an electroencephalographic laboratory can stand on its own feet financially after the first year or so, when initial expenses, organization problems and lack of clinical material are met.

TRAINING AND QUALIFICATIONS OF PERSONNEL

The following are the recommendations of the American Electroencephalographic Society in regard to training:

1. The heads of laboratories or those responsible for the clinical interpretation of the electroencephalograms should be supervised by a person holding an M.D. degree.

2. Twelve months is the minimum of training in clinical electroencephalography for a worker to be able to carry the responsibility of clinical interpretation.

2. Six months is the minimum of training to enable a technician to work in a laboratory as a qualified electroencephalographic technician.

Experience has adequately shown all of us in this field that the minimum of six months for the training of a technician is sound and practical. Most laboratories will no longer accept the "three afternoons per week" of an x-ray technician who wants to broaden his interests as well as his income. Such casuals usually drop out after a few months and do such a wretched job with electroencephalography that they are regarded as a disgrace and discredit to the laboratory on which they impose their visits.

The interpreter of the records and chief of the laboratory requires at least six full months of special training and, in most situations, one year. If he can be closely supervised for a year after three months of preliminary training, this in some cases may be adequate. There should be no excuse for short-cut, inadequate training in a field as complicated as electroencephalography. His training should cover some of the fundamentals in electronics, neurophysiology and the art of clinical interpretation of laboratory data.

THE DILEMMA OF PH.D. OR M.D. IN THE INTERPRETATION OF THE CLINICAL ELECTROENCEPHALOGRAM

This problem was fully covered by the following address* not previously published:

We are taking more seriously each year the qualifications of those who interpret the electroencephalogram. The early pioneers in this relatively new field were psychriatrists, physiologists, physicists, psychologists, and engineers. Now, as more and more clinically trained men have entered the field, there has been talk, writing, and feeling that the interpretation of clinical records should be restricted to men with M.D. degrees, who have the legal responsibility and *perhaps* the clinical experience to make a diagnosis of a disease. On the other hand, some of the best clinical reports, and certainly a good proportion of the clinical research in electroencephalography, have been done by non-medically certified workers with Ph.D.'s or even no degree beyond their college work. Some of our colleagues, who are not physicians, feel that they are being pushed out of the field or restricted to a limited scope within the field.

There are, of course, those scientific workers, not physicians, who rather welcome the relief from routine clinical burdens and a greater opportunity for experimental work.

Now, before going any further into the electroencephalographic field, let us look about in other fields of medicine and see how similar situations have been handled.

In the field of bacteriology, an integral part of every large hospital, we find both medical and non-medical investigators working rather smoothly together. In their national society, some forty per cent are not M.D.'s. I need not dwell on the achievements of bacteriology from the non-M.D., Pasteur, to electron microscopic descriptions of viruses, largely due to engineers and physicists.

On the other hand, in roentgenography, we do have a large group which has kept within the clinically trained sphere. Without depreciating their meetings, or clinical contributions, we have a feeling that the progress in x-ray diagnosis and treatment has been relatively slow and restricted. What progress there has been, seems dependent on physicists and vacuum tube engineers. They, as a group, have suffered from over-routinization and multiple complications of clinical correlates.

The same may be said of electrocardiography. The string galvanometer devised by the non-M.D., Einthoven, still serves most places and apparently the only way to get the newer vacuum tube and cathode ray recorders into clinical use, has been to smother their more faithful recording by filters and devices, so that they reproduce the characteristics of the *old string*.

* Presidential Address before the Eastern Association of Electroencephalographers, New York City, May, 1947. The remarks still apply to the situation in January, 1950.

The problem before us as to who shall interpret a clinical test on a patient is obscured by legal terminology and tradition.

In the eyes of hospital administrators, *opinions* must be backed by appropriate signatures of M.D.'s, but descriptive facts may be entered by anyone at all. A high school graduate may enter the leukocyte count that she has done in the record; a second year medical student (unqualified), may write a history implicating the gall bladder; eventually the surgeon operates and that organ is removed. Yet the most skilled of x-ray technicians may not write in the record that she sees a fracture of a bone which requires attention.

Returning to electroencephalography, is there really any significant difference in these three reports:

"The record shows 3-per-second waves and spikes, described by Gibbs and Lennox as characteristic of petit mal";

"The record shows the wave and spikes we have previously seen in petit mal";

or "The record is typical of petit mal."

If the non-M.D. is limited to a pure description such as the "record is filled with 5 to 10 second paroxysmal groups of 3 cycle waves and spikes," invariably the referring doctor calls for an explanation. It is here, I believe, where the problem lies. The basal metabolism technician or metabolism physiologist need write no more on his report than the fact that the BMR is plus 40 and the test was satisfactory. The physician makes the diagnosis of hyperthyroidism from this report plus his own clinical history and findings. No one ever calls up to ask what a BMR of plus 40 means.

In x-ray and electrocardiography, however, a simple description is not enough. The ordinary physician is often unable to assess the meaning of a PR interval in the EKG of .24 seconds hence the cardiologist does this for him.

In EEG work, the average neurologist or psychiatrist would call for help if he has only a descriptive report. In spite of the fact that electroencephalography has been in use in this country since 1936, only ten per cent of the candidates for certification in neurology and psychiatry, whom I saw recently, could state that they were familiar with such records, let alone interpret them.

Many internists interpret their own EKG's, and most neurosurgeons proceed on their own opinion as to the air studies, yet ninety per cent of the neurologists and psychiatrists depend on another person's evaluation of the brain's electrical activity. This, I am sure, is only a passing phase. More and more neurologists and psychiatrists are spending some time, at least, in electroencephalographic work. There will be less dependence on their physiological friends.

But what about the present situation? It is close to being deplorable. There are not anywhere near enough neuro-physiologists to go around and the few that there are are not interested in *clinical routine*. Apparatus is rolling out like new automobiles and every hospital wants to be up to date with such a laboratory.

The clinician adequately trained in neurology, psychiatry and physiology, is so rare that he would only end up as a professor with administrative tasks. The ordinary neuropsychiatrist has to get his income from private practice and is burdened with teaching and ward visits. He tends to allow his technician to run the laboratory, if he is responsible. The field is temporarily badly over-expanded.

The neurologist, psychiatrist, neurosurgeon and internist had better join up with the best physiologist he can find, secure a technician and with timidity and reticence try to learn from a few hundred records what is going on. Since patients may die during a convulsion or injure someone during a confusion period, it seems wise for every laboratory to have *medical* supervision. Since the diagnosis of epilepsy is a *serious one to make,* a medical opinion on the report would be better than avoiding responsibility by ambiguous phrases or a clinically unsatisfactory description. Eventually, we all hope enough clinically trained men will be available to take over the interpretation of these records.

INTERPRETATION OF THE RECORDS

Referring physicians often feel that the electroencephalographic record should be interpreted with no data as to the history or clinical findings available. They argue that, if this is done, the interpreter will be more honest in his conclusions and the value of the report increased. In short, it turns into a type of game to see if the electroencephalographer can find out the answer with his new "toy," without any coaching from the audience.

This is ridiculous, since electroencephalography has been firmly established for fifteen years and does not require the constant proof of its value by such methods. The true worth of this diagnostic test to clinical problems rather lies in the closest correlative effort in obtaining all the facts, not only electroencephalographic, but also clinical and other laboratory data about each patient, and building up the final interpretation from them.

We have stated that 15 per cent of normals show mild electroencephalographic abnormalities and that some 15 per cent of patients with verified brain subdural hematomas have normal records. If the mild degree of voltage asymmetry found at a certain examination is to be used to aid the surgeon in lateralizing his lesion, a correlative report is essential and intelligent.

A study made by the author in 1947 illustrated this point. An unselected group of 100 records were taken as they came through the laboratory and interpreted first without any knowledge of the patient's clinical state or history. This report was called the *absolute electroencephalographic interpretation.* Then, at a later date, the records were pulled out and the reports were gone over again in the light of the clinical history and findings, and a second interpretation, called the *correlative interpretation,* was made. In 90 per cent of the cases these two interpretations were the same. In 10 per cent of the cases the original absolute interpretation would be modified, sometimes considerably, by correlating the findings with the clinical history and other material available in the record at the time of the examination. This additional 10 per cent of correlative information would have been of value to the clinician referring the patient.

It is important, of course, for the interpreter to know how to read the record without the history, and he should be familiar enough with the procedure to do this without any difficulty in most of the cases, but in certain situations where every bit of help must be given to the referring physician, it is far better to put all the material together to see if the interpretation in the light of this material cannot give the answer. After all, our problem is not whether electroencephalography is 90 per cent correct in its diagnosis or only 60 per cent, but whether this procedure is of any help to the referring clinician in diagnosis which may lead to better or earlier treatment by surgery or medication. In most laboratories the localization of intracranial lesions by means of the electroencephalograph runs somewhere around 75 per cent correct. In other words, 25 per cent of intracranial lesions are not localized by means of the electroencephalogram. This percentage is satisfying enough, but it is not as high as can be obtained with air studies. If correlative interpretations are used more extensively, the percentage of electroencephalographic localization will be considerably improved. See Figures 102 to 105.

	Clinical	EKg	Activated
Heart Dis.	Precord. Pain Murmurs Size Decompensation Dyspnea	Dis. T. Waves Cond. Delay Volt. Dist. Dysrhythmia	Tachycard. Pain Dysp.
Epilepsy	Seizure Hist. of seizures Focal N.E. Injuries & F.H.	EEg Seizure Patterns Ab. Waves Focal Spikes Dysrhythmia	Overbr. Metrazol Photo Audio Comb.

Fig. 102. A diagrammatic comparison of the relationship of the electroencephalogram in the diagnosis of epilepsy with the electrocardiogram in the diagnosis of heart disease. In the first column are listed the clinical points that a physician would use to make the diagnosis without the aid of laboratory tests in these two conditions. With a good clinical history a clinical diagnosis is clear in approximately 80 per cent of both of these conditions and the electroencephalogram would only corroborate the diagnostic decision.

In the second column are listed some of the findings that the electroencephalogram would produce in the ordinary recording, and above it, the electrocardiogram as it is used routinely in the majority of doubtful cases of either epilepsy or heart disease. The correlation of these findings with the clinical history would make the diagnosis obvious.

In the third column would be the additional findings obtained if the electrocardiogram is used during the performance of specific exercises. Additional diagnostic data in the small number of patients will be obtained. The same is true in the use of activated electroencephalography.

The chart emphasizes the importance of correlating clinical history with the electrical findings and never depending on any one alone.

An example of the value of this type of correlation of the electroencephalographic record with the clinical findings follows:

A thirty-seven year old man was referred to hospital because of severe headaches, inability to concentrate, a certain amount of vertigo, and inability to hold his job. He gave a history of having been in an automobile accident a year before. The first electroencephalogram was done before there was any clinical history available, and the interpretation of this record was made in this light. The record was within normal limits as far as frequency and voltage went, but there was a definite asymmetry. This could have been found in a number of normal persons. The record showed, over the right temporal region, a few low voltage 5- and 6-per-second waves, not seen on the left temporal region. Other areas showed normal 10-per-second alpha with normal voltage, and in the frontals there was a normal 18- to 20-per-second beta of normal voltage. There was no change with overbreathing. The report given by the interpreter at this time was nearly a normal record, and no localization was described or mentioned.

A week later the neurosurgeon and the electroencephalographer went over the patient's history, neurological examination and electroencephalogram together. The questionable increase in tendon reflexes in the left arm was noted, and the slight

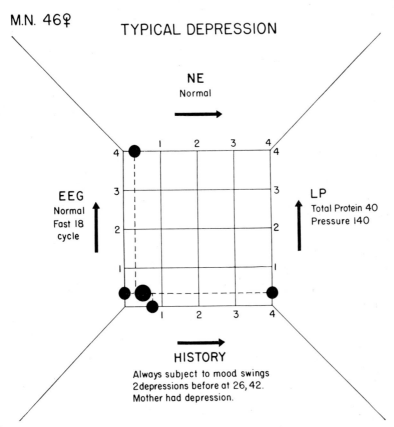

Fig. 103. A graphic method of showing how the electroencephalogram can be correlated with the history, neurological findings and other laboratory tests to make the diagnosis clear. The degree of abnormality is listed numerically from zero to 4 and the arrow indicates the direction of the abnormality. Each of the 4 factors is placed in its appropriate position on the square and they all fall in agreement in the left lower portion of the square. In this particular case the electroencephalogram corroborates the other negative findings to make a diagnosis of a nonstructural condition.

asymmetry of the record in the right temporal region fitted in with this. It was agreed that these two findings, although not significant alone, might, when they occurred together, be due to a lesion in the right temporal area. On the strength of this a pneumoencephalogram was done and a questionable increase in air over the right temporal lobe was seen. The ventricular system was neither displaced nor enlarged. The neurosurgeon felt that there was enough to warrant an exploration; so a small bone flap was turned down, exposing the right temporal lobe, where a small scar, over which there was a collection of subarachnoid fluid, was found. The scar was removed, the fluid evacuated, and the patient made an uneventful recovery.

In this case the correlative interpretation which the neurosurgeon and the electroencephalographer achieved established a correct diagnosis, and proper treatment was instituted. This illustrates the best way to utilize in full this new electroencephalographic diagnostic aid.

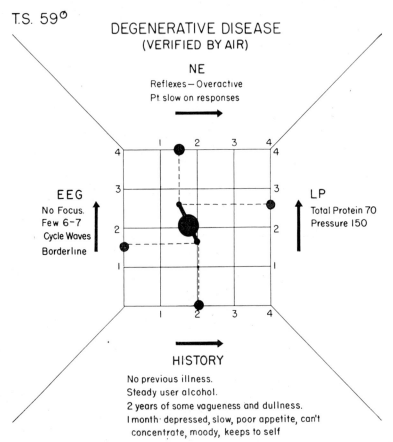

Fig. 104. The same diagrammatic pattern is followed as in Fig. 103. Here there is a mild abnormality of the electroencephalogram and the spinal fluid; history and neurological examination are not clear as to the diagnosis. All fall in the middle of the square and leave the final decision uncertain. It required an additional procedure—the pneumoencephalogram—to settle the diagnosis in this case. Again the correlation of the electroencephalogram with the other findings is emphasized.

Five sorts of electroencephalographic reports are usually found in hospital records, and an example of each should be of interest.

The first type of report is the shortest, and one might call it the terse report. For example: "EEG normal" or "EEG abnormal." No other data are given. A great many clinicians like this sort of report, which may make the record of the patient a simple one to compile. Other clinicians feel that they would like to know more about the nature of the examinations and findings as well. Of course, the interpreter of the electroencephalographic reports must know something about the physicians referring cases to be guided as to how often he turns in this kind of "terse report."

The second kind of report is purely descriptive. This is the sort of report mentioned earlier in this chapter that some non-medical people might be forced to give. It would simply describe, either minutely or in general terms, the record and leave the clinical interpretation to the

CLINICAL CONDITION	Specifically Valuable Alone	With Clinical Correlation		Total Valve	No Valve	Misleading	Total Failure
		Positive Confirmatory Valve	Confirmatory Valve by Exclusion				
EPILEPSY	15%	70%	5%	90%	5%	5%	10%
HEADACHE	0	10	75	85	10	5	15
MISC. NEUROL. DIS (M.S.- ENCEPH.)	0	20	50	70	20	10	30
VASC. ACCID.	0	50	30	80	15	5	20
HEAD INJURY	5	50	25	80	10	10	20
SUB DURAL BRAIN ABSCESS	5	65	20	90	5	5	10
BRAIN TUMOR	5	70	10	85	10	5	15
SUSPECT BRAIN TUMOR	0	20	70	90	5	5	10
NEUROSIS	0	10	70	80	15	5	20
BEHAVIOR DIS.	10	35	25	70	20	10	30
NON-ORGANIC PSYCHOSIS	0	10	60	70	20	10	30
ORGANIC PSYCHOSIS	10	50	10	70	20	10	30
	5	CLIN CORRELATION 75		80			20

Fig. 105. This is a table of the summary of the clinical value of electroencephalography in a number of conditions. This table represents data from numerous laboratories as well as estimates of different workers. A number of surveys of our own data are reported too. It is a composite picture. All techniques of electroencephalography such as activation are included in these estimates.

referring physician. An example of such a record is as follows: "The voltages on both sides of the head were between 30 and 50 microvolts. The rhythm at the anterior part of the head was between 18 and 20 cycles per second and the rhythm in the posterior part of the head was around 9 and 10 cycles per second. No waves slower than this were seen in any part of the examination. When the patient was overbreathing, there was no change in the frequency or voltage during the three minutes of overventilation." This report could be more elaborate if disturbances were seen or if a focus were found, but it would essentially describe the record as the recorder took it, and there would be no clinical interpretation at all. The referring physician would have to

pick up this material and be sufficiently acquainted with electroencephalography to incorporate this descriptive report into a clinical opinion.
Few referring physicians would be satisfied with this kind of report.

The third type of report would be the uncertain or "on the fence"
report. These are usually given by those inexperienced in electroencephalography or by people who are afraid of being wrong or who
dislike committing themselves. For example: "The rhythm in the anterior part of the head is nearly normal, but not quite normal. A few
borderline waves are seen in the parietal and temporal regions and in
the occipital region, but the rhythm is very close to normal limits and
the few suspicious waves here and there are probably of no significance.
The record would be classified as almost normal or borderline." A certain number of records are just that; they are no different from this,
and must be given even though experience is adequate. They represent
about 10 per cent of all reports.

It is possible, if beginners are unwilling to commit themselves, that
this percentage would be as high as 40 or 50 percent. Unless the person
rapidly changes his style, he will find himself subjected to considerable
criticism and ridicule by his colleagues.

The fourth type of report is the statistical one, an example of which
follows: "The record is normal in the anterior part of the head and
slightly abnormal on both sides over the temporal regions, and there
are some slow waves produced by overventilation during the second
minute. This type of record in a patient with a head injury in 70 per
cent of the cases indicates that there is some structural damage present.
If this type of record is found in an adult of forty-five, it indicates some
tendency towards a convulsive state," and so on. This would go on for
several paragraphs or pages and would inform the clinician of the status
of the electroencephalograph and its correlations with a lot of different
disorders. On the whole, this sort of report is not satisfactory. It takes
a tremendous amount of time, is boring to the average doctor, and has
no place in the clinical record of a patient.

The fifth type of report is one in which the interpreter tries to guide
the patient's clinical course. This type of report has produced a good
deal of criticism on the part of the referring physician toward electroencephalography and is obviously improper. As an example: "This
patient showed an abnormal record with paroxysmal runs of 3-per-
second wave spikes coming from both sides of the head, lasting one
or two seconds, which were increased by overbreathing to ten to twelve
seconds in duration. This is typical of petit mal epilepsy. The patient
is on phenobarbital, which is the improper type of medicine for this
form of epilepsy, and instead should be given tridione 300 mg. four
times a day." The patient, incidentally, was told to ask his doctor for
this prescription, which adds insult to injury.

In my opinion, the following report or some modification of it is the proper type of report that should be submitted to the physician: "The patient was examined with the usual nine electrodes. The patient was cooperative, was off medication, and had eaten one hour before the test. The resting record (i.e., when the patient was breathing normally) showed frequencies in the anterior part of the head around eighteen to twenty per second with voltages between 20 and 30 microvolts. This rhythm was symmetrical on both sides. The posterior part of the head showed normal type of 9- and 10-per-second alpha symmetrical on both sides. Overventilation produced no change in the record either in the voltage or in the frequency, and no abnormal delta waves were seen anywhere in the record. This record is within normal limits."

Here there is a brief description of the record. Voltages and frequencies are mentioned, asymmetry is discussed, the patient's cooperation noted, time after eating, and the number of electrodes are stated. No diagnosis is made, and there are no suggestions as to treatment. The statement as to whether the record is normal or abnormal is mentioned either at the beginning or the end of the record for the purpose of summary. It seems that most referring physicians would be better satisfied with this type of report. They may not be interested in the details in the first paragraph or two, but such details are available if desired.

In concluding this chapter, some comment may be made about the form on which the report is made. It is generally agreed that reports should be in duplicate, one of which remains on file in the electroencephalograhic laboratory. This is essential for comparative reports of future recording, for the purpose of research, and in case the first copy is misrouted or lost.

The report may be written directly in the record, or a card or form on which it is typed added to the record. A representative sample may be sent with the report. This is a nice gesture, and some referring physicians really appreciate it, but it involves sample selection and marking each sample with electrode placements, calibration and other data. This really adds to the burden of the interpreter. Some laboratories use a punch-card type of report (Fig. 106), which carries on the carbon copy punching arrangements whereby any particular category can be pulled out and assembled for study. Each laboratory works out its own requirements and special preferences, so that no particular type of report form is recommended.

Since each electroencephalographic record averages 100 pages of recording paper and each sheet is 12 by 5 or 8 inches, after a year or two the storage problem and record file are considerable. Records may all be thrown out and only the duplicate report retained. The record may be discarded, except significant portions, thus greatly reducing the storage problem. Records may be thrown away after two or three years, though then the mass must be regularly sorted to get at the old ones. The records may be microfilmed in their entirety at a cost of eighteen

ELECTROENCEPHALOGRAPHIC LABORATORY

KEEP THIS SPACE FOR FINAL TYPED EEG REPORT
This is a preliminary description for convenience of physician and not the
final report

NAME: *Eve Dawn*   ROUTINE ✓   LOCALIZATION   OTHER
DIVISION: *OPD*   UNIT #: *406-92* AGE: *17*   DATE: *7/21/50*

1. Was the patient cooperative? ✓   If not, describe.

2. Were eye movements or other artifacts controlled or all marked? ✓
3. Was the test perfectly satisfactory as far as technician was concerned? ✓
   If not, why.

4. If done, was overbreathing satisfactory? ✓
5. Was the patient clear mentally? ✓   If not, describe.

6. Was the patient tense or worried about procedure, uncomfortable, or in pain? *no*
7. Did the patient do anything unusual during the test?   If so, describe in detail.
   Short, blank look with flicker of eyes - during test.
8. Did the patient become drowsy? *no* Could this be controlled?
※※※※※※※※※※※※※※※※※※※※※※※※※※※

In opinion of technician, did the test indicate:
   a. A normal record — An asymmetrical normal record
   b. A borderline record
   c. An abnormal record
   d. A grossly abnormal record (diffuse)
   e. A record with paroxysmal activity ✓
   f. A record with difference between the two sides
   g. A record with positive localizing data
REMARKS:

*3   7 sec spike and wave bursts on both
sides during overbreathing and once
before. See p. 841,* Signed: (technician)
869, 871
                                      Anne Tureen

A

Fig. 106 A. The type of "log" kept in duplicate by the technicians in our laboratory. A good deal of interesting information about each test that the clinician might find of value is included in such descriptions. The technician who takes the recording (recordist) makes the preliminary descriptive report in the manner shown in the Figure A. A certain copy of this sheet is immediately placed in the patient's hospital record for the preliminary and tentative guidance of the physician in charge of the patient. The final written report is typed on a sheet as shown in B. This is signed by the clinical electroencephalographer and appropriate tiny squares in the margins of the report are checked off at the time he makes his report. The carbon of this appears on a punch card shown in C which is kept in the laboratory for research and other procedures.

The value of the technician's description, which in no sense is a clinical report, is two-fold. It makes the work of the technician-recordist far more interesting and stimulates him to more careful operation of the equipment. The second advantage is that some form of preliminary evaluation of the record is immediately available

cents per record, and each 100 feet of 16 mm. film containing twenty to twenty-five records kept as a permanent record. If this is done, the

B

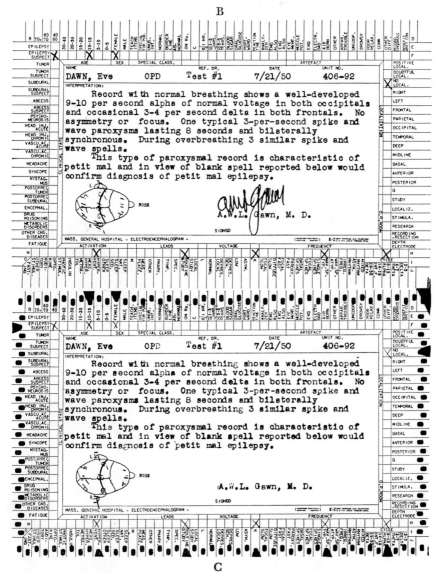

Fig. 106 continued.

to the doctor to guide him in the handling of the patient. It is in no sense a clinical opinion and this does not appear until the electroencephalographer makes out the final report. The combination of the two which appear in the record keeps the clinical as well as the descriptive report in one unit.

reverse side of each record may be used over again at a saving of twenty cents per record, which just pays for the cost of microfilming.

Charge slips, requisition forms, budgets, schedules, and so forth, are too varied and depend on too many special situations to be discussed here. All these problems are usually solved to fit the special needs of each laboratory, and no one system satisfies everyone. The general rule is to model the electroencephalographic laboratory as to reports, filing and storage of records along the sound experience of x-ray, electro-cardiographic or other older departments of the institution.

Glossary

A battery	The source of electricity, usually a storage battery of 6 volts, to heat the filaments of the vacuum tubes.
Activity	A broad term to mean the changes in electrical potentials recorded from the brain.
Activation	Various techniques of altering the physiological environment of the brain or stimulating it by light, sound or electricity, in order to produce hidden or latent abnormal activity in the record. See Chapter IV, page 66.
Active electrode	One of the electrodes of a pair that is closest to the source of electrical activity being measured.
Alpha rhythm	A recurring wave pattern resembling a sine wave in the electroencephalogram that lies in the frequency band of 8 through 13 per second. See Chapter III, page 21. Many feel that the word alpha rhythm should be restricted to the 8 to 13 per second waves that are recorded from the occipital parietal region and which are diminished or eliminated by sensory stimulation such as a flash of light or opening of the eyes. They feel that this frequency when encountered under different circumstances should be identified only with a number.
Alternating current	(symbol, AC). An electric current which reverses its direction of flow. The usual commercial alternating current reverses uniformly 60 times per second (U.S.A.) and 50 times (Europe).
Ampere	(symbol, I). The common unit of current or flow of electricity per unit of time. When the voltage is 110 and resistance is 11 ohms, the amperes flowing are 10. (E 110 = I 10 (R) 11, shown by Ohm's Law.)
Amplification factor	The ratio of the output of an amplifier to the input. In electroencephalography this may be as much as 10,000,000 times.
Amplifier	One of the units in an electroencephalographic apparatus consisting of vacuum tubes, resistors and condensers designed to increase the applied voltage a sufficient amount (at least 1,000,000 times) so that these signals can operate a recording instrument.
Amplitude	The peak amplitude of a wave is the vertical distance on the record from the peak of the wave to the baseline.

To peak amplitude is the vertical distance from the peak of the wave to the adjacent trough below the baseline. Electroencephalographic amplitudes are usually defined in terms of peak to peak amplitude. This can be compared with the measurement of a signal of known voltage that enters the same amplifier and thus be read in microvolts instead of millimeters.

Analysis   The recorded distribution curve or plot of the data produced by an analyzer. An analysis can be done manually, but is, of course, exceedingly tedious.

Analyzer   An instrument attached as a separate unit to the electroencephalographic apparatus for the purpose of determining the frequency and amplitude components of a particular channel or channels of the electroencephalographic record. Such auxiliary equipment may write out such an analysis on the electroencephalographic record for certain fixed intervals of time.

Anode   The positive pole or electrode of a battery or vacuum tube.

Artifact   Any fluctuation of the recording unit that is *not* caused by the potential difference of the phenomenon being measured. See Chapter IV, page 58, for types.

B battery   A large number of small (flashlight type) dry batteries all connected in series so that their individual voltages are added together to make a value of 90 volts or more.

Balance   The adjustments required so that both sides of a push-pull amplifier operate equally.

Band   A number of adjacent frequencies in a spectrum grouped together for convenience under a name or letter, also grouped by some according to physiological characteristics and anatomical location. See *Alpha* and *Theta rhythms*.

Basal activity   The electrical activity of the under surface of the brain as recorded by basal leads.

Basal lead   An electrode so placed that it records the activity from the under surface or base of the brain.

Base line   The straight line made by the pens of an ink writer when no signal or waves are being recorded. It should bisect a sine wave whose positive and negative components are equal.

Base line swing   The very slow swings or waves, one per second or less, of the pens such as caused by skin sweating; hence an artifact.

Beta rhythm   The frequency band of the electroencephalogram from 18 to 30 cycles per sound. See Chapter III, page 21.

Bilateral synchrony   The simultaneous appearance on two sides of the head in homologous points of some normal or abnormal activity. Usually the form, polarity and components are similar. There is evidence that such activity originates in a central deep structure such as the thalamus.

Bipolar recording   Recording from two electrodes both over electrically active parts of the brain. See Chapter III, page 55.

Blocking (amplifier)   The effect of too large a signal applied to the amplifier input so that the degree of amplification is too large. This causes a sustained plate current cut off owing to one grid becoming too strongly negative. The result of this is an inability for the electroencephalographic signal to be transmitted for a short period of time which may be as long as several seconds. When this occurs the input wave signals have the appearance of flat top waves. Lowering the gains prevents this.

Blocking (activity) The phenomenon of repression or elimination of certain electrical activity in the brain because of the arrival of a sensory stimulus, e.g., blocking of the occipital alpha rhythm by light.

Calibration A signal of known voltage (amplitude) either in the shape of a square wave or sine wave that may be sent into all channels of the apparatus simultaneously. Such a signal has two functions. One is to test the balance, pen function and amplifier setting of each channel to see that they are identical. The other is to provide a convenient visible scale on the record which is used to measure the amplitude of the electroencephalogram about to be taken. The calibration signal should be used before and after each test and whenever the various gain *controls* are altered.

Cathode The negative pole or electrode of a battery or vacuum tube.

Cathode ray tube A vacuum tube oscilloscope that uses a beam of electrons as the moving element which registers on a fluorescent screen on the face of the tube. When a camera is used to photograph the electrical events on the oscilloscope the entire apparatus is called a cathode ray oscillograph.

Channel A unit of an electroencephalograph which consists of two sets of electrode selector switches, one for grid 1 and one for grid 2, an amplifier (some apparatuses have a pre-amplifier and a power amplifier as separate units in each channel), one of the ink writing oscillograph units and pen. Each channel has its own gain control, filters, power switches and pilot lights.

Complex A specific combination of fast and slow activity in the electroencephalogram that reoccurs enough times to be identified as a discrete phenomenon. See *Wave and spike.*

Component The various frequencies or impulses that compose a mixed rhythm or complex. For example: the slow component of the wave and spike.

Condenser An instrument for storing an electric charge. In its simplest form it consists of two conducting metal plates separated from each other by an insulator. Direct currents cannot pass across a condenser; alternating currents can. Also called *Capacitor.*

Condenser coupled As applied to an amplifier this means that the direct current component of the electroencephalogram is blocked by condensers in series with the input to each grid but the alternating components are transmitted.

Coupling The type of connection between the input and the grids of a vacuum tube in an amplifier. See *Condenser coupled, Direct coupled.*

Cut-off The points on a frequency response curve of amplifier and recording unit where the amplitude of the output signal has fallen to 50 per cent of its correct value. The slow and fast cut-offs are due to filters in the circuit as well as specific limitations of both amplifier and oscillograph.

Cycle

The complete upward and downward excursion of a single wave, complex or impulse. The number of times a cycle occurs in a second is the frequency, and the time from beginning to end is the duration.

Delta rhythm

A wave pattern in the electroencephalogram that lies in the frequency band 1½ to 4 per second. There are some who restrict the meaning of delta rhythm to pathological waves produced by impairment of function in the brain and regard this same frequency in infants or normal adults asleep as a different phenomenon and use the frequency number instead of delta to identify them.

Diffuse activity

An electroencephalogram that shows similar patterns in all leads.

Direct coupled

As applied to amplifiers this means that a direct current path exists between the input and the output circuits so that direct current components of the elecroencephalogram may be amplified. Resistors are used instead of condensers and transformers in such an amplifier. Both direct and alternating currents are amplified by this type of apparatus. A poorly constructed or connected amplifier of this type might pass a dangerous high voltage direct current back to the electrodes on the subject.

Direct current

An electric current that flows in only one direction. All current from A, B or storage batteries is direct.

Dominant frequency

The particular frequency in any electroencephalogram that occurs most of the time. In any automatic frequency analysis the amplitude of the waves contributes to the determination of the dominant frequency.

Driving

The appearance of a frequency in the electroencephalogram as a result of a sensory stimulation of this frequency. A flashing light at 8 per second may produce 8-per-second waves in the electroencephalogram.

Duration

The time usually expressed in milliseconds from the beginning of a wave, impulse or complex to its end. It may not necessarily be related to the frequency.

Ear lead

An electrode placed on the ear lobe which at one time was thought to be indifferent. Mastoid leads are sometimes regarded as equivalent to ear leads. The right and left ear lead connected to one wire of an input is still regarded by some as an indifferent or remote electrode.

Electrode

The terminal of the electroencephalogram that is in direct physical contact with the subject. There must *always* be two electrodes for each channel. They are always of some form of metal. This metal can be solder; many prefer silver; and there is some evidence that if the silver is chlorided and covered with a saline pad less artifacts are introduced into the recording.

Electrode box

A shielded extension of the selector switches of the electroencephalogram to which the various electrodes are attached. This permits each electrode to have a light,

	short connecting wire. The box is usually next to the head of the subject.
Electrode holder	Any device, clamp, cap or fixture which holds the various electrodes against the scalp or brain of the patient.
Electrode paste	A conducting material to decrease the resistance between skin and electrode.
Electrogram	Any record on paper or film made by an electrical event; used by some to mean both scalp and cortical recordings of brain potentials, by others as a short word for electro-encephalogram.
Epoch	A fixed period of time during which an automatic analyzer obtains the electrical activity for one analysis. In the Walter machine it is ten seconds.
Evoked response	An alteration in the electrical activity of a particular part of the nervous system produced by an incoming sensory stimulus. In recording from the scalp or cerebral cortex such responses have a specific and well-recognized pattern.
Faraday cage	An enclosure whose entire surface is composed of a conducting metal or metal screen that is connected to ground. Most external electrical waves causing artifacts are drained to the earth in such a shielded room and therefore are not picked up by the electrodes on the patient.
Fast activity	Electric potentials from the brain of short duration. They may be as brief as 0.5 millisecond up to 50 or 60 milliseconds.
Fast speed	A recording speed of above standard on most ink-writing oscillographs, often twice standard.
Fast waves	A wave pattern in the electroencephalogram that lies in the frequency bands above thirteen cycles per second. See Chapter III.
Field	A field is the distribution of current flow, and hence also of gradients of potential difference around a source of current.
Filters	A variety of combinations of condensers and resistors so arranged that it attenuates or eliminates certain components of a given signal and passes other components. For example, the muscle filter will pass the brain wave frequencies of $1\frac{1}{2}$ to 30 per second, but attenuates the short duration 10 to 12 millisecond muscle potentials.
Flat-top waves	Activity in the electroencephalogram that has a pattern that suggests a flat top. In reality such an appearance is caused by downward impulses or spikes of short duration with a free period of no activity between. They are regarded by some as specific of temporal lobe discharges in automatism or psychomotor epilepsy and may occur four to six times a second. Blocking of the amplifier produces an appearance of flat-top waves which are an artifact.
Focus	A source of electrical activity in the scalp, usually referred to some region in the brain.
Frequency	The number of times per second that an event occurs. Only in *continuous* wave pattern is it a reciprocal of the duration in milliseconds.
Frequency response	That part of a frequency spectrum which is recorded with less than 10 per cent change in amplitude, and is regarded

as the range of adequate frequency response for the apparatus.

Frequency spectrum
A transformation of the amplitude-timegraph of the electroencephalogram to an amplitude-frequency graph or to a percent time-frequency graph. The amplitude as percent time will be the ordinate. This transformation may be done manually or by frequency analyzer machines.

Fundamental frequency
In an analysis of a complicated wave form the slowest frequency component is called the fundamental. Twice this frequency is called the second harmonic (see Harmonic). For example, the second harmonic of a fundamental at the alpha rate of 10 per second is the frequency 20 per second.

Gain
The number of times that a signal entering an amplifier is increased in strength, usually in voltage, but some stages include amperage as well.

Gain control switch
The switches or dials which increase or decrease the amount of gain.

Grid
That part of a vacuum tube between the filament and the plate. The incoming signal is connected to the grid of a vacuum tube and a push-pull circuit with vacuum tubes on both sides of the system. One grid is called g^1 and the other g^2.

Ground
That part of any electrical circuit that leads to a connection to the earth; it may be a water pipe.

Harmonic
A frequency which is an integral multiple of some other frequency, usually defined in terms of sine waves.

Indifferent lead
An electrode which is so located or connected that the potential recorded between it and the active electrode is due primarily to the activity of the latter. Also called a remote lead.

Ink writer
An oscillograph that activates an ink-writing pen.

Instrumentation
That part of electroencephalography dealing with the assembly, operation, principles, calibration and care of the apparatus.

Intensity
The relationship of the amplitude of a particular activity to the calibration signal or to other activity in the electroencephalogram.

Interference
The appearance of so much artifact in a record that it obscures the potentials being studied; also used when one activity has so much more intensity that it hides another.

Intermediate fast activity
The activity of the electroencephalogram that lies in the frequency band 14 through 17 per second.

Intermediate slow activity
The activity of the electroencephalogram that lies in the frequency band 4 through 7 per second. When this activity is in the region of the temporal lobe and is related to emotional activity, Walter calls it *theta,* but others use this term regardless of location or state.

Interval
The period of time between the appearances of certain electrical events.

Lead	The term applied to any one of the electrodes in use in an electroencephalographic examination. Sixteen electrodes on the scalp is called a 16-lead study.
Linked amplifier	Two amplifiers so arranged that one electrode is common to both grid 1 and one channel and grid 2 of the other. See technique page.
Master gain control	A single dial or switch that can raise or lower the gain setting in all channels of the apparatus at one time.
Micro-electrode	Two electrodes, usually less than 0.01 mm. in diameter in a fine needle or glass tube, that are less than 0.1 mm. apart and can therefore record from only a few cells or a small area.
Microphonic	Artifacts produced in the circuit from mechanical vibration directly affecting the vacuum tubes or electrodes.
Microvolt	One *millionth* of a volt—the standard voltage unit in electroencephalography. Symbol: Micro V. or μ V.
Milliampere	One thousandth of an ampere; also called *mils*.
Millisecond	One thousandth of a second; also called *sigma*.
Millivolt	One thousandth of a volt, the standard voltage unit in electrocardiography.
Monopolar recording	Recording in which one grid of each channel is connected to a common indifferent lead and the other grid of each channel to an individual active electrode. (Chapter IV, page 53.)
Nasal lead	An electrode that is introduced through the nose and which rests against the posterior pharyngeal mucous membrane to pick up activity from the under surface of the brain. See Chapter IV, page 46.
Negative	The conventional sign to represent the cathode terminal of a battery or power supply. The upward deflection of the recording pen in most apparatus is so arranged that grid 1 is negative to grid 2. Also used by clinicians to represent a report or examination that is within normal limits.
Noise	A term to describe an artifact in the electroencephalogram that obscures the record because of its high frequency. It is usually continuous and due to 60-cycle alternating current. Consult electronics manual for term noise level and electron noise.
Ohm	The standard unit of resistance. When the voltage and amperage are numerically equal according to Ohm's Law, resistance will be 1 ohm. 15 volts = 15 amperes $\times$ 1 ohm; $E = I\,R$.
Ohmmeter	The electrical measuring device to determine the number of ohm's resistance between any two electrodes.
Oscillograph	The recording unit in each channel. See *Ink writer* and *Cathode ray*.
Paroxysmal activity	Any activity in the electroencephalogram that occurs suddenly, lasts but a short time, and then disappears. It is usually identified with epileptic discharges.

Pharyngeal lead   An electrode placed against the posterior pharyngeal mucous membrane; usually the same as nasal lead.

Phase   The relationship in time of the components of one wave to that of another one of a different source. If the alpha waves from each occipital lobe rise and fall simultaneously, they are in phase. If one source is one quarter of a complete wave behind the other, they are 90 degrees out of phase.

Phase reversal   A special arrangement of two amplifiers so that the source of a wave is between the first grid (g^1 of amplifier I and g^2 of amplifier II and the pairs of grids of each amplifier face in the same direction. In such an arrangement the recorded waves will appear to be 180 degrees out of phase or mirror images of each other. Each amplifier will be recording from opposite sides of the electric field of the source. See Chapter IV, page 55.

Polarity   The sign, either positive or negative, of an electrical event.
Polarization   The accumulation of electrical charges on an electrode from chemical changes in it or its medium. Such charges usually build up slowly and act as a direct current. They have little effect, therefore, on condenser or transformer-coupled amplifiers. With direct or resistance-coupled amplifiers they introduce large artifacts.

Positive   The conventional sign to represent the *anode* of a battery or power supply. The downward deflection of the recording pen in most apparatuses is so arranged that grid 1 is positive to grid 2. A term used by clinicians to indicate a record or examination that is *abnormal*.

Power amplifier   An amplifier operated from the lighting current that increases both the voltage and amperage of the input signal to a strength sufficient to move the recording system.

Power supply   A piece of apparatus that produces (from the lighting current) the correct amounts of voltage and amperes to operate the various vacuum tubes. It also may include regulators to insure that such sources of electricity are constant and unaffected by changes in line voltage from other apparatus in use.

Pre-amplifier   Some amplifiers are built in two sections. The first part which receives the input signal and amplifies it the first thousand or so times is called the pre-amplifier. Such amplifiers usually increase only voltage, must be exquisitely well built, and often operate from batteries to avoid the weight of the power supply sufficiently perfect to run them efficiently.

Push-pull   An amplifier circuit which has vacuum tube amplifiers in both grid 1 and grid 2 systems. In such an arrangement the top and bottom of a wave signal across the grids are both increased at the same time, whereas disturbances within the system cancel out.

Reaction time   The time between a stimulus and a response in any subject being tested. This may be recorded on the electroencephalogram by the signal pen. In alert normal human beings it is 0.170 second for light and 0.150 second for

sound or between a fifth and a sixth of a second. It is greatly increased in states of impaired consciousness.

Recorder   The same as *Oscillograph*.

Recordist   The person operating an electroencephalograph.

Repressed activity   Any potentials in the electroencephalogram that are reduced in amplitude by pathology within the skull or by physiological alterations; usually localized.

Resistance   The number of ohms, as between two electrodes.

Reversal   See *Phase reversals*.

Rhythm   A regular recurrence of an electrical event. The alpha rhythm is composed of waves of 100 milliseconds' duration that re-occur ten times in a second.

Selector switch   The pair of switches in each channel with sixteen to twenty-four points on each switch. Each point is connected to one of the electrodes and moving terminal leads to one of the two grids of each channel. By turning these two switches appropriately any two electrodes can be connected to this channel.

Setting   Any specific position of a variable switch or dial.

Sharp wave   A wave form that appears to have a sharp or peaked appearance in the electroencephalogram at the standard recording speed of 3 cm. (2.5 cm.) per second. This is a relative term, since different filters in the circuit and changes in recording speed will alter such appearances. It is usually compared as sharp to the rounded top of most alpha waves in the same part of the record. See *Spike*. It is usually described as fast rising with a slower fall.

Shielding   Metal or metal screen covering of apparatus, cables or rooms that are connected to earth. See *Faraday cage*.

Signal   Any electrical impulse or wave that enters the input of an amplifier.

Signal pen   An extra pen on an ink-writing oscillograph operated by a magnetic relay to record time or other signals made by the patient or recordist.

Silver; Silver chloride   A silver electrode covered with a layer of deposited silver chloride that rests in a sodium chloride solution in contact with the subject. Such an electrode produces a minimum of polarization currents.

Sine wave   A smooth, regular recurring wave form whose mathematical formula can be expressed by the sine of the angle of rise. The 60-cycle alternating house current is a sine wave, and alpha waves closely resemble sine waves.

Single ended   An amplifier circuit with vacuum tubes on only one grid. See *Push-pull*.

Slow wave   A wave form in the electroencephalogram slower in frequency than the alpha.

Spike   A brief electrical event of such short duration that on the electroencephalogram the appearance at 3 cm. per second standard speed is that of a rising and falling vertical line or an extremely sharp wave when compared to the alpha wave. As with sharp waves, such appearances are relative (see *Sharp wave*). Spikes also resemble the discharges of the muscle in activity and the nerve-action potential. Their duration is usually 3 to 25 milliseconds.

Square wave	A sudden non-biological direct current signal that remains flowing at the same amplitude for a period of time.
Stage	One of the sets of vacuum tube circuits in an amplifier with a certain amount of amplification. Most electroencephalographic amplifiers have several stages of voltage amplification and one stage of power amplification.
Standard conditions	An arbitrary set of conditions to insure uniformity of recording. See Chapter III, page 23.
Standard speed	3 cm. per second on the ink-writing oscillograph paper in most laboratories but some use 2.5 cm. per second.
Surge	A slow rising and falling of the amplitude in the electroencephalogram; usually an artifact.
Sweep	The term for a repetitive excursion of the beam of a cathode ray oscillograph that can be varied at will to spread out or narrow the apparent duration of an electrical event.
Synchrony	The simultaneous appearance of two separate electrical events.
Theta rhythm	The frequency band in the electroencephalogram from 4 to 7 per second; also called intermediate slow, or psychomotor activity (Gibbs). See Chapter III, page 211. Defined by Walter, who first used the term, as "a rhythm most common in the parieto-temporal areas and sometimes associated with emotional activity."
Time constant	The time taken for the recording pen to return to 37 per cent of its initial value with a square wave calibration signal. With different filter settings on the usual electroencephalographic apparatus it may be as short as $\frac{1}{5}$ second or as long as one second.
Time signal	Marks on the record indicating the elapse of a specific period of time. In the ordinary electroencephalographic record it usually represents one second of time. With faster recording units $\frac{1}{10}$ second or $\frac{1}{1000}$ second may be used.
Transverse linkage	A line of electrodes connected together across the scalp.
Transient	A non-recurring and non-continuous electrical event.
Tympanic lead	An electrode that is placed against the tympanic membrane in the external auditory canal for the purpose of recording basal activity in the electroencephalogram. See Chapter IV, page 46.
Unit	A term used to identify apparatus built or assembled together, usually on a common chassis.
Vacuum Tube	A vacuum tube is an amplifying device containing a heated source of electrons—a positively charged plate (anode)—and a grid for modifying the flow of electrons. (See any college textbook on Physics for details.)
Valve	The same as *Vacuum tube,* the term used in England, Australia, New Zealand, etc.
Volt	The common unit of potential or strength of electricity whereas the amperage is the flow per unit of time.
Voltage regulator	A piece of apparatus to insure an exact even level of voltage delivered to apparatus in spite of fluctuations of the voltage on the power lines.

Wave   The complete change of a source of energy in respect to
                              time. In the electroencephalogram the wave is essentially
                              a voltage-time graph. Waves may be pulses—periodic, con-
                              tinuous, aperiodic, complex, sinusoidal or square. In elec-
                              troencephalography some restrict the term to periodic
                              or continuous functions with respect to time such as alpha
                              waves, and call spikes or single occurring events impulses
                              or transients. Whatever usage is followed, the essential
                              difference in property of transients and periodic waves
                              must be kept in mind.

Wave and spike   A complex of a slow wave and fast one, giving the appear-
                              ance of a "dome and dart," usually seen in the electroen-
                              cephalogram in petit mal seizures. More accurate to call
                              it *Spike and wave.*

Wave analyzer   An apparatus that can take a complex mixture of wave
                              forms and separate out their component frequencies and
                              indicate their distribution on the record.

Wave form   The spacial appearance of a wave in respect to time on a
                              record.

Index

NOTE: Page numbers which refer to illustrations are set in *italic* type.

Meyers, 50
    depth electrode, 50
Migraine, EEG, 134
Military service, and epilepsy, value of EEG
    in, 100, *100, 101*
Mongolism, EEG in, 131
Monnier, 155
Monopolar recording, 52
Montreal electrode placements, 50, *51*
Muscle artifact, 64, *66*
    cell, 9
    contraction on electric stimulation, 1
Muscular activity in convulsions, 87
    atrophies and dystrophies, EEG in,
    131
Musicogenic seizures, 71
Myasthenia gravis, EEG in, 131
Myers, 130
Myoclonic seizures, 84
Myotonia congenita, EEG in, 131
Myxedema, EEG in, 132

NARCOLEPSY, EEG in, 130
Nasal electrode, MacLean, 46, *47*
    Schwab, 46
Needle electrode, 41, *42*
    Jasper, 46
    ventricular, Walter, 50
Nerve action spike, 11, *12*
Nerve cell, 8, *10*
    axones, 9
    communication, types of, 10
    dendrites, 9
    internuncial, 9
    nucleolus, 8
    nucleus, 8
    size, 8, *10*
Nerve impulse, 11
    along axone, diagram, *13*
    duration, 15, *15*
    electrical phenomena, 12
    frequency, 15
    various, diagrammatic representation,
    17
Nerve loops, 13, *13, 14*
Nervous system, central, nutritive elements,
    9
Nervous tissue, types of communication, 10
    time periods, 11
Neuritis, EEG in, 131
Neurosurgical problems, EEG in, 104–135
Neurones, 9
    loops, 13, *13, 14*
        rate, 15
Neurophysiology, relation to electroenceph-
    alography, 8–19
Neurosis and epilepsy, 138
    case history, 138
Neurosurgical problems, EEG in, 104–135
Nucleolus, 8
Nucleus, 8

OSTEOCYSTOMA, case history, 122
O'Leary, 140
Overbreathing. See *Hyperventilation.*
Oxygen, low, effect on EEG, 70

PARETICS, general, EEG in, 145
Parkinson disease, 129
Patient, preparation for examination, 41
Personality, normal, types of, and EEG, 136
Personnel requirements for laboratory, 163
    training and qualifications, 164
Petit mal, 80
    akinetic seizures, 84
    aura, 80
    brain wave pattern, 4
    description of seizure, 80
    duration, 80
    EEG, 81, *81*
        voltage distribution, *82*
    myoclonic seizures, 84
    respiration lapse, 80, *82*
    seizure, reaction time, 76
    spirogram and EEG, *82*
    tridione in, effect on EEG, 97
    vasovagal seizures, 81
    wave and spike pattern 81, *83*
    waves, relation to induced respiratory
    changes, *94*
Pharyngeal electrode, MacLean, 46, *47*
Phase reversal technique, 54, *55, 56*
Pituitary disorders, EEG in, 132
Pituitary tumors, EEG in, 132
Poliomyelitis, EEG in, 129
Potassium ion concentration, electric charge
    and, 9
Prognosis, in epilepsy, 95
    in head injuries, 113
Psychiatry, electroencephalography in, 136–
    151
Psychic equivalents in epilepsy, 88
Psychoanalysis, brain wave pattern after, 137
Psychomotor seizures, 85, *85*
Psychoneurosis, EEG in, 137
    in epilepsy, 99
        case history, 99
Psychopathic behavior, 140
    EEG in, 140
Psychosis, EEG in, 141, *142*
    in epilepsy, 88
Pyknolepsy, 81

RAGES. See *Automatism.*
Reaction time in EEG recording, 18, 78
Recording, bipolar, 52
    monopolar, 52
Records, description, 173
    interpretation of, 167
Remond tripod electrode, *45*
Research, EEG in, 152–162
Respiratory changes, induced, relation to
    petit mal, *94*